6-5-18

Sharon, Hope you enjoy the book

RAISING
THUNDER

RAISING
THUNDER

MICHAEL BOOK

Copyright © 2018 by MICHAEL BOOK.

Library of Congress Control Number:	2018903848
ISBN: Hardcover	978-1-9845-1811-8
Softcover	978-1-9845-1812-5
eBook	978-1-9845-1860-6

All rights reserved. No part of this book may be reproduced or transmitted in any form or by any means, electronic or mechanical, including photocopying, recording, or by any information storage and retrieval system, without permission in writing from the copyright owner.

Any people depicted in stock imagery provided by Getty Images are models, and such images are being used for illustrative purposes only.
Certain stock imagery © Getty Images.

Print information available on the last page.

Rev. date: 03/27/2018

To order additional copies of this book, contact:
Xlibris
1-888-795-4274
www.Xlibris.com
Orders@Xlibris.com

768727

Contents

Introduction ix
Abbreviated Background xi

Chapter 1   A Shot Was Fired 1
Chapter 2   Why Me? 5
Chapter 3   A More Formal Education 8
Chapter 4   Thunder Scores First 13
Chapter 5   Welcome to Wild, Wonderful West Virginia 16
Chapter 6   Personal Hygiene 23
Chapter 7   April Fools' and Counting 29
Chapter 8   Freedom at Last or the "Great Escape" 31
Chapter 9   Thunder Moves Out 37
Chapter 10   Thunder Receives Other Human Guests 45
Chapter 11   Depression Creeps into Training Camp 50
Chapter 12   The Change from Feasting to Fasting 54
Chapter 13   Batter Up 60
Chapter 14   A New Beginning All Over Again 66
Chapter 15   On to Second Base for the Trainer 72
Chapter 16   What's in a Name? 79
Chapter 17   Verbal Communication 84

Chapter 18	Sight versus Sound	91
Chapter 19	Trust versus Instincts for Survival	95
Chapter 20	Our Third Christmas Together—Already	109
Chapter 21	Preparing for Our First Offsite Presentation	118
Chapter 22	Presentation Variables and Substitutes	132
Chapter 23	Who Is Thunder?	138
Chapter 24	Feather Development and Aging	141
Chapter 25	Thunder Goes to the Beach	146
Chapter 26	Feathers and the Molt	167
Chapter 27	Roadkill and More	174
Chapter 28	Tennessee Trout	183
Chapter 29	Thunder Flies to New Orleans	187
Chapter 30	A Favorite Hotel	207
Chapter 31	More Time and More Questions Yet Fewer Answers	219
Chapter 32	On the Road Again	221
Chapter 33	Next Stop—Orlando Florida	230
Chapter 34	Kids "R" Kids	235
Chapter 35	Thunder and Blackberry 6210	242
Chapter 36	Respect in the "Swamp"	249

A Thunder/Spot Poem 253

To my parents, Esther and John Book, who were always proud of me and encouraged the off-centered outlook I had on most subjects.

Unfortunately, my father did not live long enough to enjoy the wonders of Thunder. He did, however, teach me about the outdoors from an early age by including me in his fishing and hunting adventures. Respect and understanding of each creature, whether a prey species or not, was expressed by both his words and actions. Disrespect for any creatures, including man, was not tolerated.

My mother, who emptied frogs and worms from my dirty jeans, fortunately, knew to check early and often while I was still wearing them to make sure the critters were released alive. Her patience and quiet "pat on the head" support were warm indications of approval for and acceptance of my youthful antics. She was always a big fan of Thunder and was very proud of the accomplishments that Thunder and I shared. We'll always have that last photo of the three of us shortly before her passing at the age of ninety-three. She always gave me her total support, although because of height differences, the pat on the head had been replaced with a pat on the hand. It translates the same.

Introduction

In the fall of 1992, an eight-month-old female bald eagle was migrating southward from its nest area along the Delaware River in New York. She continued to follow major waterways while traveling in a southerly direction. While this provided a vital food source, it also, unfortunately, led her to the Ohio River and into West Virginia. It was early morning, and she was still perched in a tree along the river, where she had stopped and rested for the night. It was a chilly morning, and the warmer waters of the Ohio River produced a thin fog that drifted onto the shore of the adjoining bottom lands.

Suddenly, a shot rang out, breaking the early morning tranquility. It was the early morning on December 1, 1992, and this young bald eagle was struck with the bullet. She dropped from the branch to the ground below, where she was quickly found and ultimately taken to the West Virginia Raptor Rehabilitation Center for triage and condition assessment. Thus began the rare but wonderful relationship between Mike Book, the founder and director of the WVRRC, and his partner, Thunder, a magnificent female bald eagle who was deprived of her freedom by a single thoughtless act.

Over the next twenty-one years, Mike and Thunder struggle to communicate with each other as they travel over one hundred thousand miles on back roads and interstates, both locally and nationally, to convey a message of environmental awareness and responsibility. The relationship between man and giant bird deepens as they learn the meaning of tolerance, trust, and mutual respect. Mike's dedication to the well-being of Thunder and all she represents is clear as they educate young and old, from Boy Scouts to members of Congress, spending nights together in rustic cabins and five-star resorts. Thunder teaches Mike a thing or two about the nature of bald eagles and their nobility (or lack thereof), wicked sense of humor, intelligence, and refusal to be anything other than wild.

Please join Mike and Thunder in their journey through years of tears, laughter, hard work, frustration, and perseverance, culminating in their first public appearance on Earth Day 1995. Somewhere along the way, Mike and Thunder establish a bond like none other, sharing years full of surprises and scientific revelations. Thunder learns to drink from a cup, while Mike discovers she suffers from occasional car sickness as each falls into their special role of ambassador for environmental education.

Abbreviated Background

Work Experience
- Grew up in rural America, where the outdoors and farming were part of everyday life
- Vietnam veteran, captain in U.S. Army as aerial intelligence officer
- Wildlife biologist for seven years with a state agency
- Started and managed two small businesses (total of forty employees)
- Developed business plans, including marketing analysis, as well as all management, training, and safety procedures, including employee policy manuals
- Directed investments and growth while supervising operations directors
- Founder and current director of the West Virginia Raptor Rehabilitation Center, located on Bunner Ridge, Fairmont, West Virginia [a 501(c)(3) tax-exempt all-volunteer organization]

Education
- Bachelor of Science
    Wildlife Biology/Forestry, West Virginia University, Morgantown

Skills
- Problem Identification and Resolution
- Project Management
- Production Efficiency

- Strategic Planning
- People Skills
- Raptor Behavior and Care (over forty years)
- Public Speaking (with emphasis on Environmental Education)

One Man and One Eagle

Chapter 1

A Shot Was Fired

Once upon a time, seemingly eons past, a young bald eagle, while making its way south for the winter from where it hatched in New York state, arrived at the Mason–Dixon Line. Shortly after passing this point, it probably began following the Ohio River. After all, not only did it head in the same general direction her instincts were pushing her, but also, the river would provide a source for fish, a favorite and necessary food staple.

At some point during her migration, she decided to take a food-and-rest break in the area south of Parkersburg, West Virginia. This was a huge mistake. Although details of exactly what happened are not fully known, many can be surmised. This is what likely happened.

It was early December 1992, and antlerless-deer season was just winding down in the state. Meanwhile, the eagle had found a nice tree to roost in for the night. Later that evening or very early the next morning, an alleged hunter armed with a rifle spotted the large brown bird. Bald eagles do not have the traditional white head and tail until they reach the age of five or six years. Had this been an adult, it might have been spared. From the ratio of young to adult bald eagles shot that we know about, I theorize that not being able to correctly identify these birds (ignorance) is a significant reason so many more juveniles than adults are being shot. This is by no means justification for these dastardly deeds, but it might give us some insight as to the reason it is happening. Once we suspect this, we can direct and have directed our educational efforts accordingly.

Things were likely slow for the hunter, and here, perched high above, was this large target. A shot was taken, and the bird was hit. Fortunately, it was not a fatal wound. The bullet had passed through the left thigh, missing the bone (femur) and continuing on and through the tip of the left wing, severing the wrist at the last joint (equivalent to your hand). The bird was definitely down but not dead. It was later found, probably by a responsible hunter, and the authorities were notified. Someone had just committed a federal migratory bird law offense, as well as violating the Endangered Species Act. The eagle was ultimately transferred to the special agent with the U.S. Fish and Wildlife Service, who then turned the bird over to the West Virginia Raptor Rehabilitation Center (WVRRC) for care and rehabilitation.

This bird was banded on both legs. The right leg had a blue aluminum band with the markings X-62 inscribed on it. This band was the state of New York's identification bracelet, so to speak. The left leg carried the traditional U.S. Fish and Wildlife Service band. It was from this band that her age, sex, and hatch location were determined. This particular bald eagle, while migrating from where it hatched along the Delaware River in New York State only eight months earlier, was found suffering from a gunshot wound in Jackson County, West Virginia.

This was a big bird, nearly forty-one inches long with a wingspan of six feet and eleven inches. Even with her large size, being mostly hollow bones and feathers, she only weighed twelve pounds. Her weight was hardly what most observers would have guessed. However, anyone who has worked with raptors will not be lulled to sleep by the minimal weight factor when handling or even attempting to handle a frightened wild predator such as this one.

Thunder—she had no name at that time but, for our records, was referred to as Bald Eagle 604—was taken for emergency treatment to one of the volunteer veterinarians who worked with the WVRRC. She had two wounds from one rifle bullet. It entered her left thigh from below and in front, missing the femur, and passed through the leg before hitting the wrist in the left wing and severing it at the joint. This meant that all ten primary flight feathers that grew out of what would be our hand would never grow back. It was the same as having your entire hand amputated at the wrist. We would lose all our fingers, and she would lose all her primary flight feathers. Otherwise, her health appeared good, but this would not be one of our success stories where we treated, rehabilitated, and released the bird.

After the minimum necessary stay at the veterinarian hospital, she was transported to the facilities at the WVRRC. Here, she would receive daily care, which included injections and medicating and dressing her wounds as well as feeding and monitoring her general health. Shock was always a possibility that must be considered, especially in bald eagles that were very high-strung. Handling very large wild raptors that were not sedated could be and usually was very traumatic for them. Care and precautions to minimize this trauma would go a long way in increasing the odds of a successful rehabilitation process.

At this time, although we were not yet aware of it, she was beginning to lay the groundwork for us naming her. The next twenty-one days went something like this. Usually, three of the volunteers (the larger, the better) gathered at the center, where they dressed for battle. This included as much heavy leather covering the hands, arms, and chest area as could be found. Then a hard hat with a face shield was worn to protect the head and face. Unlike most other raptors, bald eagles would use their beaks as weapons.

Countless attempts to convince her to be cooperative on the basis that this was going to be for her own good were offered but summarily rejected. Being a young, large, extremely frightened, and powerful wild bird, she would have no part of even the most pleasant bedside manner. Two of the volunteers would secure her powerful wings and large, sharp, and potentially hazardous talons, while the third volunteer would do the necessary medicating of the wounds. For this procedure, her head was kept covered in what usually resulted in a futile attempt to keep her calm.

After the first two days of this, we noticed that we now had another problem. She had not yet eaten on her own since we received her. We thought at first that with the injury to the leg, she could not tear her food, so we had cut her fish into bite-size pieces. She still didn't eat, so after her medical treatment was completed, her head cover was removed, her mouth was pried open, and food was forced to the back of her throat, at which point she had no choice but to swallow it. This was a traumatic but necessary practice considering the obvious alternative of starving. The forced feedings and the medical treatments went on for twenty-one days until her wounds had healed sufficiently and all immediate danger of things like infection had passed.

Twenty-one days—think about it for a moment. It's been said that any habit can be formed or broken in that length of time. If you take the most bold and shy puppies from a litter and subject them to this same type of treatment, you might expect different responses immediately, but the long-term effects it would have on their general demeanor would likely be very similar. Looking back, I'd have to say that we definitely did not have a shy puppy. This eight-month-old bald eagle may have been extremely frightened, but retreating or cowering was not among her behavioral traits. And despite her aggressive attitude and low or no tolerance for humans, her wounds healed to the fullest extent possible.

Chapter 2

Why Me?

Thunder's injuries were nearly healed, and we now had a decision to make. Since Thunder could never be released back into the wild, we had two choices. We could either turn her over to another center or zoo or keep her and condition her to be used as our own educational bald eagle. Keeping her would provide us with our first bald eagle that we would have to use in our environmental education programs that we offered to the public. We chose the latter option. Since I had been rehabilitating raptors for the last fifteen years and I was the founder of the WVRRC, it was decided I would be the most logical choice to work with this unknown quantity.

This is where the story really gets interesting, funny, sad, rewarding, frustrating, and always hopeful. Before we venture too far down this long and winding path, a good starting spot may as well be with my interest in raptors, which started a long time ago, so long ago that some of the volunteers at the WVRRC accuse me of being so old that I was working with raptors when the Dead Sea was still only sick. Granted, I have been doing this work with raptors for many years but not quite that long.

My interest and curiosity in raptors began at a very young age with the influence of the old Westerns on television. Some poor cowboy, oftentimes the ultimate hero, was left to die in the scorching heat of the endless desert. He would be horseless and waterless, of course, and sometimes even staked to the ground with rawhide straps (I guess a version of the jesses we use now on our education birds). I was never really concerned with that aspect of the show as much as I was always waiting, looking, and listening for the vultures to appear. I later learned that the vulture's scream was actually that of a red-tailed hawk (which also is dubbed in for the bald eagle), and without a voice box, the vultures cannot actually vocalize. Vultures were and still are associated with death. I knew that even then, but my real interest stemmed from my basic curiosity about their ability to fly. They seemed to be able to fly endlessly in those nice circles with all their companions. I was impressed that not once did I see any of them collide with one another. I also wondered how they happened upon that prospective meal, the lone cowboy. At the time, I didn't know that these birds really weren't there at the site where the cowboy was. Had I known the vultures were filmed separately and were circling actual carrion elsewhere, I would likely have been devastated and my youthful curiosity much less engaged.

At any rate, my childhood was shaped by these bits of information and my willingness to lie on my back in our freshly mowed hayfield and play dead, hoping I would attract a turkey vulture. Back then, I was around eight or nine years old and likely referred to them as "buzzards." This was the name given them on the TV shows. I can remember doing this many times. One time my mother saw me lying there and yelled out to me to make sure it was me and that I was okay. I dutifully acknowledged her inquiry and politely asked that she please go back inside so she wouldn't scare the buzzards I was trying to fool. She went back inside, shaking her head and likely wondering what gene pool this son was derived from. It's likely she never quit wondering that either.

Only one time was I patient enough—or lucky enough—to have two vultures show a real interest in me. They got fairly low and made passes over me as I peeked out of one small slit in each eye. They hung around for a few minutes but likely concluded they would probably starve before I would be a meal for them. When they did give up and finally flew away, I must admit that I was quite relieved. They were flying low enough that I could see the tiny feathers from the body near where the wings attached, gently rippling in the wind, and I could hear the wind rush through their wings as they tightened their circles of flight.

That was many years ago, and I remember it like it was only yesterday. I really was nervous; after all, some of the cowboys staked to the ground were, I suspected, ultimately eaten by these birds. My fear passed quickly as the birds departed, but I definitely remember standing and brushing the grass from my clothing, and the next thought that came into my head was something like *Wow, those birds were so close. I'm glad they didn't poop on me.*

Then I likely ran to the house to report to my mother about the close encounter I just had with the hungry buzzards. She seemed interested and excited for me at the time. I later learned that in this country, a reference to a buzzard really means a turkey vulture, and everywhere else in the world, the old world, buzzards are indeed really the hawks.

Chapter 3

A More Formal Education

My interest and curiosity continued through those young and innocent years. I ended up with part of my formal education, including a degree in wildlife biology from West Virginia University. There, I learned from some of the best, including Dr. Ed Michael, Dr. David Samuel, and Dr. Robert Leo Smith. As much as I did learn, I was taught more significantly how to find the answers to unaddressed questions. They were also modest in that they realized we were dealing with many life-forms, most of which we merely scratched the surface of knowing and understanding. I think the only thing I didn't learn and wish I had is that creatures other than humans have the ability to think and reason. This was a hard lesson to learn for some reason, and most still think that is a determining difference between humans and other "lesser" life-forms. If you feel that way now, you might have your mind changed before finishing this book.

During school, I maintained my interest in birds of prey, although there was no significant future to be had chasing that discipline. I did, however, get a job as a wildlife biologist with the West Virginia Department of Natural Resources (DNR) and was assigned to McClintic Wildlife Station, located in Mason County, West Virginia. This was the home of the legendary Mothman.

This was a great place to work in—lots of wetlands and quite a diversity of other habitats. This was a field office but also served as the District 5 headquarters. It was here that I had my first significant one-on-one experiences with raptors. Since this was a field office, the public was more willing to be walk-ins. This included the DNR conservation officers, now referred to as DNR police.

After I got to know the two local officers, they thought, for some reason, that I would be a good person to bring injured wildlife to. So they did. They brought birds, mammals, reptiles, and amphibians as well. I enjoyed helping where I could, but my real interest seemed to migrate to the injured birds, primarily raptors. I could get the local veterinarians to help where possible, but when it came to raptors, they were very reluctant to treat them. Veterinarian schools back then didn't do much (if any) training with birds, let alone wild raptors. They were potentially dangerous, and there were no formal protocols for treatments or even anesthetics and dosages. It was a new world out there. I'm certain there were exceptions, but they must have been very scarce.

Regardless of this, I continued to work with these birds, and from time to time, I managed to successfully release some of them, likely less than 10 percent. I'll never forget my first release, a big ole great horned owl, the ones they call the "hoot owl." I think I became hooked after that, not just on the release part but also on learning about the different species and the way each had to be handled and treated so differently. My early raptors were kept in small flight cages constructed of chicken wire, an absolute no-no today. Wire is the enemy of wing bones and feathers as well. It didn't take me long to realize these basic facts.

In 1979, I was promoted to another position and transferred to the District 1 office, located in the north-central part of the state. I moved, and the birds followed. Moving to a less rural area increased the number of raptor encounters. Could this mean that humans were the cause of the problem or just a larger part of the solution? This would be addressed more equitably later on.

The birds started coming in larger numbers to the point that finding food for them was becoming more difficult. That was when I started soliciting help from my coworkers with food-acquisition requests. I handed out garbage bags for them to collect fresh roadkill. This was a great help. It was after dozens and dozens of birds were healed in my basement garage that Thunder would begin her healing process there as well. As a result of this growing need, it was in the spring of 1983 that the WVRRC became an official nonprofit 501(c)(3) organization. It was and still is run by an all-volunteer staff that takes care of the sick, orphaned, and injured birds of prey while providing environmental education to the public for the benefit of all living things. As in the beginning, our slogan remains—"Man is *a part* of nature, not *apart* from nature."

Now back to patient 604, Thunder, who had just completed twenty-one days of medical treatment administered by staff members of the WVRRC. It was decided that we would keep her as an educational bird and that I would be the one responsible for her domestication and training. I had no experience of this type with bald eagles, so I did some reading—lots of reading. Looking back now, I am not sure I learned as much as I had hoped. I have always believed that reading was the most effective way to learn (and I still do), but I quickly found out that this would be an exception.

I had lots of experience dealing with other raptors with what we wanted to accomplish with Thunder, but none were as large, strong, and potentially dangerous. The closest thing to Thunder, who was a very big girl, would be the great horned owl or the red-tailed hawk. I had lots of experiences handling them, but the difference would amount to fighting a brushfire versus fighting a thirty-story building engulfed in flames. There is no comparison, and the differences are just that great. A small person can handle a red-tailed hawk, but they would not likely be able to comfortably hold Thunder, let alone handle her. Federal permits with the U.S. Fish and Wildlife Service require that raptors used in educational situations be handled only by those able to safely secure the bird for the sake of the bird and to protect the audience from that bird. These situations are not the same as when we train in areas where the environment is totally controlled.

Thunder was brought to my home late on December 21, 1992 (Merry Christmas). She was placed in a rather small custom-built four-by-four-by-three-foot cage, which took the place of my vehicle parking area in the garage. It had a large perch stretching from side to side, a rubber floor to help keep the cage cleaner with less effort, and a small tub/pool for water that measured twenty-four by sixteen by six inches deep. Water is very important to eagles, not just to drink but also to bathe in as well. All this was done intentionally to allow her some freedom to move about but not so much that she could bang into the walls and possibly reinjure herself. She still needed some medicating of her wounds, even though they were healing quite well. The smaller area would make this solo job much easier for both of us. She had also been force-fed before being brought to me, so that was not a concern that first day, but I was curious as to how I would accomplish that task by myself if it became necessary. I would worry more about that if I could not get her to eat on her own.

She entered her new home reluctantly. She was extremely alert and, I would say, equally frightened. This cage was placed inside my basement garage, which would provide moderate temperature for her as well as for me. I anticipated spending countless hours with her. Here, she would have natural light as well as afternoon sun coming through the garage door's windows. Raptors are much calmer in subdued rather than bright light. This was as good a setup as I could have hoped to have had.

I knew this was not going to be an easy job, so whatever actions I could take ahead of time to make the task easier for me and more bearable for her, I did them. Nearly all the birds we used for education programs were once wild animals. In fact, they are all still wild animals that cannot be released. If we could fix the problems that each of our education birds have, we believe without doubt that they could survive in the wild if released. Our birds are not trained with food as a reward. We develop a trust with them and a routine of familiarity. This takes time, lots of time, but our methods must work pretty well since we have had one education bird with us for over twenty-five years.

She was left alone for the remainder of the afternoon, and I looked in on her only once before dark. She was doing okay, but I quickly found out that you cannot sneak up on this bird—at least not yet.

Chapter 4

Thunder Scores First

We both survived the first night. December 22 started as a bright and sunny morning. I went to the basement quietly, but she was quite alert, rested, and, if possible, more frightened. She began hopping around on her perch and threatening me with open beak while making a loud and hideously nasal snorty squawk. She was not a happy camper and most certainly was not interested in visitors. Much to her displeasure, I made myself comfortable on a stool at the door of her cage. The cage had a solid top and bottom, but the four sides were wire. She always knew what was going on around her. After almost one hour, she became fairly calm but far from relaxed. I was sitting with my head only three feet from hers, and the slightest movement from me caused her considerable anxiety.

I slowly began to move around. I got up and moved away from her cage but would remain in sight. She was no less irritated by the increased distance between us, but her fear seemed less immediate. Another hour plus passed, and I thought she had had enough. I did decide to leave her with a fish before I left. That act did not score any points with her either. She was in good physical condition, and I am sure she viewed the situation such that starvation was not her most immediate threat.

One more visit later that day and two more the next produced similar results. This morning's breakfast had gone untouched as well. Now she has not eaten on the twenty-second, the twenty-third, or the morning of the twenty-fourth, Christmas Eve. *I can solve that problem*, I thought.

Now it was Christmas Eve midmorning, about thirty-five degrees and wet from the morning rain. I had an idea. What if I offered her a live fish in her pool? My neighbor had a small pond with lots of fish in it. I would get some of them for Thunder. This could be the icebreaker.

I began gathering my fishing gear and went outside into the landscape and dug up some worms from the mulched bed. As I was doing this, the temperature began to drop drastically; it began to snow, and a strong wind was now blowing. The air was really cold, so I decided to add coveralls to my layers.

The thirty or so minutes it took me to get everything together was time enough for the weather to really change. When I walked out the garage door, the wind hit me from the west, carrying snow horizontally across the ground so thick, you could hardly see. I walked toward the neighbor's pond with the gale-force winds at my back.

By the time I had walked the quarter mile to the pond, a skim of ice had already covered it. I cast my worm, hoping it would break through the thin film of ice . . . but it didn't. I looked to the ground for some rocks I could use to break through the ice, just to make a little opening to drop the worm into the pond. The wind was blowing so hard now and snowing even harder. I didn't dare turn toward the blizzard. I tried to free a small rock from the ground but could not. I kicked it and found it was frozen solid. Finally, I did kick one loose without breaking any toes. I tossed it onto the ice, and it didn't break through.

By now, I was freezing. The rock was lying on top of the ice about twenty feet out into the pond. I was so cold, I was not sure my brain was even working as I almost stepped onto the ice to push the rock through, but I didn't. I did find another rock, which I had managed to break free from the frozen grip the ground had on it. I tossed this one onto the pond, and this time, both rocks fell through the ice. Now was my chance. I quickly cast my now-frozen bait onto the ice and dragged it back toward the refreezing hole. I pulled the worm across the ice, and it dropped into the hole but set there a moment before sinking into the water.

My bait set in the water for nearly fifteen minutes. By now, the wind chill was surely well below zero. I was really cold, and the fish were not biting. The once small hole in the ice was no longer open water; it had refrozen almost as quickly as I had made it. I decided to give up. This whole ordeal was what I called good initiative and poor judgment. The only success I could lay claim to on this excursion was that I neither fell into the pond nor suffered frostbite. I did almost succeed at both though.

I walked the quarter mile home into the face of the biting wind, a defeated fisherman. My only hope was that the weather was so foul that nobody had seen me. After a failing two-hour effort, I finally got back to the house and entered the basement as white from the snow as a snowshoe hare in its winter coat. I stomped and shook to try to remove as much of the snow as possible.

I removed my outer layers of clothing before walking into sight of Thunder. When I finally did, I found to my surprise that my freezing efforts had been for naught. It seemed that while I had gone on my tundra trek, Thunder had eaten the fish I had placed in her cage earlier that morning. I guess she wanted to see what stupid lengths I would go to, thinking she was hungry.

It being only the third day together, already, a score sheet began to develop, and it didn't look good for me. As of Christmas Eve 1992, it read, "Thunder—1, Mike—0," just the first seventy-two hours of what would end up an extremely lopsided and embarrassing score. After just 0.000391 percent of the time we would spend together, she had taken a lead that she would never relinquish.

Chapter 5

Welcome to Wild, Wonderful West Virginia

At this time, the bird had no real name, not that she wanted or needed one. I did, as I do with about everything, start calling her Spot just because, as I said, I call almost everything that hasn't a name or has one I don't know Spot. I did believe that I needed to call her something just for reference's sake, and I surmised that the more I said one thing, the more there might be some association for her there too.

In 1992, there was not a lot of research on the behavior—or much else, for that matter—of our national symbol. We did know about DDT and that its effects resulted in this bird being as rare as hen's teeth in the lower forty-eight states.

When we found Thunder in 1992, during a twelve-month period from 1992 to 1993, there were twelve bald eagles shot in West Virginia. Of the twelve, Thunder was the only survivor. Only one of the twelve was an adult bird with white head and tail feathers. Also, in 1992, there was only one known nesting pair of bald eagles in West Virginia. Thunder was banded on the Delaware River in New York, so we knew she didn't come from our nest. We found twelve shot birds, but it was more than very likely that we found far less than a quarter of those shot.

So for the sake of this example, let's assume there were forty-eight or so of these birds killed in 1992 in West Virginia.

Look at the larger picture, where, in the lower forty-eight states, the total bald-eagle population was estimated to be about three thousand pairs of nesting birds located east of the Rocky Mountains. Now if we take the total square miles east of the Rockies (1,904,064 square miles) and compare that to the size of West Virginia (twenty-four thousand square miles), we could project that West Virginia's share of the population might approximate seventy-five birds. Now this estimate will be no better than the numbers I'm working with. I also question the estimated population, but it does demonstrate, to some degree, the extent of eagle shooting in West Virginia in 1992. So it might even be somewhat accurate to assume that we might have shot every visiting bald eagle that crossed into our state during that period. While these numbers would not likely pass scientific scrutiny, they do shout out that there is a definite problem here, and it needs to be addressed. We will get to that later as well.

There wasn't a lot written, but I read every book or study I could find about bald eagles. Since I was going to be working with this bird, I was particularly interested in any information dealing with the species' behavior. Two things stood out from my readings. First was that the wild bald eagle was difficult to tame, and the larger female had possibly the nastiest and most aggressive attitude of all the raptors. Part of this reputation could easily be attached to them merely because of their size. I also read a great deal about golden eagles. It seemed they had a much more pleasant disposition than the bald eagle and were about the same size. The bald eagles were also one of few birds of prey where the beak was as much a weapon as the talons. The other thing I read was a documented and authenticated account of one bald eagle taken to England in the late 1800s that lived to be eighty years old. The report did not specify if this was a wild captured bird or an imprinted one taken from the nest at a very young age, not all that surprising when you consider some of the large tropical birds live as pets for that long or longer.

I kept searching, but most of my behavioral readings referred mostly to falconry. We didn't want to teach our bird to be used for falconry or to do any other tricks. We thought that a wild bird that could represent the species and do so with no more stress to it than the handler would suffer would make for a better and more authentic education bird. So far this practice has proved—in our case, anyway—to be excellent for the bird's extended well-being.

As a rule, our education birds are well adjusted when handled properly and do not suffer excessive stress. Our birds also seem to live long lives. You might wonder how a human can determine stress in one of these birds. Well, with the experience our volunteers have, it is very simple to recognize these signs and just as easy to avoid the situations that cause increased stress. Believe it or not, the most significant stress comes from a handler who truly lacks the confidence in what they are doing and lacks a basic understanding of raptors in general. Just because someone really, really wants to be a professional baseball player doesn't mean it can happen. Some people can practice till the cows come home and still not get it, baseball or an understanding of raptors. That is a difficult trait to teach some volunteers. As a result, most who think it is "cool" to handle the birds don't get to. It's sort of like a person who fears or has apprehensions around dogs, especially large ones. Some people never get over that, so you can imagine how difficult it is to overcome this fear of a creature much less familiar than a house pet. I learned a long time ago that a genuinely healthy respect for Thunder was much more beneficial to possess than any amount of fear. In her case, that was easy to say but much more difficult to convey to the bird. This subject will be discussed in great length throughout these chapters.

Most references to bald eagles being used in captive situations where the bird needed to be handled were negative. Golden eagles were used for falconry around the world, but likely, at least in large part, the bald eagle's attitude limited its use. A factor could also be that bald eagles are limited to North America, where the golden is cosmopolitan and exists in the birthplace of falconry. I looked to other raptor centers for assistance, but no one seemed to handle their wild bald eagles. Why did I think we were any different? I didn't. In, fact this was going to be a trial to see if it could be done without harm to man or beast. Only time would tell.

Back in the garage, Thunder and I spent countless hours together. I kept stacks of notes, but there was little that I could observe that I could draw any meaningful or useful conclusions from. Her seeming inability to relax and her keen awareness to anything or everything that moved amazed me. It was like she was on guard duty 24-7.

There was one intriguing observation I made one day though, and it had no correlation to my attempt to get this bird to relax. Well, I inherited this very nice large white cat from my parents when they moved to another state. Nick the cat was more like a dog, following me almost anywhere and sitting to wait until I finished whatever I was doing. Nick was an inside/outside cat. He stayed in the house for the most part but liked the cool basement garage just as much. In fact, he spent so much time there, we had a litter box and feeding station in the garage as well as upstairs.

The first three days that Thunder was with me, the weather was so bad that Nick never went out or came to the garage. I was there when he made his first trip over to the area where Thunder's cage was set up. All was normal until he glanced up and saw this massive bird. Thunder saw him at the same time or likely sooner. Nick froze in place, not a motion or twitch for several seconds, and then he slowly backed away. Thunder did nothing and seemed more relaxed with less tension in the eyes. For a moment, she seemed fixed on Nick but not in a predatory way. She seemed calm. You might question how I would describe the look on her face or what I saw, and I would not be able to describe it. Even today, after twenty-plus years with her, I can't describe how I can tell what sort of mood she is in. But I could. As a result of this encounter, I had to move the litter box and food and water bowls to an area not visible to Thunder, not for Thunder's sake but for Nick's.

This was the first moving object of any description that did not generate a reaction from Thunder. *Interesting*, I thought. This aroused a bit of hope and even more curiosity. What else was there that I couldn't see? I decided that I needed to do some more experimenting. I was curious about sounds and likely reactions to different ones and was hopeful that if I played a radio—soft music, rock, country, classical, or just talk radio—I would see a preference and would be able to use that information to understand a bit more about the problem that lay before me.

That last statement likely did more to help me on the road to understanding than any other single thing I did. In that last statement, I referred to the "problem" and my understanding it. What exactly was the problem? Remember that you can't solve a problem until you can clearly identify what it is. Most will get tangled up with the symptoms and lose sight of the real problem, for example, when you see a sign before crossing a bridge that reads Caution: Bridge Freezes before Road Surface. The fact that the bridge might be slick and the road is not is not the problem but merely a symptom of the problem. The problem is getting across the bridge safely. Thus, it was now my task to identify the real problem with Thunder.

My first hint came from Nick's and Thunder's reactions when they first met. Nick expressed both fear and, I would say, a great deal more respect for Thunder. He hadn't panicked and run away but calmly backed away from what he must have thought to be a no-win situation. Thunder was just as indifferent as Nick was concerned. From this, I decided that the real problem was that somehow Thunder and I had to develop, truly develop, a mutual respect for each other.

What I thought at the time was the easy part. That was akin to entering that ice-covered bridge at ninety miles per hour. Knowing what the problem was in this instance wouldn't make it any more likely I'd get across the bridge in one piece.

I started documenting Thunder's reactions to different sounds I could produce on the radio. Each day when I did this, I had to be able to dedicate not less than two hours at a time. This way, I could play the different sounds for at least twenty minutes each. I included talk radio, classical music, country, rock, instrumental, and plain static. Each time, I began with ten minutes of me reading aloud while I set near the door of her cage. I began and went through the entire list of preselected radio stations. I kept the volume at a level that I would be listening to. I repeated the same order each day. I did it on five different days.

The different sounds effected no visible changes to her behavior. She would sit there like a stump on a log with no reactions at all. Some of the music was easier for me to listen to than others, but the static nearly drove me nuts. I tried to read to keep my mind otherwise occupied. Thunder didn't respond at all.

The only noticeable change to her behavior came only when I leaned away from her and toward the radio to change the station. Movement, not sound, was what stimulated her. I knew she could hear, but her vision was so important that what she heard didn't really matter. Sound had never provided her with a threat or food, but her eyesight did. By now, there were two things I knew for sure. I needed to develop a mutual respect with Thunder, and only vision would come into play.

On January 2, 1993, I needed to rearrange some things in the area where Thunder was kept. The first thing I started to move made her very agitated and filled with panic, even though I was moving slowly. So I decided to completely cover her cage with a large blanket while I did the moving. We always covered the heads of birds we were working on to help keep them calm, and we did this with the travel cages of our education birds as well.

I covered Thunder's cage, and as soon as the lights went out, so to speak, she calmed down. I was making a fair amount of noise, but she didn't move. It was like I wasn't there, and I found out later that in her mind's eye, I wasn't there. After I finished my moving, I removed the blanket from over her cage. She didn't like that a bit. I have handled hundreds of raptors up to this point, including the very high-strung accipiters, and have never had a bird so easily upset. This was the main reason that few wild bald eagles were used for educational birds other than in display situations. And as I said earlier, the females were generally much worse than the males and much larger as well.

I needed to do something differently. The bird was on edge. She was young and strong, but this much stress was definitely unhealthy. If this continued with no progress, we would be forced to turn her over to a zoo or another organization where she would be used for display only. She'd been here just over a week, and while we had made some progress, it seemed we had gone backward even further. I certainly was not making any strides toward realizing a mutual respect, the necessary ingredient to making this project successful.

One more thought crossed my mind. I felt that for her to relax, she needed to feel more secure. And for her to feel more secure, she needed more security, another simple statement not so easily realized. I had, only minutes ago, almost put her to sleep by covering her entire cage. What if I covered the three sides and left the front uncovered? Even if I sat in front as I had been doing, she might not feel quite so threatened. It seemed at the time to be worth a try. I pulled the blanket out and covered the entire cage and then folded the front back to expose the front. I wasn't standing in front of the cage when I pulled the front back, and she didn't make a peep. She had a fish, and her pool was filled with fresh water, so I decided to call it a day. She likely would have appreciated it if I had left two hours earlier.

Chapter 6

Personal Hygiene

The next morning, I was up early. It was still dark. I planned on visiting Thunder after sunrise, which was almost seven forty. It was a clear and sunny but cold winter morning. By eight fifteen, it was really bright outside. Thunder's windows didn't get morning sun, but there was plenty of light for her nonetheless. The house was quiet, no TV or radio going.

I had finished eating breakfast and was doing some everyday household chores when I heard this unfamiliar commotion coming from the basement. *Good heavens*, I thought, *what could create this noise?*

I rushed downstairs, expecting the worst, and, to my surprise, saw water all over the floor, and it was still running out from Thunder's cage floor. Thunder was standing in her pool, soaking wet. She had to have submerged her entire body to get this wet. She stopped as soon as she saw me, which was before I saw her. She stood quietly in the water, and I slowly backed away. She acted like I had walked in on her taking a bath and she had no towel to cover herself. I went back upstairs and gave her some privacy.

After a bit, I heard some more splashing, and then it stopped. I gave her another half hour and then went to see what had transpired. She was sitting on her perch, wet but no longer dripping. Her pool, which held about eight gallons, was nearly empty. The area around the cage was wet in all directions. It looked like two five-year-olds had just finished a water battle in a bathtub. Her fish was gone as well, and there were just small pieces scattered about the cage floor. This was a great day, I thought.

In retrospect, I could just kick myself for not having this great day more than a week ago. She was more relaxed than I had ever seen her but still more tense than I had hoped for by this time. She just needed security. I was pleased. It had been at least since December 1, when we received her, until now, when she was at last able to get into the water.

Now that she was eating about one pound of fish per day and bathing regularly, I realized I would have to address the issue of sanitation. For a while, she hadn't been eating, so the sanitation wasn't initially a concern. But a pound of fish a day in a twelve-pound bird could and did quickly become an issue. Now what? Will the challenges ever end? Let me cheat and jump ahead and assure you that they haven't ended yet. When Thunder had a full tank and excreted her bodily waste, it wasn't pretty. In fact, she could project a stream about three quarters of an inch in diameter for eight to ten feet. That equaled a third to half a cup—big bird, big mess.

After her big bubble bath, I would need to clean and refill her pool. Until now, that hadn't been necessary, and the only time I would open her cage was to remove and/or add fish. Now I needed to open it far enough to fill the pool with eight gallons of water. I figured that since I needed to go this far with activities in her cage, I might as well figure out a plan for cleaning.

Remember that her cage floor was already covered with sixty millimeters of roofing rubber. The cage was designed sort of like the hand railings on a deck. There was a space between the bottom of the railings and the deck surface. This would allow water to run off freely or make it easier to sweep debris or even snow from the deck. I made both sides and the back the same way. The corner posts went to the bottom of the floor, but the back and side walls were raised about one and a half inches from the floor to allow for easier cleaning. In hindsight, this had been one of my better plans. This way, the rubber could extend out and down the back and sides. I had covered her back and both side walls to give her a more secure feeling. I had changed the temporary blanket with the same rubber I used on the floor. I cut a piece that would reach from the front left corner around the back and up the right side to that front corner. I made it wide enough to go from the very top to about two inches above the floor. I fastened it with staples.

I filled two five-gallon containers with water and got a small plastic pail that held a bit more than a gallon. I turned all the direct lights off to dim the area. It was still light outside but not enough to interfere with my efforts. I filled the small pail and opened the door to the cage slowly and only far enough to reach my left hand and the pail into the front right corner of the cage. Thunder moved as far away as possible and was noticeably irritated, but she didn't leave her perch. As I poured the water in the pool, she just watched very intently. She looked as though she wasn't certain how much displeasure she was experiencing. I continued pouring, refilling the pail and pouring again until I had her pool filled. She still didn't like me being there, but as long as she didn't leave her perch, I considered that a success. And while I was already in her space, I decided to pour some water on the cage floor to see about cleaning it.

Some of the newer excrement washed out the back of the cage onto the very large piece of roofing rubber (approximately ten by twelve feet) I had placed under the cage and over a floor drain. I had cut a hole in the rubber to expose the drain and placed two-by-four boards under the rubber along all the edges to contain any spilled and splashed water. This had worked well while she took her first bath and appeared to work with the small mess I had just flushed from her cage floor. The garage floor was sloped toward the drain, which helped immensely.

I still needed to come up with a plan for cleaning and some place to sit while I would likely be spending long hours in this location. I found another five-gallon bucket, the heavy kind that paint or wall plaster came in, set it upside down, and placed a small piece of carpet on the top. The height was perfect. My shoulder came to about the lower third of the cage, and my head had a total view of the entire cage. In fact, my head and Thunder's head were at the same height, sort of eye to eye.

At this time, I did remember one of the things I had read about eagles that was also supposed to apply to gorillas—that is, don't look them directly in the eye. Keep your gaze down. Well, I'll tell you what. All the things I had read years before about raptors' vision had me pretty well convinced that we didn't really know that much about what they did or didn't see and how it equated to the vision of mammals. I could believe that a territorial gorilla might resent you staring it down and take it as a challenge, but that was where I drew the line. This bird had no territory yet, and her eyes were on the side of her head and not on the front like mine, so I honestly, then and now, haven't a real clue what and/or how they do see. *I'm going to look her in the eye. I might learn something.*

Now that I had a practical—perhaps not so comfortable—seating arrangement decided upon, I could now find nonaggressive cleaning implements to tackle the floor issues. I chose a light blue hand towel and cut it in half. The cage was four feet across and deep. I had a pretty long wingspan myself but not that long. I would need some sort of extender for my towel. I got a putty knife that I thought could double as a scraper and two pieces of thin-walled aluminum tubing about two and a half feet long. I pounded about four inches of the ends of each piece flat with a hammer. I placed each one on the top and bottom of the handle of the putty knife and then duct-taped them together. *This will work*, I thought, silently praising the multifunctionality of duct tape.

I'm taking a moment here to briefly discuss duct tape. One of my sources informed me that it was invented in 1942. That may be so, but I will always believe it was invented before the wheel. Imagine pterodactyls circling over the mouth of a cave where some man was inventing the wheel. He had a large square stone, a small club about two feet long, a hard stone that resembled a chisel's edge, and a roll of duct tape. You can fill in the rest of the tale.

Now I could try out the wheel I had just fabricated. I got a full bucket of water and placed it to the left of my seat. I sat down gently. I never tried to sneak but to move smoothly and slowly yet deliberately. This seemed to work best for Thunder. I dropped the towel into the water, soaked it, and picked it up from the bucket to allow it to drip. Thunder made no major response but kept an eye on the still-dripping water-filled towel. I opened the cage door about ten inches or so, transferred the towel to my right hand, and raised it up toward the opening in the cage—still not much reaction. I moved my hand into the cage with the towel in tow. She scooted to the farthest point on the perch away from the pending invasion. I slowly set the towel down with my hand on top of it. I began swirling the towel in small circles at the entrance of the cage. I did this for minutes, removed the towel to the bucket, and went back for round two.

I continued this process for over an hour. By now, the entire cage floor was wet, and over half of the water was gone. I had moved my hand and the towel inside the cage to where my elbow was now inside the cage. That was as far as I could reach without moving my body any closer. I filled the rag again and placed it about a foot inside the cage. I grabbed my caveman extender and slowly brought it into the cage but mostly hidden under my right arm. I placed my hand at the end of the scraper on top of the towel. I slowly moved my hand back, leaving the scraper on the towel. When I go about a foot back, I took a grip of the handle and pressed down to secure the towel under the end of the scraper. Now I again began to move my hand to create a circular motion for the scraper and the towel. I also extended my reach to other areas of the cage floor. Unfortunately, the messiest part of the cage was also the farthest away from me. The extender and rag did the trick though.

My entire session took more than four hours, but I can gladly report that Thunder, although ill at ease the entire time, did remain on her perch. For the record, having my exposed hand and arm in the cage had me ill at ease too. I finished by pouring a couple of gallons of water on the cage floor and through the back of the cage to make it spotless. I gave her a fish and left her alone. She was nearly dried out by the time I left. No more visits today. I was so pleased and even a bit optimistic with a tad of realistic cynicism included. I thought I was a patient person. This would be a good measuring stick for reality.

A milestone had been reached regarding Thunder's adjustment to a new life in captivity. As the days turned into weeks, she became much easier to work with in her small cage. Cleaning was never a problem, and bathing was more regular with her than with some humans I have encountered. She was still shy and always did her threat display when I first approached her cage. Nick, my white cat, was also much more adjusted to the shared space. While he wasn't as spooked as he once was, he did not roam around but would hang around me while I was sitting at Thunder's cage.

With each passing day, things had improved, and her wounds were no longer noticeable. By now, we had almost developed a relationship of sorts. When I was cleaning her cage, she had grown so accustomed to my routine that she didn't even pay any attention to me. I would even walk away from her cage to grab something while leaving the cage partially open. She was no longer stressed. As long as she had her food and water, she seemed content.

Chapter 7

April Fools' and Counting

It was April 1, 1993, and Thunder had spent a hundred days in this cage. I believed it was about time to be thinking of where she went next and when. I spoke with others from the center, and they agreed with me that before she was put into a flight cage, it might be beneficial to introduce her to others while she was in a familiar environment. I felt completely new surroundings and new faces, plus the instant splash of nature and its sounds and movements, might be a bit overwhelming.

I decided on the location for her flight cage, and we even had a chain-link fence company that would donate the materials. Remember, this bird would never fly again. The tip of the left wing that contained all the primary flight feathers was now missing, and not unlike an amputated hand, the wing would not grow back either. This cage only had to facilitate her need for healthy exercise. The birds with injured wings that we rehabilitated with the hopes of releasing were initially housed in similar cages. The natural instinct of all these birds was to get as high as they can. We would place perches high with lower ones until a bird could use the higher perches, sort of like ladders, to climb to the top. They would be placed so as to require the bird to use its wings to assist reaching that next lever. It was simple to get them down—just put their food on the ground level of the cage. They'll come after it on their own. But Thunder wasn't quite ready for the new cage yet.

This same day, I was in Thunder's cage, cleaning. The door was open more than halfway. Nick, the cat, was in a particularly frisky mood, running back and forth in front of the cage and then back behind me. At one point, I removed the cleaning rag from the cage and had dropped it into the water bucket. Just as I did this, Nick jumped onto my right shoulder from behind and took one small leap for cat-kind right into Thunder's cage.

I reached into the cage as quickly as possible to rescue Nick from a no-win situation. But before I did, my mind was conjuring up all these bloody scenarios, none of which would have a good ending. I snatched and scooped up Nick, and an instant later, he was out of the cage and safely on the floor. When I looked back toward Thunder, she was giving me a look as if to say, "What's the big deal?" Nick seemed to project the same sentiments.

After I got my wits back, I realized that had I not snatched Nick from there, nothing might have happened. They both seemed totally indifferent toward each other. I did not expect one to attack the other, but I did think that with the sudden move into the cage, Nick would at least send Thunder into a panicked retreat in a place where there was no room to retreat, nothing but indifference. I believe it only because I saw it, but to this day, I still don't understand it. I guess Nick and Thunder had been spending more quality time together than I had realized.

Chapter 8

Freedom at Last or the "Great Escape"

During the first weeks of April 1993, I arranged for several controlled visits by other humans. At the time, it seemed that she responded to each visitor in a way that likely indicated her mood the time of the visit. Later, I would find out that was not the case, at least not with this bird.

Sometimes she was extremely calm and quiet, while other visitors caused quite a stir that always began with her open-mouthed nasal squawking. It almost sounded like a snort but generated from an exhale and not an inhale. It was one of those sounds you needed to hear for yourself to fully appreciate it. But it would not likely be identified as a normal vocalization made by a bald eagle had you never heard it before. For that matter, the normal vocalizations of a bald eagle would not be recognized by 99 percent of our population. On television, when an eagle makes a call, it is a dubbed red-tailed hawk call.

The following weekend, we had guests at our house, and among them was a young lady in her mid-to late twenties. Cindy was definitely a city girl, and she would even "yuck" at the possibility of stepping on an ant. Walking on grass was even an unnatural act for her. Birds flying too near her would drive her back inside. She was a nice person but a bit out of touch with nature and all its offerings. As a result of this information, I was very surprised that Cindy had an interest in even seeing

Thunder. There were three visitors, and I explained the object of the visitation was a form of conditioning for Thunder more than for them to see her, but that could be a worthwhile secondary mission. I also explained that the visit could be cut very short depending on her response to the small group. They understood. I asked them to give me about twenty minutes to get her warmed up to the idea. I would go down and spend time cleaning her cage so a visit wouldn't be quite so overwhelming.

I went down and began my routine with the water, rag, and extender. She was fine with it. I left the rag on the cage floor and stepped away from the cage to get my notepad ready for visitor observations. I had left the door about half open, and as I turned back toward the cage (I was only five feet from it), Thunder hopped down from her perch, out the door, and onto the floor. There we stood, each in amazed wonderment, asking, "What now?"

Believe it or not, she seemed very nonchalant about the entire escape . . . or did she think I was releasing her? I took a small slow step toward her, and she ran like a turkey with long strides right past me toward the back of the garage. She went back to my workbench, flapped once, jumped, and was on top of the bench. I sort of herded her on around, continuing the counterclockwise direction. She was on the floor now as she ran past the stairs and once again flapped her giant wings, which put her to rest atop my golf bag. She just sat there.

I paused and waited for her next move, wondering about my next move to get her back into the cage. She stayed put. Since I didn't have a capture plan yet, I thought I'd go upstairs and tell my guests that the visit was off. As I got to the stairs, I assumed she would move farther away. Again, I was wrong. She held her ground and a grip on the golf bag cover. I walked up the steps to within four feet of her as she watched.

I told everyone that we would not be able to go downstairs since she was sitting on my golf bag like a century. The one lady, the one who hated all forms of nature, said she wanted to see her. Something about the way she asked made me believe that she really did want to see. I said okay and then slowly opened the door. I wasn't sure where Thunder might be. As I cracked open the door and looked down, she was still sitting in the same place. I let her look. She asked if she could go down the steps.

I thought about this one. My first thought was that it was potentially too dangerous. My second thought was that neither the bird nor the girl seemed unsure about the situation at hand. I decided I would let her begin down the steps and see what reaction was generated. She walked down two steps and sat down. She did this on her own, and that's what I would have done too. She sat for a second, speaking to Thunder in a soft reassuring voice. Then she moved down another step without standing. Again, she waited a bit and then moved down two more steps, paused, and moved down another two. I was still motionless at the top of the steps with the door open. I thought she had gone far enough, but Thunder was extremely calm, as though she were all alone. Cindy had her feet on the third step up from the floor.

Before I could say anything, she confessed that this was far enough. I agreed. I stood above them both and observed the interaction or the lack of it. There could have been some nonvisual interaction that I could not perceive. Needless to say, Cindy was almost at eye level with Thunder, who was still sitting on top of my golf bag. That would put her head at nearly six feet and Cindy, sitting on the fifth step, at about forty inches plus about another three feet from the step she was sitting on to her eye level. Everyone was relaxed, almost too much so.

Then the unexpected happened. In one motion, Thunder hopped down from the bag to the floor directly in front of the stairs and, in the same instant, hopped onto the bottom step—just two steps below Cindy's feet. Her head was at or above the height of Cindy's feet, which were definitely within her reach. Cindy did not flinch during the entire episode. She seemed to enjoy it, and Thunder . . . well, honestly, I still haven't an idea what she had in mind, unless it was nothing more complex than simple curiosity.

After thirty seconds or so, Cindy backed up one step while still sitting. Then Thunder moved up one step, and then Cindy followed, and then Thunder again until Cindy was now sitting on the landing at the top of the stairs. Thunder was still only two steps below her feet. I had moved back into the hallway, and then Cindy got up and backed through the doorway. As we were closing the door, Thunder hopped onto the landing that Cindy had just left.

Where did she think she was going? To this day, I still haven't a clue why she would put herself into a dead end like this. Granted, it was higher than any surrounding places, but the stairwell had closed sides above halfway.

The door was closed, and I thought the episode was over, but Cindy did not agree. She lay on her stomach and cracked open the door. There, just inches away, was Thunder, staring back. The door was cracked open so slightly that Thunder could not have gotten her beak through it. Cindy was in heaven, really enjoying whatever they were having together. And I would be the first to admit that Thunder had come a long way over the past 133 days, but this was an unexpected surprise. Maybe there was some hope for our relationship yet.

I asked Cindy if she wanted to help me get Thunder back in the cage. She gave me a look like "Sure, but what can I do to help?" I asked her to entertain Thunder while I went into the garage from outside, turned off the lights on the steps, climbed the stairs with a blanket in front of me, dropped it over Thunder, and snatched her up. We did it, and it worked as planned.

Since I had her secured, I wanted to take advantage of the situation and get her current weight. To do this, we just put the bird and blanket into a large box and put it on the scales. I recorded the weight of everything, and then I removed Thunder and put her back in her cage. I then weighed the box and blanket and determined that Thunder's weight was now just one ounce greater than when she was last weighed on December 21, 1992. Her weight today was twelve pounds and one ounce—perfect.

She would only be in her small rehabilitation cage for about another week. That would make her one year old plus a few days when she got to move into her new flight cage. She would have spent 140 days inside. Her hatch date was calculated from her banding information to be about April 28, 1992. She was scheduled to go outside on May 10, 1993. She had already established a fairly regular diet of mostly fish. I have been fortunate enough to be able to get trout from the hatcheries plus other fish such as carp, bass, bluegills, suckers, and shad from fish surveys where the DNR would conduct aging studies. The fish were sacrificed anyway, so this made good use of them. The larger fish, mainly the ten-to-twenty-pound carp, were good for keeping her beak worn down.

I had been rehabbing raptors for sixteen years, ten of them formally with the WVRRC. On my travels, I would always visit other raptor rehab centers so I could see what they were doing that we might be missing. The two significant things I observed were that a lot of trimming of the beaks and talons was necessary for their long-term patients but especially for the permanent education birds. This was something we never had a problem with, and I quickly discovered the reason. The beak and talons grow sort of like your fingernails do. If you dug in rocks all day, you would likely never need to trim them. If you didn't, as most of us don't, manicuring to some degree will be necessary. It was obvious why raptors at some of the other centers I visited needed their talons trimmed. The perches were far too small for one. Each species would have their own sized perch, but when the bird perched, which was always, they only lie down when incubating eggs or are very ill; the points of the talons, for the most part, hardly ever touch anything. As a result, they would continue to grow and, in some cases, could actually grow back into the bottom of the talon or foot. This would be crippling.

The solution is to select perches more of the size each species might select in the wild.

At one rehab center, they were actually boasting about the fact that they did pedicures for their birds. Not being very nice, I suppose, I asked if they had many wild birds come in to have their talons done. Then I did explain that we simply used larger perches wrapped with rope. The size allowed the talons to wear and self-sharpen naturally, and the rope made it virtually impossible for them to sit in exactly the same spot, which could provide a constant pressure point on one spot on the foot pad. If this happened, a bad case of bumblefoot could possibly occur. It was often not curable, and in extreme cases, the birds had to be put down. Fortunately for our birds, we have never had a case of bumblefoot develop. The perches get all the credit.

The beaks are a different story. Rope won't keep the beaks worn down, but the right kind of food that contains bones and other materials like the hides of mammals will. Diet is important to rehabilitating birds anyway, so if natural food is available, that's the winning ticket.

CHAPTER 9

Thunder Moves Out

It was finally going to happen. I would get my garage back today. Oh yes, and Thunder was moving to her flight cage. The cage was ready. One long perch went entirely across the width of the cage. At about the midway point, another perch was connected to the main perch at ninety degrees and ran to the back wall of the cage, where it was attached. Since she couldn't really fly with the shortened wing, it would be tormenting her to have perch systems she could only look at. The main perch was about four and a half feet off the ground. This was too high for her to fly to from the ground, so another perch a bit over two feet high was placed in front of the main perch. She could hop and fly to this perch and from here to the main one.

All perches were wrapped with half-inch hemp rope. The diameter of her perches was about five inches. The cage itself was an inch-and-a-half chain link. I custom-made a top using netting and one-inch PVC pipe bent from back to front to form an arch, making the cage almost two feet higher. I covered the back down to within one and a half feet from the ground. The sides were covered from top to bottom about halfway to the front, and a roof covered the main perch but left the lower perch in the weather. Her pool was placed near the front center of the cage. Bald eagles spent a good deal of time on rocky or sandy beaches of rivers and lakes, feeding or bathing, so I made the floor of her cage (the technical term is *mew*) with river stone. They are smooth but range in size, from a standard marble up to four inches in diameter. Everything, including me, was ready. Thunder might not yet have been aware of it, but she was ready too. The question now was to see if she was aware of it.

I thought it would be nice if I just called her and she would come. That would likely never happen, so I went back to the garage and rounded up my box to transport her the sixty yards to the cage. We transport birds, wild ones, in cardboard boxes. This was the safest way to carry them. Some people brought us injured birds in wire bird cages. The wire in the closed space just shredded feathers of active birds. It was also dark, which helped keep them calm.

The box was ready, and I had a large blanket set up above the front of her cage. My plan was to open the door, stand back, and let her come out on her own. I didn't want to fight her in the cage. It might leave a bad last impression, plus if she struggled, which she would, it would be likely she would injure her bad left wing. The tip had healed wonderfully, but running it over a cheese grater would likely open it up.

Once she hopped out, I hoped she would pause for a second or two before deciding where to go. If this happened, I would lower the blanket I had stretched over a six-by-six-foot square area. It was suspended about five feet high and looked like an extended porch roof. She jumped from the cage, and if I had had an X marking the spot, she would have hit it. She paused, and I let go of the ropes. Lights out—and she didn't even flinch. I scooped her up and put her in the box. Again, I weighed the box and contents.

I took her to the new cage, set the box on its side, and opened the end of the box, and *bam*, she was out. I'll never forget the look of "Where am I, and what's going on?" rattled but not panicked. I had a hold of the box, pulled it away from her, and made my exit. I closed the door and affixed the safety latch for the first of what would be thousands of times. She had already eaten for the day, and her pool was clean and full of fresh water. The rest of the day was for her to explore the new surroundings and likely get a good wing stretch in.

It was late morning, and she still had plenty of sun in the cage too. I went back to the house, where I could observe without disturbing her. By the time I got back to my observation post, she had already made her way onto the lower perch and was looking like she very much wanted to be on the next level. She would sort of squat with her wings partially opened, but she didn't have the confidence she could make it. After several more fake attempts, she jumped to the ground, repositioned herself, facing the lower perch from about a forty-five-degree angle, flapped once more, and was on the lower perch. She immediately turned to face the upper perch, flapped those giant wings three times, and was proudly sitting on the upper perch. She had the cage under control.

Now that she seemed relatively comfortable, my concern was directed to things that went bump in the night: dogs, other birds like crows, and even the possibility of humans. Her cage was well hidden. It had evergreens partway along the upper side and all along the back and lower sides. It was nestled in an evergreen corner with a few black cherry and walnut trees sprinkled along the edge, with native dogwoods making up a good portion of the understory. It was a nice habitat for a cage but not what I would call ideal bald-eagle habitat. That didn't matter as long as she felt secure.

The remainder of the evening passed quietly, and her first night out, so to speak, had just begun. In early May, it stayed light for a while, but I still had work time after dark. I thought this would be a good time to clean things up in the garage and get the cage moved outside. I went into the garage, and there was Nick, in Thunder's cage. He was meowing and walking around in the cage. I moved him out and told him if he stayed around, he would get a bath. I turned on the hose and started cleaning. Just like the old Nick he was, he went to the steps, out of harm's way, and watched me clean. It didn't take long, and you would find it difficult to believe that a messy bald eagle had just spent 140 days in there. The place was always clean. The rubber made it so easy. I got the cage outside and moved a car in, and then Nick and I called it a night.

The next morning, there were crows in the trees around Thunder's cage. I watched her closely with binoculars. She couldn't care less. I thought about chasing them away, but my plan was to not go to Thunder's cage until later today if at all. My plan was to work with her more on dimly lit days and early in the evenings. I had already determined that she was much calmer in dim light. I looked in on her from the house several times. All appeared fine.

In the morning, I went to the garage to go somewhere, and there was Nick, still confused by the changes that had taken place. He was as disturbed as when Thunder had first appeared but now seemed like he was having trouble accepting the status quo. I ignored him, jumped in the vehicle, and drove off.

I was gone about an hour, and when I pulled into the driveway, I glanced to my right, where Thunder's cage was located. I stopped abruptly, not believing my eyes. Nick was all stretched out against the front door of Thunder's cage. Thunder was on her upper perch, as calm as she could be. *What was the cat doing there?* I wondered. Cats liked fish. Thunder ate fish, and maybe that was why she hung around her cage in the garage, but Thunder had not had a fish in this cage yet—strange but curious. In most cases, cats and birds make unlikely companions, except for dinner, of course. Nick had no hopes of ever eating Thunder, and she obviously wasn't threatened by Nick as evidenced by the trip Nick took in her cage a while back.

I never figured out the attraction, but spring, summer, winter, and fall, Nick spent a great deal of time with Thunder until about a year later when he died. I assume there must have been a developed relationship during the time they shared the garage. I'll never know for sure because Thunder was not talking and Nick took the secret to his grave.

I spent countless hours working with Thunder. That's not really true because I was counting. Training with a plan, a very loose plan, had begun, but I knew that before long, I would need a more significant and strategic plan of action. I spent time in the cage changing water, cleaning up, and just sharing her space. I was never afraid of her but had more than a healthy respect for her. Even after all this time, she continued her threat display and squawk when I approached the cage. She was still off-limits to others except from a distance.

I offered her food by hand every time I fed her. I would tear or cut off a small piece of fish to try to get her to eat from my hand. Sometimes it seemed she wanted the food, but the risk seemed greater than the reward. I knew from reading that this battle could be easily won by me. All I would need to do was to not feed her for several days. If someone were to withhold food from me for a long enough period, then I too might do most anything they might ask of me. I wasn't asking Thunder to do anything horrendous, and I had no intention of trying to break the spirit of an American bald eagle, our national emblem and symbol of freedom, strength, and spirit. If I was to develop a relationship, I wanted it to be one of mutual respect and not fear or a forced sense of dependency. I wanted her to always be the free spirit that the bald eagle symbolized. I wanted to know that the only reason I had her was because she would never be able to be turned loose to fly free again. And I wanted to keep her spirit as wild as it was when she came to us, knowing that if she could ever be turned loose, she would be a free wild bird with all the character she had the day she was shot.

I had respect for Thunder, plain and simple. Many will disagree, but our years of experience show that respect, whether training horses or bald eagles, yields great long-term results. A very good friend of mine owns a lot of horses, and is equally knowledgeable about their care, both physical and emotional.

In the horse world, he says there are two methods to train a horse. You can use the "cowboy method," which is to get on the horse and ride it until it breaks, or the "join-up method," where time is taken to maintain the spirit of the horse while developing a mutual respect between man and horse. Fear in any animal can be dangerous, be it horse, dog, or bald eagle. Everyone has heard of fear biting dogs, but I have never heard of respect biting dogs.

We would continue down the road of mutual respect. After just a few months with hardly any noticeable results, it appeared this road would be a long one. She still appeared to dislike me, but there hadn't yet been any acts of aggression on either of our parts. Just remembering handling her those first three weeks was reminder enough that if she were to attack, there would be serious injuries inflicted. When I was in the cage with her, she remained calm. She kept an eye on me, and I was careful not to introduce any new items to the cage too quickly. For instance, I raked her cage periodically. The first time I introduced the rake with a long handle, she really flipped out. I retreated and slowly, with the handle in a lower position, brought the rake inside. That effort made no difference to her. I removed the handle entirely and tried again. She still didn't like it but decided to settle with the lesser invasion.

I tried to create routines that she could trust. For instance, every feeding was preceded with the hose turned on to refill and clean her pool. I had it fixed to the cage so I didn't have to do anything but turn the water on. She liked the sound of splashing and running water. She had been exposed to that multiple times every day while she was inside. I also always brought her food to her in a gallon Ziploc bag. She would look at it as if to see if there was ever anything different. Sometimes there was fish other than trout, and a rat was thrown into the mix from time to time. She seemed more calm with me in her cage but still not calm enough to eat in my immediate presence.

As our days and weeks flew by, there were several observations that were made with this bird. This might be a great time to make a qualified disclaimer, that being, "All the information I repeat here and observations I make apply exclusively to this one bald eagle and may or may not apply to any other bald eagle." I say this and do mean it, but I also believe there will be observations made over the years that likely apply to most if not all bald eagles, but no one else has made the same observations. I will begin with a few seemingly insignificant observations.

All that I do with my training strategy is to apply the "what if" this-or-that principle and try to guess what direction to take. Now this is a simple and obvious statement, but consider that your selected next action may well be predicated on your last action. Everyone should know that. After all, there are over six billion humans, of whom all had, at one time or another, been juveniles. We have lots of experience with child psychology and millions of books that have resulted from millions of studies. The same cannot be said of bald eagles. In fact, even though this is our national symbol, there has been almost no research done on it. Why? Because there is no money to fund this type of research.

I would guess—and this is an educated guess based on personal experiences—that all original research on bald eagles could be packaged and put in boxes that would easily fit in a cargo van. The same original research on, say, African lions or white-tailed deer would require its own library. The reason is money, plain and simple. As I said earlier, what I say here applies to Thunder, but I'm willing to bet it applies to a whole bigger sample size than that. So some of the things you'll read here will be directly contrary to things you may have heard or read. Just because it is or was written doesn't make it the gospel.

I have an old Boy Scouts publication that shows that hummingbirds migrate riding on the backs of larger birds, maybe in the olden days but not today. I also have an official government publication from the U.S. Department of

Agriculture that specifically states that research conducted on the multiflora rose shows that it is the perfect plant to make living fence lines. It is self-sustaining and doesn't need repair or replacement like traditional barbed wire does, and it will not spread. If you are from an area in the east, you likely know just how it does spread, and it does not stay in the fence line. The official statements were made with little or no practical research and the application of little or no common sense. Had they really conducted any real research, they would have found that the plant produces berries, and birds eat these berries. After the digestive process, the undigested seed of the fruit will likely be deposited some distance from the plant where it was consumed. If the farmer had planted the seeds of this plant and it grew, it is nearly a sure thing that at least some of the randomly dropped seeds will germinate on that farm and likely grow there as well. And it did indeed. The only factual part of this is that it makes a good fence—well, at least cattle will not walk through it.

So here goes my first observation. Bald eagles aren't disturbed by sound, even loud sounds, but they can see, and they do that quite well. At least I think they do . . . but how sure are we? For example, I understand that vultures have a very keen sense of smell. They can follow the scent of carrion for miles and find a decaying carcass. I have seen decaying carcasses in wooded areas that are not found by nearby vultures. This may just be a coincidence, but I often wonder, if I were to place a deer carcass in a large open field and construct a roof of sticks and branches about four feet above it but block its view from all angles from above, would they still find it? I'm not sure. My point is that during my time with these birds and Thunder, I and lots of others have made numerous observations regarding behavior and physical characteristics that seem to differ from things we had been previously led to believe. More of these observations will be addressed as the story continues.

Chapter 10

Thunder Receives Other Human Guests

It was early fall, and by now, Thunder had received many guests. All whom I knew about were quite controlled. People would visit her, and she would squawk. The closer they came, the louder she protested. But her protests did not seem to include children. In fact, she didn't care in the least if a five-year-old approached her cage alone. Strange—the child was a moving object, and something moving is something moving . . . so it would seem.

One day a little boy who had visited before was wearing a red jacket. Again, he was allowed to lead the group and say hi to Thunder while the adults stayed back. He and all visitors were only allowed to go to a yellow rope I had up as a boundary. It was about fifteen feet from her cage. This day, before he was anywhere near the rope, Thunder squawked first, but as he continued to approach the rope boundary, she flew in a panic into the side of her cage and finally to the ground. I got the boy to retreat quickly, but the damage was done. Thunder had been scared more severely than she had been since being in this cage. I was puzzled, but she had never had this reaction to this little guy, who had visited many times. The only difference I could see was the red jacket.

It was cool but not cold, so I asked his dad and mom if he could remove the jacket and try again. They said okay, but the little guy was reluctant. I convinced him that he and Thunder would both be okay. Again, he moved toward the cage, but he hesitated somewhat. I didn't really blame him, but he really did like Thunder. He got to the rope, and Thunder didn't move.

He turned and said, "I don't think she likes my red jacket, Mike."

I asked him to come back, and then I gave him the jacket to carry in one hand as he returned for the third time. He walked four or five steps from us toward her, and she began to squawk. He asked if he should stop, and I told him to take a few more steps. After three more steps, I asked him to please stop. Thunder was about ready to go ballistic on us again. I asked him to put his jacket down and continue walking. He went to the yellow line without the jacket, and Thunder was as calm as she could be. We repeated the same sequence, and he got to the same spot and had to drop his jacket again. He came back to us, and I told him he could put his jacket back on. He said he promised that he wouldn't wear his red jacket when visiting Thunder anymore.

About that time, there was a loud ear-ringing boom that came from nearby. We all jumped. Thunder didn't react at all. A few seconds later, there was another and then a third boom. Thunder never flinched once. It was a neighbor that lived about 150 yards from me who was sighting in a deer rifle. He wasn't aware that this was the first of many examples where sounds didn't faze Thunder at all, but red jackets sure did.

She also had a great fear of hats and glasses. I figured that out but not the red. This went on for over five years before I finally got her used to red. The hats and glasses, I think, were a fear response we taught her in those first twenty-one days we had her. Remember, we wore hard hats with face shields every time we handled her. It took a really long time to get over those two fears, but she did finally. After these observations of her behavioral preferences were identified, I would not let anyone near, within twenty feet or so, if they had a hat or glasses on. Usually, they would kindly remove them if possible.

The slow training continued, but I was still getting squawked at every time I approached her cage. I would always talk to her, not that I figured she cared, but if this could possibly be a small part of her recognizing me, the effort would be worth it. I had a daily routine, and lots of time seemed to be spent with little results. I wasn't all that concerned though because things did seem to be going in the right direction.

One day it was cooler than normal in early October, and I had on a pair of camouflaged coveralls. I had Thunder's fish in tow and was strolling toward her, talking as I went. When I got about thirty feet from her cage, her squawking grew more intense, and she finally flew into the side of the cage. I turned to see what could have caused this reaction but saw nothing. The closer I got, the more violently she reacted. I quickly backed away, figuring I was doing something. The only thing I could figure was the coveralls. The bird definitely recognized me when I approached. She probably even knew my stride, but something was making her react to me the same way she did to any stranger who came too close. I ducked out of sight behind one of the evergreens that bordered her cage, and she instantly calmed down.

The coveralls, I thought. I removed them and walked into her sight, and she was as calm as though nothing had happened. I left my coveralls on the ground and entered her cage, and we conducted business as usual. All this time, I thought I wasn't getting anywhere with her, but I was at least beginning to understand her—so I egotistically thought.

Another twist to the story began with the realization that my once-excellent eyesight was no longer what it once was. It wasn't bad, but the ophthalmologist determined that I had an astigmatism in my right eye, and the left was a bit farsighted. I wanted to wear contacts instead of glasses, especially since working with Thunder at this critical juncture might cause major setbacks with the glasses. I got my contacts, but since they were tiny gas-permeated ones, I needed to practice wearing them for short periods.

It took about a week of "in again, out again" before I got the go-ahead to wear them full time. So one morning in mid-November 1993, I got up, put my new contacts in, and headed toward Thunder's cage. At the time, the only aberration here was the new contacts in my eyes. As I entered, there was no problem, but as soon as I glanced up and we made eye contact, she flushed off her perch as though she was frightened by something. I looked around and saw nothing anywhere. She was still clinging to the cage in a panic. All I could think of was my new contact lenses, which were only half the size of a dime and almost clear. I turned my back to Thunder and removed my six-hundred-dollar contacts and held them securely in my hand. I turned and faced her, and she became calm. I turned around again and replaced the contacts in my eyes. This time, when I turned around, I tried to avoid eye contact with her. I stayed in the cage for an extended period, giving her an occasional glance. When we made eye contact, she reacted adversely, but as soon as I turned away, she would relax. When I left the cage, I made a point to position myself about twenty feet from her and then make eye contact. She could still see them but reacted much less.

I stayed in that area until almost dark, looking at her from time to time. I would often do it while I was moving laterally. This seemed to have less of an adverse impact on her. Once again, my vanity got the best of me as I thought I had won this standoff by simply enduring the cold evening air in an attempt to get her used to seeing me with the contacts. It was actually just short of twenty years later that we determined that it wasn't my "stand my ground attitude" that relaxed her to my new eye ware. It was that we determined that all non-owl raptors have a significant decrease in their ability to see or judge objects moving perpendicular to their perched or flying direction. This will be addressed later in much more detail.

So the next day, I strutted out to her cage, wearing my new invisible sight correctors. As I got closer to her, she was definitely studying me. I knew this because I was studying her at the same time. This meant eye contact, which, in her case, meant danger. She started moving from perch to perch but did not fly away from them. She was disturbed but not violently like yesterday. She still didn't trust that I was really me. In this case, the "eyes" had it. I tried to go about my chores without making eye contact. I even managed to hand her a trout without raising my eyes toward her. Before I left, I made a point to make eye contact as I was backing out the gate. She started to bate (fly) from the perch, but I turned my head in time to reduce the pressure; she didn't bate this time. After I was a distance from the cage, I turned and faced her again. She was agitated again but only enough to let me know she still didn't trust the new eyes. I told her I was sorry about the contacts, but she was going to have to get used to them, another adjustment we both had to make.

CHAPTER 11

Depression Creeps into Training Camp

I never wanted to do anything to stress her out, but since the day she was brought to us, it was unavoidable to save her life. This stress was drastic and harsh, but the alternative for her would have been death or perpetual sedation. This is a free-spirited wild bald eagle we are talking about here, and the stress she had to endure was tiny considering the alternative. Me, on the other hand—well, I chose to stress myself out for the long-term sake of this particular bird's future well-being. I knew she could never be turned back into the wild, so her future would be best spent helping other bald eagles and other wild creatures from suffering the same fate she did. It was at about this point on the timeline that I decided the direction of our mutual fates.

I was approaching the end of my first year of working with Thunder, and I asked myself, *Is this all the progress I have made? Was I going to have to deal with such things as new contact lenses or a different change of clothes like the coveralls for the rest of our lives?* I had to make a choice. Would I be able to commit enough of my life to this bird's future well-being to be fair to this magnificent creature, or should I throw in the towel and turn her over to a zoo, where she would end her days as little more than a visual object to be admired or just casually glanced at by the passing masses? I was glad I had thought about it in this way. My mind was made up, even though I realized that Thunder still had stress to deal with and likely always would. But I also realized when thinking back on situations with the contact lenses or the coveralls that while she didn't yet trust that person, she was beginning to trust me, the real me without the contacts or the coveralls. Everything and everyone has to deal with stress in their lives, but I was determined to make every effort to minimize Thunder's stress levels while ensuring she maintained a high quality of life. Although she would never again be able to soar thousands of feet into the sky, she still deserved a quality life. At that point, I dedicated myself to ensuring she would have the best life a flightless bald eagle could have.

The days of November grew colder and shorter. I still spent lots of time with her but was not yet able to formulate what I considered the perfect plan. I would still offer food bits by hand, wondering too what I would do if she decided to take it from me. Could I resist flinching? Doubtful. Perhaps the time I was spending with her was not so much to acclimate her to me but perhaps more the other way. Respect is earned, and to this point, she had done very little to instill trust to that degree. What if she missed? Would I be shy a finger or two? I think that this was part of the learning process. If I were to withhold food from her using "operant conditioning," the "reward system" technique, I would only learn the obvious—hungry things will do what is necessary to survive. If certain actions will quell this hunger, well, then why not play the game? I just wondered how much will and spirit would remain after this seemingly heavy taxation.

Just as a side note, though, I still have all my fingers, eyes, and ears. I also kept trying to handfeed her. By late November, she was so accustomed to sharing her space with me that she would sometimes almost ignore me. All I would need to do to change that behavior or flip the light switch was to move toward her with an extended appendage. I never jerked my arm out toward her as the simplest movement in that direction caused an avoidance-type response. She wouldn't leave her perch, but she would draw back in preparation of doing so. There must still be strong memories from almost a year ago when we were physically handling her during her medical treatment. I'm certain that had a huge impact, along with her natural wild instincts. But I continued to try to befriend her with trout treats.

Then one day she seemed to be in a less aggressive and distrusting mood. She still addressed me with mild disrespect when I approached her cage. I cut off a small quarter-sized piece of fish. The quarter size really was small, relatively speaking. I later found out that she could swallow a ten-inch trout whole. I stood as close to her as possible when I was tearing the fish. It was difficult to tear fish with your bare hands. I always used a knife to cut it, but she was not trusting me with a knife in hand. Maybe she saw the person use a knife to cut off her dangling wing when she was found. I can't say for sure either way. So since the view of the knife disturbed her, I had started to do just a small slice with the knife while I had my back to her. Then I would turn and rip a piece off. Sometimes I would only get the meat with the skin still hanging on to the fish. It seemed to disturb her less, seeing me rip at the fish. Maybe it too mimicked the way she tore fish. I didn't really believe this, but then can anyone say for sure what she does and doesn't think? My attitude concerning her thought processes was wide open. It seemed like, in the past, every time I had made an assumption based on I don't know what, I ended up being wrong. I still throw out all the what-ifs I formulate, but I know that more often than not, disappointment looms right around the corner. I didn't quit though, maybe because of the old saying I heard somewhere: "The more you know, the more you know you don't know." That definitely held true for this bird. But I continued to try to strengthen what trust she did have in me.

I offered her the fish piece slowly but deliberately. I held it about a foot from and below her beak. It was definitely within reach. I held it motionless for quite a while with no response. She was watching. I rolled it in my fingers, and she seemed a bit more interested, so much so that she began to slowly smack her beak together and salivate as well. According to Pavlov's study with dogs, it appeared that she was drooling with anticipation. At that, I decided to, for once, quit while I was ahead. I put the piece of fish beside her on the perch and set the other fish next to it. Both were about three feet from her. That was the first line drawn in the sand that I had to respect.

Chapter 12

The Change from Feasting to Fasting

Her first Thanksgiving in captivity was approaching. As a special gesture, I gave her the classically wrapped and stuffed turkey parts. I also included the neck. I had no idea what her reaction, if any, would be. As usual, the food was taken to her inside a gallon-sized Ziploc bag. As I approached, she had an unfamiliar look on her face. She knew this was something different but wasn't adversely concerned. She seemed curious. When I got to her cage, the water had already been turned on, so she had her soothing sounds of a waterfall to accompany her curiosity. First, I removed the gizzard and heart and placed them on the perch to her right. When I removed the long, almost meatless neck, her interest was piqued even more. Her expression now seemed one more of interest than curiosity. Perhaps this was the day for advancement. I slowly extended the neck toward her, this time even closer than the twelve inches. Her mouth was watering even more this time. I held it only briefly and then placed it on the perch. I backed away, but she still would not yield her sovereignty. I left the cage, and I had taken not more than three steps away when she reached over and snatched the neck. I watched over my shoulder as I moved away, and then the crunching of turkey-neck vertebrae began to fill the cold fall air. I was pleased and, from her actions and sounds, would say she was too.

Thanksgiving was over. December started with cold temperatures and some snow. Each day, when it was cold, I needed to dump the frozen block of ice from her pool and refill it. That was the way December started. It also started with fish skins and tails, along with parts of heads being left uneaten. Every day the food fed to her was weighed. Her average consumption for a week usually ran at about nine pounds. That made close to one and a quarter pounds per day. Her feeding schedule was never at a set time in an attempt to mimic her eating habits in the wild. They ate if and when they were hungry and can find food. They are not hoarders other than what they can stuff into their crop. When feeding, they do not likely select by size, and they don't seem to catch what they don't intend to eat.

Thunder's leftovers were also weighed. I'm not certain why I began doing that, especially since there was never much variation to her eating habits for the biggest part of a year now. As the month continued, I kept track of all her leftovers. They were considerable. Her eating habits began to resemble that of a five-year-old: just the meat, mac and cheese, and a glass of milk. Forget the beans, potatoes, salads, and anything else that might be construed as yucky.

As the month moved along, I became concerned. From consuming approximately twenty ounces a day, she was regularly down to eight to ten ounces. Her behavior was normal. She looked good and was as defensive as ever, but she wasn't eating like she had been for the past eleven months. The days passed, and I avoided the inevitability of weighing her again. This was a monthly routine, one she hated me for doing, but I felt it was necessary considering the possible alternatives. I would wait until it was almost dark, and then I would enter her cage with a large blanket. I had a platform of boards and a digital scale sitting on it. I preweighed the box and blanket. I would, as quickly and cleanly as possible, drop the blanket over her, scoop her up, and put her into the box. I was, of course, wearing my own protection in the form of heavy gloves. I would grab the box and put it on the scale and off again just as quickly. To date, she had always weighed within an ounce of twelve pounds.

Today was the one-year anniversary of her being here with me. I didn't like what I was about to see. I subtracted the weight of the box, gloves, and blanket from the total, and her net weight was now ten pounds and two ounces. That was a significant weight loss, close to 16 percent in twenty-two days.

I talked to the veterinarian, and we set a time to meet at his office. I assured him that the weight was correct and her behavior, except for the amount she was eating, seemed normal. We met and did an exam but not until he had confirmed her correct weight. It was correct. He checked for obvious things, including parasites, took blood samples, and poked and prodded down her throat. The test results were back in about three days, and they showed nothing abnormal.

I weighed her again on January 1, 1994, and her weight was at an even ten pounds, still eating but high-grading like a five-year-old. We waited and watched—nothing new. Food consumption remained down almost 50 percent, behavior just the same. She might have been a bit more annoyed with me because of the extra handling, but that was understandable and not even that obvious.

January snows and freezing weather came and stayed, as did the growing pile of ice accumulating not far from her cage. I desperately wanted to check her weight at midmonth, but the veterinarian and I decided that since everything had come back negative and she exhibited normal behavior, it might be as well to avoid the extra stress.

When the end of January rolled around, eating remained unchanged. I couldn't wait to weigh Thunder. I did, and now she weighed eleven pounds. She was still eating at the reduced rate, and the month of January had been colder and snowier than normal, but she had somehow gained a full pound. How was this possible?

I am a classic skeptic. If I had read that last entry from someone else, I would have challenged it right off. And I did that very thing. This was some sort of aberration, I thought, that could have been caused by any number of unidentifiable situations. I pored over past notes. The veterinarian and I looked at the lab work from late December. There was nothing we could recognize. This was, remember, a bird that was just under two years of age. Maybe this was part of the answer.

For those of you who wonder or are just nonbelievers, I want to help you save some time by skipping ahead. Thunder has repeated this same eating phenomenon year after year, including 2012. The only change might be a small gain in her weight over the past twenty years. She, however, doesn't like to discuss either her age or her weight. Every year after Thanksgiving, she begins the same "picky eater" behavior. Nothing changes but her weight, where she loses those two pounds almost exactly every year in the month of December and gains one pound back during January while consuming the same reduced diet. Normal eating resumes in early February. Here's what I think might be happening, and I'm not certain any testing can prove or disprove this theory.

If you are at home and someone says, "Would you go get a gallon of milk, please?" your brain immediately tells you where the milk supply is located and even the shelf it sits on, not a problem within your home range. Now pick a vacation place you had never previously visited and then go get that milk. You will no doubt be successful eventually, but the process is far more deliberate and requires more time to actually get your hands on the milk. That is understandable; after all, you are in a strange place, out of your home range.

So with the birds that grow up in one area and eventually abandon their nesting home range and migrate to other locations during the postnesting periods, nature could have evolved a metabolism that changes during those lean and migratory times. Perhaps millions of years ago, the only birds that survived these leaner times were the ones that could adapt. All these changes would have been very gradual, and weather changes could have easily impacted these results as well. I'm not even saying that this is common among all raptors, let alone all bird species. I can only say that the WVRRC experienced it with two long-term residential education birds. One was a wild bird, Thunder, and the other an imprinted red-tailed hawk, Annie, whom we had for over twenty-five years. The smaller red-tailed hawk didn't experience weight losses as great as Thunder did, but the percentage of weight loss was approximately the same. Again, this may be characteristic of no other birds in the world, but I doubt it. It makes one wonder, at least this one.

Spring was on the horizon, and I was ready for those longer and warmer days. Thunder seemed to enjoy the cold, and her feline friend, Nick, still visited. Some days he would be lying on the snow by Thunder's cage door, curled up with his long snow-white hair, barely visible unless he moved. He seldom moved except for his tail, which he would twitch from time to time. I really regret that I never took pictures or videos during these many years, but in the beginning, the technology was far inferior to today's. I had the technology to do photos. In fact, my curiosity of the birds with respect to the direction the sun was shining was brought to my attention via photography. My camera equipment was not small and compact. Thunder didn't like it from when we were inside my garage until the present day. Today she is much more tolerant of most cameras, excluding shoulder-mounted television cameras and those on tripods. My problem and the main concern for a number of years, especially in the first one, was to try to make a frightened bird less frightened. The photos and even videos would have been wonderful, but her temperament forced me to make the choice I did. I only regret not being able to share some of the special moments that could have been better described with film—video, in particular.

It was early spring, and my inherited sidekick, Nick the cat, passed away. He lived a long, interesting, and healthy life. I've never know any cat that seemingly befriended a wild bald eagle. In the end, his heart just stopped. His secrets or insights about Thunder, if there were any, were never shared with me, at least in a form I could translate. This was a seemingly strange association and one I couldn't pry from my mind. The more I dwelled on the reasons this shouldn't happen—because, in large part, cats and birds are normally like oil and water—the more I kept thinking that something was different, and I continued to relentlessly dwell on another possibly unrecognized association.

No new revelations have popped into my head, but I have determined some similarities between the two species. While one is a mammalian predator and the other an avian predictor, this is a characteristic the two of them share. Each are solitary predators and therefore exhibit extreme amounts of patience when stalking or waiting for prey. Most humans would often be heard stating just how much patience they exhibit in their daily lives. Relatively speaking, there may be something to that, but it isn't often someone has to wait patiently for their next attempt at catching their next meal. From birth, we learn ways to minimize the wait—just cry. And humans are social animals, so there is no expectation that the patience a human would exhibit should, by any means, be compared to that of a solitary predator. Humans are more like dogs; they too travel in packs or groups.

Chapter 13

Batter Up

My patience was wearing thin with Thunder's training. It was now almost fifteen months, and we had shared so much together. Unfortunately, what we shared did not include much either of us really wanted to share. Every attempt I made to advance our relationship seemed to come up short. I always thought I had the right ideas, but my presentation was lacking.

Partially out of desperation and also using some deductive reasoning, I decided to acquire a training aid for myself. I needed to understand this attribute of patience that both cat and eagle had in common. So I adopted a stray kitten. I was going to train it and apply what I would learn from that experience over to training Thunder, another exhibit of my good initiative. Whether it resulted in being another poor or good judgment call on my part, for now at least, remained to be seen.

I got the kitten, which was the offspring of a local alley cat. It was just the right age. It had been weaned and was ready to be taken from the mother. We hit it off from the first time I picked her up. I didn't have a cat carrier, and the cute little tiger-striped kitten didn't look like the pet-carrier type, at least not yet. So I took her in hand and hopped into my vehicle. I put her on the floor, but she instantly began to climb up my pants leg and onto my lap. She quickly curled up and went sound to sleep. I think we had an instant bond. She probably would have done it with anyone who picked her up. Maybe so, but my ego needed to believe that she liked me. That would make it easier for both of us.

I had yet another plan. I knew that cats liked to chase things, and kittens loved to play in general. A typical kitten would also like to eat. The veterinarian suggested kitten food. It was the dry variety. My plan was simple, but according to general consensus, cats aren't nearly as bright as dogs. I even believed that, but I had no personal experience with training cats from the kitten stage. Therefore, I had no idea of the degree of difficulty I had undertaken.

After fifteen months of almost no success with a bald eagle, I didn't see how I could be any worse off. I knew I had to start at the very beginning, but I wasn't exactly sure where that was. Most categorized cats as indifferent to their owners as well as to any other humans who might be around. I didn't necessarily believe that to be true, but it did make me question my ability to find that starting point. Granted, they are not dogs, but dogs, unlike cats, are not solitary predators. Dogs are pack animals, and that's just how they hunt. They are naturally social, and the formation of pecking orders is critical to the positioning of all dogs. To an extent, that can be said with multiple cats that occupy the same household. But in the wild, most cats hunt alone and spend most of their time alone. Obvious exceptions are mother cats with kittens, but once they are weaned, they will generally be on their own. Big cats from Africa and the like are the other notable exception since the African lions live and hunt in groups or prides. My cat is alone, with no other cats around.

When I said I had to start at the very beginning, I meant it. Not having a formalized plan completely outlined, I was not going to waste any time getting started. What once was "the kitten" was now named Mitzi, and I had decided to make a baseball player out of her. Since she enjoyed eating very much, I decided we would start with eating stations that I would move around. In fact, I wanted her to eat each meal from different places. I took four very small food bowls and placed them on small square mats on the kitchen floor. The bowls were about two feet apart and arranged in a square, actually in a diamond shape if you stood in the right place.

I put a small amount in one bowl, and as she ate it, I repeated aloud, "One, one, one!" and so on until she finished. Then I put food in the second bowl and repeated, "Two, two, two!" until she finished there. We continued this until we made it through the four feeding stations. When we finished, I collected her bowls, stood up, and walked to the sink. When I turned around, I was looking at the four mats from a different angle. Now instead of looking at a square, I was looking at a diamond. *That's it*, I thought. *I'll teach Mitzi to play baseball.*

For her next feeding, I slightly rearranged the baseball diamond. I used the same four mats, which were now called first, second, and third bases and home plate. I moved them so there was a large area behind the first, second, and third bases. This would serve as the outfield. Now I decided that the objective would be to gradually, step by step, teach her to catch a flying object and drop it on the base I would tell her to go to. I would be throwing a yet undetermined toy that we would call a ball—simple enough. I already had her eating from her four bowls/bases. They would only be referred to from here on as first, second, third, and home. As long as she would be eating from a base, I continue to repeat the name of the base she was eating from. This took a couple of weeks for her to always anticipate which bowl the food would be placed in next.

Until now, I only do them in order, starting from first and ending at home. Just as she would finish the food in one base, I would call out the next base. Then I would not put the food into that bowl until after she started toward it. This was her reward. She had them figured out. The sequence went first, second, third, and home, in that order. She had it down.

Next, I changed where I would start and say third base instead of first. I would say third, and if she even hinted that she was not going to first base, I would reward her. Now I had her starting at whatever base I wanted and would randomly alternate from base to base. Within two weeks, she would head for the base when I just started to say the word. At the beginning, they all had unique sounds. She was now taught four words and could associate a specific location with each word. Now to turn it into baseball.

The next step was to remove the bowls and just leave the small square bases. They were very thin, not at all like real bases used in real baseball. She adapted to this quickly and didn't care if her food was in a bowl or on the floor. I think she liked the floor better; it seemed to make it easier for her to pick up the treat. At first, I was concerned that her association might be to the bowls themselves and not the bases. I might have been lucky in one regard. Cats are color blind, and since all my bowls were the same color, she was associating the treat with the location. I now wonder what would have been the results had the bowls been the same size and shape but different colors. They don't see colors, but they do see degrees of shade. Maybe I'll try that with the next cat if I ever have one.

The month we were developing her English language, we also developed a fondness for these tiny little gray mouse chew toys that looked and felt like mice and had rawhide tails. The mouse was light, and she loved for me to throw it. She would run and chase it and bring it back to me to throw again, just like a dog and a ball.

She was still small and full of energy. One day I accidentally threw one quite high over her head. I was amazed to see her run back a couple of steps, leap two feet into the air, catch the mouse between her front paws, and pull it to her mouth before she hit the ground. That was great and impressive. Prior to this, I was always throwing them so far, she never had a chance to catch them. Now I could see it clearly. Mitzi would play all the outfield by herself. I would throw the mouse in the outfield in the air but where she had a chance to catch it. As she was bringing it down, I would call out "first," "second," "third," or "home" and expect her to drop the mouse on the correct base, where she would be rewarded with a single treat.

Now the first time I tried this, I thought it only fair that we perform some real warm-ups first. In real baseball, everyone throws the ball around a bit to get loosened up. So with Mitzi, I didn't throw the mouse but put her in the outfield and called off a number of bases for her to report to go get her treat. After this warm-up, which I was not certain we needed, we would commence with the real game. I had not yet thrown an object for her to catch and then asked her to report to a specific location for a treat. The addition of the mouse to the equation might cause some confusion. If so, I had no specific solution in mind. So here goes.

I threw a long one to deep right field, and as she jumped for it, I called out, "Third!"

She caught the mouse in her front paws, transferred it to her mouth, and hit the ground pointed across the field and headed to third base. She instinctively dropped the mouse on the base beside the food she then picked up. I had hoped she would just naturally put the mouse down for the treat.

Sounds simple, and it was. Just break it down into enough easy common-sense steps, and we'd be playing ball. Honestly, it was that easy. In less than a week, after she learned her vocabulary, she was playing like a pro. I think she would have done it for the fun that she was having. She was a very good outfielder.

I was convinced that cats were not the unintelligent creatures they are usually portrayed to be. I know everyone who owns a cat thinks their cat is special, and they are, but if the truth were known, not many would ever try to train a cat like a dog is expected to be trained. "Hey, kitty, go get my slippers!" I don't think so.

Anyway, Mitzi was trained to teach me how to train Thunder. That's all I wanted to accomplish. Thunder didn't have to play fetch, but there would need to be some control. She was a big girl regardless of her young age, and she would always be a wild animal that could pose some real danger.

So what does this have to do with Thunder? Patience, simply patience—but mine, not hers. Training Mitzi was merely an exercise for me, an exercise where I wouldn't get hurt. I needed to realize that this training would take a long time, and if I were to succeed, I would be the one who would be forced to demonstrate the patience of a solitary predator. That was a challenge I was up for, but I honestly was not 100 percent certain at that particular point that I would succeed. You had to have been there.

Chapter 14

A New Beginning All Over Again

Day one, it seemed, began on May 3, 1994. It was a Monday and my eldest daughter's birthday. She was just nineteen, and it was just two years and five days from Thunder's estimated hatch date. There was no special significance connected to the date other than it would mark the third phase of our training/conditioning. The first began when she had arrived from the intensive care unit at the WVRRC. The second began the following spring when she moved into her permanent flight cage. On paper, one could say that little was accomplished during those first months. I believed that. It seemed the input of time–reward ratio was way below expectations, but remember that was a time when I had little patience compared to our wild solitary predator. But now I had passed the class Predator Patience 101.

Now the seemingly lost time during the numerous past months would ultimately be the wisest utilization of time when dealing with this particular injury and bird personality. The things I did right were few, but by comparison, the things I did wrong were almost nonexistent. I just tried to get to know and understand her. My only reinforcement was how agitated or calm she would be. I was winning that one at least. Now that I was embarking on another stage of our training, I had no regrets of the first years' seeming lack of progress. A degree of respect and trust, as small as it seemed at the time, was beginning to show.

Now to teach her to play baseball, so to speak. Looking back at Mitzi's training, you'll recall that the only expectation I had of her was her desire to eat treats. Thunder was no different. Yes, I brought her what she ate, but I didn't divide it or put it in bowls on bases. I fed her as I normally would, but now I was going to force her to eat in my presence. That could be easy if I just withheld food until she did what I asked. But we weren't going to play that game. I would be patient and get her to the point that she would eat in my presence because she didn't fear me. I would leave her an entire fish, weighing one pound plus, and spend a lot of time in her cage doing meaningless and nonfrightening activities, things like changing her water, cleaning her pool, or even moving rocks around on the floor of the cage. Then I would leave and take up an observation post about forty feet from her cage. I would sit in a lawn chair and read or just watch her. I had binoculars too. They didn't seem to bother her from that distance.

After an hour and a half on the first day, she picked up her fish with her left talon and began to eat. The fish was not fresh, but it hadn't been frozen for that long. With her beak, she reached for the area near the gills on the stomach of the fish. She buried that huge beak into the fish flesh, and I could hear the puncture and rip from my location. Still standing on the head with the left talon, she made a ripping tear by merely twisting and slightly raising her head. With no hesitation, the next action had removed the stomach and the connected organs. They were not completely detached from the body just yet but were removed from it and dangling from her beak. She then dropped them and quickly selected the heart. The heart was quite small in a twelve-inch fish. I even had a hard time being sure what she ate while watching through the binoculars. To be sure it was the heart, I opened one up the way she did to be certain that it was the heart she was eating. I didn't open it up quite the same way; I used my knife and some forceps. Every feeding I observed began almost exactly the same way. The heart was the first item eaten. Some days she seemed more eager to eat than others. On those days, there seemed to be a bit of urgency, not like she was starving, but she just wanted to get started. It could also be that she was more indifferent to my presence because of other external factors that I was not yet aware of. She did seem hungrier, though, and maybe that was all it was.

    I never had a set time to feed her. I did this to simulate her less-than-predictable natural hunting success had she been in the wild. For several days in succession, I would feed her in the morning and then skip to early evening. I never noticed any signs that she would eat more aggressively on the days that went from morning feeding to evening the following day. There might have been eight hours more since her last meal on those occasions, but that didn't seem to have a noticeable impact on her aggressiveness or sense of urgency toward eating. What did remain constant was her desire to eat the heart first. If the fish was really fresh, having never been frozen, she would eat the gills first and then go for the heart. And as for the bird pecking out your eyes, it really isn't the eyes they want but merely access to the brain. So all of you who are always worried about your eyes being "pecked out," forget that; be worried about your brain.

    I watched from this distance for days and then began to move my chair about three feet closer every time I fed her. I moved the chair on the way to her cage so she could get used to it while I was doing the usual cage activity. Once I got to within about ten feet from her cage, she became a bit more reluctant to eat in my presence. I had to wait until almost dark that night, but she finally gave in. My cat patience training was beginning to pay off.

    One evening, about a week later, I entered her cage to feed her as usual. I had a nice fourteen-inch trout that must have looked very good through that Ziploc bag. As I pulled it out, she had a look and sense of aggression that she was displaying, but it appeared to be directed toward the fish in the bag and not me. Also, as I removed it, she began to salivate, yes, drool like a dog or even a person would do with certain sensory stimulation. This looked like the opportunity I was looking for. I took my knife out of my pocket, turned my back toward Thunder, and made a first incision, approximating what she always did. I pulled out the stomach and the organ loosely attached. The tiny heart was exposed. I turned to face her, and it was apparent that she had a great interest in it. I removed it while sidestepping a bit closer to her position on her perch. I pulled the heart loose and held it in the triangle formed by my thumb and index and middle fingers.

I slowly moved my hand toward her. She drew back slightly but did not move. Her mouth was still watering, and I knew that this would be a milestone if I could manage the patience to outlast her. I would hold it as long as my arm could hold that position and then drop it to rest a bit. She was still interested but didn't yet want anything to do with me and my fingers. *My fingers*, I thought, *could they be the subject of her gaze?* I thought not, yet they were my fingers, and I was making a significant wager that the heart was the proposed target.

I raised my hand again and held it motionless in front of her. She wanted it. I could tell she really wanted it. Now I wondered, if she came for the heart, could she do it without damaging the fingers that surrounded it? The longer I held it, the more concerned I became about my welfare. I had nothing else to do but stand, watch her enormous beak, and imagine the worst. I have handled hundreds of raptors and even force-fed many of them, which necessitated prying the mouth open with bare hands in some cases. I remember doing this very thing to Thunder when we first got her, but it wasn't with bare hands. We used surgical instruments to place the food in the back of the throat. Even then, we only imagined getting a stray appendage between those shear-like mandibles. We were certain they would not withstand the incident in one piece. These birds are very powerful. I knew this, but I truly believed they were not needlessly aggressive.

I held fast with the tiny trout heart, now merely a foot from her beak. Her eyes seemed glued on it. Then without an instant of notice, the trout heart was gone. She took it and drew back as though in desperation. I did the same thing, but it likely took me quite a bit longer. In fact, she took it, ate it, and then reacted adversely to my reaction, which paled compared to hers. From that day on, I realized that it would do no good to flinch. If she wanted you, she would have you long before your brain commanded that you retreat. Scary—really, really scary. I would like to think that a small bond of trust might have developed that day. A very, very small one. I handed her the remainder of the fish but instead put it down closer to her feet than I had ever been before. I considered this a victory, thanked her and my kitty, Mitzi, and left her for the night. I had been in her cage for almost an hour—a small victory for both of us.

As the days continued, I would remove the heart from the fish and briefly hold it between my fingers and thumb while positioned not far from Thunder's beak. Each day, she would salivate and softly smack her lips—really her beak—together. Instead of offering her this treat, I would place it as close to her talons as possible without her becoming too fearful. Each day, I did stay in the cage with her until she picked it up from the perch and ate it. I usually didn't have to wait very long. Each day, I placed the treats closer and closer until I was less than a foot from her. To be honest, if I put it any closer without placing it between her feet, it would have been more difficult for her to reach it. At that distance, she could reach and bend without moving her feet. This process was quite similar to the process I used while training Mitzi. It worked for her and now seemed like it would work, with expected modifications, for Thunder as well.

After several days of placing the treat next to her—and I thought I was as close as I needed to be for this phase—I began looking for opportunities to hand her another heart. It wasn't long, and this time she seemed a bit more interested at the beginning of the heart-removal process. All the signs were there, so as I rolled it between my fingers as usual and then moved as though I was going to place it on the perch, I withdrew and did a bit more rolling of the fingers. Again, she responded positively with more salivation.

I concentrated and repeatedly said to myself, *Do not flinch, do not flinch, do not flinch,* and then extended my hand slowly but confidently toward her slobbering beak.

She paused briefly, and I glanced away as though to show disinterest in her. She lunged, and in less than the bat of an eye, the heart was gone from my fingertips, which remained. This time I really held my ground and didn't flinch. I likely would have if I had been watching. She never touched me, and the heart was about the size of a pea. I was amazed but not really surprised. This would be expected of an eagle but hardly something you would or could anticipate. Two attempts now, two successes. As Mitzi taught me, it just takes patience—lots and lots of patience.

Chapter 15

On to Second Base for the Trainer

It's one thing getting this twelve-pound feathered bundle of TNT to take a couple of snacks from my hand, but it was going to be an entirely different story having her stand still while I put jesses around each of her legs. That would be the next step before I could get her onto my arm. And what would she do if she did get on my arm? I wasn't sure, but other eagle handlers had done this before, so I imagined if it wasn't particularly life-threatening for them, then I had a chance of surviving as well. Since my beginnings of working with raptors about sixteen years earlier, the largest bird I had perched on my arm was a red-tailed hawk and a great horned owl. Both could inflict pain and suffering to bare flesh but not to the extent this bird had in its power to dispense. I figured a bit more protection was called for, so I fashioned myself an elk-hide armguard that went to the shoulder. It was a simple enough design that would adjust to cover heavy clothing for those likely cold winter days. I expected that this process would not be one accomplished during one season, and even if it were, there would still be cold days that we would hopefully be traveling to perform educational programs. At least that was the plan when this project started.

I had my gauntlet extension completed. The bottom of it slipped into the cuff of my heavy glove. This extension made the gauntlet extend to my shoulder. I also had one pair of heavy yet soft jesses constructed. The problem with the jesses was complicated by the fact that Thunder wore aluminum bands on each leg, the one from New York on the right and the U.S. Fish and Wildlife band on the left. They were loose enough, I predicted, that they would slide up the leg just far enough to allow the width of the jesses to fit the leg beneath the bands. They had to fit this way to prevent the jesses from forcing the bands to abrade against the legs. This was an important consideration because if she were to bate, fly from a perch while jessed and attached to a leash, her weight pulling against the bands could severely injure her legs. This would not happen. Some things just can't afford to be learned from trial and error.

Another similar situation that had been considered to make jessing her easier was to use permanent anklets. These would be very, very short jesses made like a bracelet that would be attached around each leg with grommets. A small piece would extend to facilitate attaching the jesses. I made a set of these, but after considering the what-ifs, I decided that this situation did not lend itself to the well-being of the bird. With the bands already taking up a great deal of space, I anticipated that the necessary size of the anklets would provide enough potential to snag on parts of the cage or perches, so this idea was put to rest as well. I had seen birds in the wild get tangled in all sorts of materials, usually as a result of nesting materials, such as rope or twine—not a pretty picture—and I most certainly did not want this bird to end up in any situation that even remotely resembled these.

My next step was to introduce her to her new jesses and the leash. I would have her attached to her jesses on one end of the leash and myself on the other end. This would only be done while I was working with her. Granted, she could not fly well enough to escape, but she could potentially hurt herself or someone else if she had to be chased around somewhere.

I wore my gloves when I was introducing her to the jesses. I had not really touched her yet except for weighing and examinations, which were done while she was covered. I didn't think she would just let me strap jesses on her without a fight, and since my hands would be more in harm's way than any other part of me, I thought it best to at least protect them. In retrospect, I think that was a big mistake. I do say in retrospect, and that just means I would have considered other options at the time. If I had it to do today, I don't believe I would need gloves. Over the years, a great deal of confidence has been acquired and, along with that, equal amounts of trust and irreplaceable experience. While this was going on, I possessed little of either.

It was now June, and the one-and-a-half-year mark was quickly approaching. I had to be careful not to let my confidence in this process backslide because of the obvious lack of progress. I would catch myself saying things like, "Eighteen months—and where is the progress?" Sometimes I would seriously consider quitting and handing the bird off to another organization. Then I would think of Mitzi and my "patient predator training." That would put me back on track. It was really hard sometimes to trust what you knew in your heart and head to be true, very hard indeed. Consider the eighteen months and an average of twenty hours a week I spent with her. That would equal almost 1,600 hours. Walking at four miles per hour, I could have walked from coast to coast and back. I had too much invested in this bird to quit now. So suck it up, I did, and moving onward, I realized it was also time for our monthly weighing. Great, another trying event to look forward to. That would take place in a week.

I had an idea fresh out of my state of "whine." *Why not spend the time between now and weighing Thunder to see how well we could do with the hand-feeding? Don't worry about the jesses just yet but see what hand-feeding progress can be made till then.* By then, I would feel ready for jessing her. While she was covered for weighing, I thought it would be a great time to actually try those brand new jesses on Thunder. She didn't like the weighing anyway, so how much more could I possibly upset her? We would see.

The weighing day came—Tuesday, June 8, 1994—and I was ready. My plan was to weigh her in the box. When finished, I would leave her covered and wrapped snugly with only her feet protruding from the bottom of the cover. She was so strong, it wasn't possible for me to hold her wings in against her body. Even if she were wrapped loosely, I could not wrap my arms around her and hold her wings against her body. I have almost an eighty-inch wingspan, and at six feet and three inches and a bit over two hundred pounds, it was all I could do to restrain her.

I had learned over the months how to wrap her for a quick and effortless—well, almost—capture, weigh, and release. The trick was to wrap around the wings like a newborn baby was wrapped. As long as she had no room to leverage her powerful wings, she could be easily secured. It was like a car parked on a hill, and you could keep it from rolling, but if you let it begin to move, you would likely not be able to stop it. It was the same for her wings. So the jesses would be made ready, along with the leash, and as soon as the weighing was done, I jessed her and attached the leash to the jesses.

The leash was braided leather, about three feet long, with a heavy piece of bungee cord about a foot long added to one end. Each end was then attached to a large brass swivel-snap clip. The foot-long bungee would stretch to a bit more than three feet. Since she was so large and heavy, I thought that reaching the end of the leash after she would bate would be less shock to her legs. I quickly found out that I was right.

I put on my gear and carried her outside. She was still wrapped and her head and eyes covered. She was calm and even relaxed. Her breathing had quieted considerably. I took her to a large open area in the lawn. It was about eighty degrees, and the sun was setting behind fairly heavy clouds. It was as dark as I could have hoped for but light enough to give us at least thirty minutes.

Now as I prepared to unwrap her, I had visions of a bull calmly standing in the chute before the gate opened and the explosion happened. And that was just what happened. I had her on a very short lead because I didn't want her to fly but to sit on my arm. It almost happened that way—almost.

I let her get her feet on the ground after she got free of the wrap, and just as quickly, she was attempting to become airborne. I had given her just enough leash so she could right herself and maneuver her wings. I had expected power but not this much. It was a good thing I ate my Wheaties that morning.

Her reaction was fast and furious. There really aren't words in my vocabulary to express the obvious adrenaline racing through each of our bodies. She was off like a shot, and I allowed her enough slack to get off the ground. I got to a standing position and braced myself, and Thunder and I did our first famous "bate and loop." She didn't stop with one either. She kept going out and coming back, passing over my outstretched right arm that would ultimately, I hoped, become her perch.

After the fourth loop, I was wearing down but determined that a twelve-pound bird was not going to wear me out. And she did not. On the fifth pass, she decided she had had enough, and without the style expected of our national symbol, she came to a wobbling rest on my arm. My curiosity had been addressed about my armguard's worthiness. It was fine, but I was pleasantly surprised that her grip did not exceed that necessary to secure her to the perch.

Now what do I do with her since she is here on my arm? I thought. I knew I couldn't hold her forever, but I needed to begin walking toward her cage before she got her strength back, and my arm began to wobble like a broken branch. This is one picture opportunity I wish someone could have captured; too late for that.

Now we began moving, and as I did, I bent my arm slightly to give it a bit more strength. Unfortunately, when the palm is turned down, your arm doesn't have much strength. It's like the weak muscles of an alligator's mouth. It is easy to hold it shut but not to keep it open. Keep in mind that Thunder was weighing twelve pounds. If you want to get a small idea of the difficulty of holding her, get yourself a five-pound bag of sugar, hold your arm out to one side with a slight bend in it with the palm facing down, and place the sugar on the back of your wrist. In less than a minute, most arms will begin violently shaking. A bird won't stay long on that perch. I fortunately had done some exercises in anticipation of this weight, but I fell way short. Static weight isn't the same as moving weight. Then add the five loops that were like tying a lasso to a twenty-five-pound of dog food and swinging it around your head—no joke—and I was tired.

Thunder and I were both breathing hard, with our mutual shoulders slumped. I had no more than a minute's worth of energy left, but I couldn't pass up this opportunity while she was on my arm and too tired to be frightened. I got her to the cage with her wings partially spread to provide balance. We made it into the cage, and I backed her up to the perch and said, "Down," as she gladly stepped off my weary arm.

As soon as she was off, I kept a tight grip on the shortened leash and shoved my arm against her leg again to get her back onto my arm. I gave the command "Up" as she stepped onto my arm. I was getting my wind back, and so was she. She wanted to get off the glove, but I pulled her away from the perch, which gave her no place to go. I held her there until I couldn't hold her anymore. I placed her down on the perch, each time giving her the down command. We continued this until the sun had nearly set, but it was much darker as heavy black clouds raced across the sky in our direction.

With caution and gloved hands, I removed the leash from the jesses but maintained a firm grip on the jesses. Now to get the jesses off. I wanted so much to leave them on because I knew what would happen the next time I wanted to put them on. But I also knew that if I left them on, there was a possibility that I could find her hanging from them in the morning. So off they came. It took a while, and the sky got darker. She would hop about the perch as I touched her legs but was a lot more relaxed about it than I had anticipated she would be.

It was a long evening for the two of us but a good one, even for Thunder. She took this so much better than I had imagined. Since it was getting even darker, she would have to wait until morning for her fish dinner.

Chapter 16

What's in a Name?

Until that day—June 8, 1994—Thunder did not have a name. Like most creatures I ever had or saw, I always called them Spot. Thunder was no exception. So until that evening, she was just another Spot. After I removed her jesses, it was really getting dark, and a storm was approaching from the west. I no more than gathered up my stuff than it started to rain fairly hard. Half of Thunder's cage was covered, so I decided I'd stay until the rain let up a bit. So I backed up close to Thunder's main perch and about four feet from her. She didn't mind, and the rain was pounding onto the peaked rubber roof. Loud claps of thunder could be heard moving in our direction. Along with it were bolts of lightning hitting fairly near us.

As I listened to the thunder and then felt the strikes of the lighting, I realized then that Spot would, from now on, be called Thunder. The reason was that in the entire time I had been working with her, she had never purposely tried to hurt me. She squawked and postured but never once attacked. She was half of the storm we were sitting through. Even with her strength, wildness, fear, and physical potential, she was just a big rumble of thunder. She might have had lightning potential, but she never once showed that personality. *So Thunder it was, and Thunder it will always be.* So when I consider how long I have spent trying to get her to have even a shred of respect for me, I guess I should have looked at how long I had her before she had her own identity. A total of 531 days from December 21, 1992, until June 8, 1994—she definitely deserved better than Spot.

The next morning, when I got up, I was pretty excited about the previous day's results. I was curious as to the mood that Thunder would be in today. As I prepared her breakfast—remember she didn't eat yesterday evening—I cut it open and removed the heart so I could see if I could get her to eat from my hand. I had the heart ready to be removed, and I place the fish into the plastic Ziploc bag.

As I walked out toward her cage, I could see that she was in her normal position and didn't appear to be any different today than any other morning that I had approached her cage. As I got closer, she still did her normal squawk even after a year and a half. I had the water turned on already, and I started fiddling with cleaning her tub. She watched as I played around in her water. The entire time, it seemed as though she was keeping her eyes on the Ziploc bag that contained her breakfast. I turned off the water and turned my attention to the Ziploc bag as well. I removed the trout from the bag and grabbed the heart, which was dangling from the stomach of the fish. I pulled it away and held it on my fingers and offered it to Thunder. As I normally did, I slowly offered my hand toward her so that she could take the heart if she wanted to. She flinched only slightly, and then she started making the maneuvers with her mouth that indicated she was salivating. And it wasn't too long till she decided that she would take it from my fingers. It was a quick stab on her part and an accurate one as well. I left her to enjoy her pound of fish. It was another workday for me, so I left her, vowing to return in the evening.

It had only been one time with Thunder on my arm and with what seemed a minimum of trauma for her efforts. I was beginning to believe that my patience was finally beginning to pay off. I know that one and a half years is a long time to achieve such a seemingly insignificant accomplishment, but I would have to disagree. It was significant, not just the feat of her on my gloved arm but the way it was done. There seemed to be a trust developing. Even in people, good trusting friends are few and far between, and when that relationship is finally developed, it usually has taken a significant amount of time. That's with people, the same species that speak the same language and are relatively the same size and shape.

None of these things did Thunder and I have in common. In fact, other than that we each shared the top of the food chain, there were no significant similarities. And one and a half years might seem long, but with my expected longevity of about fifty more years and the possibility that Thunder may live as long as eighty years meant we needed not rush this relationship. Thunder living to eighty may or may not happen; we'll have to wait and see. I may never know, but some of the younger readers will likely outlive her, even if I do not.

As I wrote earlier, when I was researching bald eagles, I came across a documented and authenticated account where a bald eagle had been taken to England in the latter half of the nineteenth century. According to this report, the bird did indeed live to be eighty years old. Some seem to question this information or find it very surprising. Logic would tell you that the likelihood of a predator living this long would be slim. I would suggest we haven't had any bald eagles in captivity for that long either. I'm basing this from some of the older bald eagles I have seen in captivity that were from wild stock and did not lead very good lives. I have seen and can document bald eagles in prominent institutions that you would think would be provided quality care when, in fact, the birds are so stressed by the conditions that they live in, it is any wonder they would live ten or more years. Bald eagles are high-strung birds, and it is commonly known that the larger females are much more difficult to deal with than the males. Probably for this reason, wild bald eagles are very seldom used for the practice of falconry. The few exceptions would be those hatched and raised in captivity. Golden eagles, on the other hand, are frequently used for this sport/hobby.

I had no intention of using a technique of "operant conditioning" or those employed by falconers. I have far too much respect and behavior knowledge from my years of observations to withhold food from any bird being trained for the purpose of expedience. What I had hoped to accomplish with Thunder would take time, time I had to give, and the results would benefit not only me but Thunder as well. Thunder was a large, strong, and proud bird. She required and deserved the respect of time and patience. Our trailblazing had been slow, I will confess, but the highway we were building from the start would make it much more likely that Thunder would be traveling this super highway with little effort for many, many years to come. Only time would tell, but I'm putting my money on Thunder.

As the next two weeks passed, I worked with Thunder inside the cage only. I would spend time putting her jesses on, hooking her leash to the jesses, and she would begrudgingly sit on my arm. Inside the cage, I would rest it on her perch for long periods. Usually after about twenty minutes, my arm would begin to go to sleep. This wasn't from her grip as she would grip no more than necessary to stay perched. It was from her massive talons and the mere weight she applied while standing there. Remember too that there was heavy leather protecting my arm, which dissipated the weight from any significant pressure points. At one point, I wondered if there could be any lasting effects from years of my circulation being cut off so frequently—a passing thought only.

Chapter 17

Verbal Communication

The next phase of the training was to teach word commands, just like I did with Mitzi. I wanted her to get on my arm upon command. I had no intention of fighting this huge bird every time I wanted her to do something with regard to handling. So I devised a modification to the plan used for Mitzi.

I had noticed that when I was with Thunder in her cage and a guest came to visit me, really to see Thunder, she would squawk her threat display, but if I allowed the person to approach more closely, she would move along the perch to be closer to me. The first time she did this, I wondered why, but after the third time—I'm a bit slow, I guess—I noticed that this was intentional on her part. She spent more of her days on the left portion of the perch (left if you are facing her) but would roost on the right side. So if I was standing on the right side near the perch and someone came, she would move closer to me, almost to the point of having her wing against me. When I was at the left side fiddling with her perch, she would move to the other end. If I then had someone walk toward us, she would move toward the left side of the perch, where I was standing. She would continue to squawk until they stopped walking toward her. I think she assumed that they stopped because she was telling them to with her squawking. She finally quit squawking at me when I wouldn't stop. I would continue into her cage. After a while, she figured it was a waste of her efforts, so for the most part, she stopped, unless she was having "a bad hair day."

So this was the training technique I intended to employ to get her up on my arm on command. *Sounds reasonable*, I thought, and you will too in a moment, I hope. I called a friend of mine and asked him if he had an hour or two on Saturday morning. The weather was warm, and I didn't want to work Thunder in the midsummer heat. He had visited Thunder on a few occasions, so when I told him I wanted him to assist me with training her, he immediately said that he refused to get in the cage with her. I explained that he need not get anywhere near her. He was puzzled but agreed to come over at 8:00 a.m. on Sunday, July 17, 1994. His Saturday had already been spoken for.

Sunday morning, Dave pulled in a bit before eight. He had a worried look on his face but was willing to help if he could do it safely.

"Not a problem," I assured him and then told him all I wanted him to do was to sit in the chair I had placed in one of my equipment sheds. I had placed another lawn chair in the lawn where I had gotten Thunder on my arm the first time. There was a crabapple tree there that would provide a bit of shade. The grass in the lawn was about three and a half inches long and very thick and green. The plan was for Dave to sit in his chair, read or whatever, and wait for verbal commands from me. He would be about 150 feet from me and Thunder. He went to his seat while I got Thunder jessed and ready. This would be the first time I would be taking her out of her cage while on a leash.

It took almost twenty minutes for me to get the jesses on her. The jesses, remember, were pieces of strong yet limber leather about ten to eleven inches long and nearly three quarters of an inch wide. Both ends were cut, so they came to a point, and about one inch back from the tip of each end, a slit was made, moving away from the end about one and a half inches long. The idea was to put them around her leg and stick one end of the jess into the slit on the other end of the jess and pull it snug.

The leash with a swivel clip was then hooked to the slits in the opposite end of both jesses. The gloves I wore were very heavy leather, and I would not want to do surgery on anything wearing these things. It was difficult to put the jesses on while Thunder would not stand still. Once they were around her leg, the trick was to thread one end into the other end and then situate it comfortably below the aluminum bans she was wearing on each leg when she came to us. At the time, it was much easier to write about doing this than actually accomplishing the feat.

I had the jesses on Thunder, so I informed Dave that I would be coming out with her soon. I returned to the cage and, after a brief time, did manage to get the jesses hooked to the leash. By this time, I had taken off the left glove, which I anticipated I would not need. Just in case, I folded it and stuck it into my back pants pocket. I opened Thunder's cage door as far as it would go and secured it there. This was to be another first, and I wasn't sure how to begin. Logic would say that it would be just the reverse of the time I put her back into the cage perhaps, but I wasn't too sure of that. The time I brought her back, she was tired from our handling, and I think she felt relieved knowing she was going back there. Today she was not tired, and maybe she didn't want to leave. I wondered what she could possibly do to prevent me from removing her from the cage.

About then, she adjusted her nearly seven-foot wingspan. *Sure, just open your wings, and we would have a difficult time getting them through a thirty-six-inch opening.* I had already decided that whatever she did, I was not going to reward her by allowing her to get to the ground. I don't think she was being forced to do anything she greatly objected, but I doubt it was clear to her just exactly what I wanted her to do. We clearly spoke different languages. At this point, I decided to confidently go for it. I nudged her until she stepped onto my gloved right hand.

I said, "Up!" as she did it, but that wasn't the reason she did it. I merely replaced her perch with my arm. And no, I didn't get Thunder to perch on my fist as most hawks do. She used almost all of my arm from the wrist to the elbow. That placed her body about a foot or less from my face—with her beak pointing toward me.

I held her with my arm resting on the perch, making sure she was relatively calm. I had the jesses hooked to her legs coming over the back of my glove and under my hand. That would make it easier to hold her in place if she tried to bate. I picked her up and thought, *What a load.*

I moved toward the cage door. I backed through it, and she followed on my arm. That went fine. She must have considered the width of the door too and realized that any flapping activity at that time could be hard on the wings' feathers. She did wonderfully until I got turned around, facing the direction we were going. I took four steps, and she decided she had had enough. Her wings opened up in a flash, and the left one, the one that had been amputated at the wrist, started beating against the side of my head. It wasn't her feathers doing this either; it was that bony stub left from the amputation.

I raised my arm and straightened it as far as possible at the same time, moving my head to the left and down. Now I was clear of her flapping wing. I couldn't hold her on the glove any longer, so I relaxed my grip on the jesses and let her fly to the near end of the leash that I had secured with the left hand. I had brass swiveled clips on both ends, and they were large enough that I could hook my little finger through the loop that was attached to the leash. This would be the ultimate safety should the leash itself slide or be pulled through my hand. She was strong, but she wasn't going to pull my finger off.

When she got to the end of the leash, I gently leaned back to turn her direction of flight back toward me. She came around the first time and gently landed on my outstretched right arm. The loop wasn't perfect, and she was a bit wobbly on the landing. She settled, and we continued to walk the forty yards we needed to go.

It was a nice sunny morning, and other than the realization that I really needed to strengthen that right arm, we had a calm but guarded walk to our destination. Once we arrived at the lawn chair that was set up near the tree, I maneuvered myself to my knees, and just as she jumped the last foot and a half to the ground, I barked out the command "Down!" I could see I would likely never have difficulty having her obey that one.

We were in the shade of the tree, but I had no intention of having it interfere with the scheduled plans. I was holding the other end of the leash. I had another ten-foot line in my pocket. I connected it to the main leash and gave Thunder a bit more slack. I sat down in the chair, and she just stood there, about six to seven feet from me. She wasn't doing anything in particular that I could observe, but I was sure she was alert. After just a few minutes, she seemed to be in a neutral state, and I figured it was time to begin the training.

I was in my chair, Thunder was to my right, and Dave was still in his chair. I called to him and asked him to get up and start walking slowly toward us. As soon as he got up, Thunder directed her attention toward him calmly but intently. He came about twenty yards, and I asked him to stop. After about thirty seconds, I had him begin again—no response from Thunder other than her original reaction. Then I told Dave to walk about five yards at a time straight toward us and then stop for about ten seconds and then continue until I said otherwise.

After his third stop and start, there was a nervous reaction from Thunder. She started to look around and began moving her feet very slightly. I asked Dave to stop. I stood and moved my chair about five feet to have Thunder directly to my right. She was now definitely on edge but hadn't really moved from her starting position. I shortened up the slack on the leash just a bit and told Dave to continue without stopping but to come slowly. He was taking a small step about every two seconds. I hoped I could get the timing right so she would not panic yet accept me as her only safe escape from this intrusion.

I told Dave to totally stop as soon as she moved, which wasn't going to be much longer. About then, she looked all around in a state of desperation, and I knew she wasn't going to tolerate much more.

I extended my right arm out to and in front of her and said, "Up!" just as she flapped her way to the only safe perch she could get to. I had Dave retreat quickly but without haste. He went back to his chair and sat down.

I let Thunder stay on my arm for a couple of minutes and then lowered my arm and said, "Down!" Instantly, she was on the ground, convinced that she was now safe.

After a short time, I once again extended my arm, and said, "Up!" Like she had done it a million times, she obliged without hesitation.

We did a few more ups and downs over the next few minutes, and I decided we had accomplished the desired results. This was a tiny step, necessary yet tiny.

I had her on my arm, and as I stood, she remained calm and stayed on my arm. As I slowly but deliberately began back across the lawn, I asked Dave to stand and slowly come toward us, not so fast that he would startle her into bating but just enough to make her realize I was a safe zone for her. We did this all the way back to her cage without incident. Dave never did get closer than twenty yards. That must have represented a safe distance for Thunder.

I got her back into her cage and spent the next ten minutes or more removing her jesses. Finally, she was free, but I needed to come up with a better method for jessing and unjessing her. I didn't have any ideas just yet, but I didn't trust Thunder enough to even remotely consider doing the jessing and unjessing with no gloves. This bird and I were developing a mutual respect and even a little trust thrown in there, but there was no way this wild animal was going to be trusted to that degree, at least not yet.

Wild animals are and will always be wild animals. As humans, we like to think we can accomplish anything we set our minds to, and I'll likely almost always agree with that. We have one flaw though—we usually think everything thinks and perceives things the same way we do with similar or like priorities. An animal having tolerance for you doesn't mean they are your most trusted friend either.

A baby raccoon is the cutest little thing when found along a roadside, crying over its dead mother. Take it home, and it will be your friend . . . only because you have rescued it and are feeding it and taking care of it. This would happen in the spring, the only time you'll find baby raccoons in this hemisphere. When fall arrives, things change. They aren't babies anymore, and they may be friendly until something triggers that unexpected transformation to a ferocious wild beast. Sounds pretty extreme, but it's true more often than not.

Thunder was already a wild, crazy beast by human standards when she was found. If it weren't for the severity of her injuries, I wouldn't be writing this today; she would be free in the wild, where wild animals belong. I trust Thunder too but only about as much as she trusts me. I would imagine she trusts me about as far as she can throw me. She did trust me more than Dave, but I think that's not much of a compliment. I was just the lesser of two evils. It was a start though, and if I wanted to use her at public venues, it seemed the road would be long and the going very slow.

Our expectations for Thunder were quite simple. We wanted her to be the ambassador and spokesbird, I guess, for all creatures living in the wild. She, as our national symbol, would help instill pride and respect in our youth so as they mature, they remember and respect what Thunder and the other raptors used in our environmental education programs really stood for. We wanted Thunder and the rest of our raptor ambassadors to help bridge the gap between all species and mankind, with the intent of illustrating that "man is a part of nature, not apart from nature."

From this, we should see our species as just another of the millions that inhabit this planet, all of which are directly or indirectly connected to one another, with each species having their own basic needs/requirements for survival. This is where the difficulty really begins—with understanding.

Chapter 18

Sight versus Sound

As an example at hand, Thunder, our national symbol, was not understood at all. With the basics of sight and hearing, it has not been too many years ago that the species was endangered. Protective measures were put in place by the U.S. Fish and Wildlife Service and the U.S. Congress to help protect the birds that remained. One of the items of concern was the disturbance of nests. The nest sites were protected for obvious reasons, and it was a good thing that these measures were instituted and enforced. As late as 2001, the regulations were still in place and justly so.

A navigation regulation required large boats or other water-going vessels of a certain size to sound their horns when pulling or backing into a dock. This safety measure has been on the U.S. Corps of Engineers' books for years. It had nothing to do with eagles; it was and still is done for safety reasons. In one instance that I knew of, an exception to this regulation was made at a site of an active bald eagle's nest. The fear was that the loud sound of this ferryboat's horn would cause a possible abandonment of this nest. The facts are that sounds, including reports from gunfire, do not disturb these birds in the least. If the truth had been known, they would have eliminated the ferry moving about from around the nest site. Birds of prey do not seem to care about sounds. They are very visual and trust only what they see. Had the ferry been too close for the nesting pair to be comfortable with the invasion, they would have abandoned the nest site. The horn was sounding while they were building their nest, so why would they abandon it afterward?

It is a fact that the more time invested in a nesting episode, the greater the likelihood that the pair will not abandon the nest. For instance, just like chickens, free range or not, you can take their eggs every day, and they will lay others tomorrow. You think these birds are laying eggs for your consumption, but in actuality, they are laying eggs in a primal effort to reproduce and ensure the existence and survival of a species. You have nothing to do with it. The eggs aren't fertile, but given the chance, one hen left alone would lay about a dozen eggs and then stop so she could sit and incubate them, hoping they would hatch. The hen doesn't yet know the eggs are infertile; she is just doing her part. The fertilization of the eggs is left up to the rooster. If a rooster had been in the chicken house with this hen, she would have had each egg fertilized prior to the forming of the egg as we recognize them. Each sex knows what to do and when to do it. This would be required for each egg prior to it being laid. So if you were to remove the eggs from a chicken, it would continue to lay that clutch of about a dozen. If you did this to a bald eagle, it would try to lay another egg as well.

This could go on for a short time but nothing like the chicken. Eagles would give up after a reasonable effort has been made. The same is true if a nest is disturbed. They would make an effort to repair it. Once the nest is completed and eggs are laid, the only reason they would abandon the nest this late in the game is if they felt that their survival was threatened. Even after the young hatch, they would do all that is possible to protect them without giving up their own lives. Some instinct must tell them that if they fail today, they can move on to another site and try again. In a way, it is like they are saying that they are adult proven reproducers, and it is quite possible that the young might not even survive to the point of sexual maturity. In a sense, the adults see themselves as proven entities, and the young do not bring nearly as much to the table as they do. They may represent hope for the future, but that alone does not ensure the existence of a species. I don't really believe that they think this way, but their natural reproductive instincts, which have occurred for millions of years, generally yield these results.

All birds that I have ever seen are adamant about completing the nest during this fever-pitch time. I had a truck once where, every morning, a robin would have started to build a nest on the top of one of the rear tires. I would remove the nest every morning just to find another attempt back the following morning. This went on for over a week. I figured if the bird was that determined, I would go out of my way to help the poor creature. So I constructed a platform similar to the wheel and fender arrangement. The next day, I placed the partially built nest on the fake tire. That evening when I came home, there was a nearly completed nest on my recently made nest site. The following morning, there was no nest on my tire, but six feet away was a female sitting on a nest. She was probably laying her first egg. This is an example of the tolerances most species will endure to facilitate that primal urge of reproduction.

Understanding all things about all species is akin to my contemplation of infinity. I can't wrap my head around that one, and I believe that the millions of possibilities of interactions involved are beyond our ability as a species to not only identify but also to incorporate into a concise plan. We see parts, but the whole picture won't begin to fit on our fifty-inch flat screens. I too think that we oftentimes look too hard for answers that are right before us. I will say that my years with Thunder have provided answers when I didn't even know there was a question. My study of her, one sample of one species of millions out there, has given me an insight on the enormity of our efforts of looking for and finding that one particular needle in that enormous haystack. But it is essential to begin somewhere, and I think the first and most logical place to begin is with effective education. Thunder will help with this, I am certain.

Chapter 19

Trust versus Instincts for Survival

Our training continued on a daily basis. It was, however, no longer just the two of us. After we got past the "up" command with such success, it was time to move on.

I did discover one very interesting thing regarding this training episode though. During the next few weeks, every time I asked Thunder to go "up," she would get on my arm—every time. I had a very smart and well-trained lab a long time ago, but it took him hundreds of repetitions to get that one command down perfectly. I still don't understand the difference. But it was once and forever for Thunder. Now to tackle new things.

Now that I could get Thunder on my arm, I could weigh her inside her cage. That would improve trust by me not needing to wrap her in a towel and put her in a box. That certainly cut down on the stress, mine as well as hers. I also began introducing new things to the cage, like the scales I use to weigh her. That was important. Anything I brought into her cage that wasn't in a Ziploc bag was foreign matter to her. At one time, the Ziploc bag was foreign to her as well (more patience shining through). She spooked very easily. From time to time, I would leave her food with her, leave the cage, and return holding something as insignificant as a small twig less than a foot long. I would need to hold it almost out of sight as I entered the cage and then squat down so I was as far from her as possible. Then I would lay it on the ground, move it to another spot, and so on until it didn't matter to her anymore. I would leave but would leave the stick in the cage.

The one salvation that was almost as effective as a sedative was her water. She had gotten so used to the splashing sound of water that she would almost calm instantly when I would slosh my hand around in her pool. That was something she grew used too from the days in the garage. I think she found that so nonthreatening since she made the same splashing while bathing. Perhaps she took it as a sign of safety. It seemed that everything about her was about safety, which translated into the most basic instinct: survival.

June and July of '94 were very satisfying regarding Thunder's and my progress with the training. At that time when I thought that to myself and made that note in the log book, I began to wonder if that was, in fact, an accurate and correct definition of what was going on here. Had we really been training? I recalled when I got Mitzi (my little kitten) at six or seven weeks of age. When I put her in my vehicle for the first time, she went across the floor and between my legs, climbed up my pants leg and curled up on my lap. That was after meeting her less than an hour earlier. Let's see . . . yes, that was exactly the way it happened with Thunder. Sure, it was. While Mitzi and I had mastered baseball in a couple of months, where had I gotten with Thunder? That's right. It'd been twenty months, and she was still somewhat reluctant to sit on my arm, and I still spent fifteen to twenty minutes each time I put the jesses on her. I'd say we definitely had not been training.

My realization of this fact didn't improve the process, but it certainly made me consider other objectives and goals. It was obvious that Thunder was far more intelligent than I had given her credit for. I didn't really need to train her but, rather, instill trust in her as I introduced new situations to her. This might seem like a six of one, half a dozen of the other concept, but really, it wasn't. She was a wild and frightened animal. The genetic and psychological makeup of a female bald eagle is vastly different than that of a domestic kitten. To have the same or even similar expectations of the two of them would constitute a very narrow view of life. At that point, my view wasn't that narrow, but it wasn't as open as it should have been.

As a comparison, take a female bald eagle that is hatched and raised in captivity by humans and draw comparisons to Thunder, who spent most of her first year in the wild. They are both female bald eagles that have similar dispositions and the same general genetic makeup. The difference here would seem obvious. One was raised by humans and had no natural or acquired fear of humans. The opposite is true of Thunder. The hand-raised or "imprinted" one can be trained using food as a reward just as Mitzi was, but Thunder cannot be trained in the same manner. To receive food as a reward, she would have to be so hungry and lose so much weight that the only remaining instinct would be to not starve to death. I know many folks who train birds of prey refer to their training technique as "operant conditioning." I discussed this technique earlier and don't approve of it any more now than I did earlier. Let me tell you a true story as an example of what a strong training aid starvation is for these wild birds.

I still work with the WVRRC as a volunteer. I was there when the center began, and I have more than four decades of experience working with injured, orphaned, and sick raptors. I have facilities and federal permits to provide care for raptors, including Thunder, at my home. I have a six-by-eight-by-ten-foot temporary holding cage for raptors. I use this when folks drop off birds at my house that have been found injured or orphaned and can be held in a cage instead of a smaller confined area for those birds requiring intensive care.

One day in February, three guys I happened to know were looking at some property to purchase. As they walked along one of the fields, they came to a pond where they found a red-tailed hawk caught in a trap. A hawk wouldn't normally walk into a trap, but if it was set with exposed bait, the raptor would see it and launch an air strike, leading with its talons, thinking it was prey. This was what happened here, and fortunately, the bird had only one talon caught in the trap. One of the guys knew to throw a jacket over it to calm it before removing it from the trap. Had he not known to do this, the bird could have and likely would have sustained much more damage to the talon.

They brought it to me, and I examined it while they were there. The foot did not appear to have any damage, and the hawk had plenty of grip in both talons. Before they left, I was given precise directions to where it was found so it could ultimately be returned to where it was found. I told them I would keep it overnight and see if it showed any adverse signs of injury to either foot, leg, or wing. If all was well—and I expected it to be—I would turn it loose the next day.

I went ahead and weighed it and examined the keel. Both were fine. The keel that I examined was the bone running up and down the breast of the bird. If you visualize the breast of a chicken that you eat, you are aware of the raised bone running down the center of the meat you will eat. The keel rating goes from one to five. Five would constitute a very healthy bird, with the breast meat running to the top of the keel. If it is rated a one, well, you and the chicken are both on your way to starving to death. A one would be a case where there was maybe 10 percent of the meat on the breast that would be present on an otherwise healthy bird. A one is indicative of severe emaciation. In a case like this, we would be treating a very weak and dehydrated bird. Protocol normally dictated tube feeding to rehydrate and provide much needed nutrition, with a minimum of energy being burned by the bird digesting it. When a bird was that bad—it was possible to have them expire trying to digest solid food—they were hand-or force-fed. It's sort of you eating celery where the caloric count is so low, you burn more calories eating and digesting it than you gain from eating it.

I have three six-by-eight-by-ten-foot-high cages at my house for cases like this and for the general temporary holding of birds brought to me. I put this bird in the one closest to my house, situated on my patio right off my porch.

That night there was a five-to six-inch snow, and even though the bird's foot was fine, I decided I'd hold on to it until the weather cleared a bit. I fed it mice while it was with me. The snowy weather continued, and three days later, we had an additional seven to eight inches of snow.

That morning I went out to the cage. The roof was made of netting so the birds could get plenty of light and the back third was covered to provide shelter from the weather. I greeted the red-tailed hawk when I approached the cage. He sat motionless as I entered the cage with four mice, each weighing about an ounce (twenty-eight grams) apiece.

I had to duck down a bit to get through the doorway, and as I did and began pulling the door shut behind me, I saw something move out of the corner of my eye. The caged bird had not moved, but as I focused my attention to the back of the cage, I witnessed a wild red-tailed hawk fly from the tree line about thirty yards away and land on the outside top of the cage. I tried not to move so I could watch it and try to figure how I could get to my phone to take a picture of it. I stood stooped over for a considerable period, trying to figure out how I could do this without scaring the new visitor away. I had mice in my right hand and the door in my left as I decided to slowly place the mice on the perch in front of me so I could reach for my phone.

I set the mice down slowly, and immediately, the visitor raced across the netting the length of the cage, not two feet from my head, and desperately tried to reach through the netting to get to the mice. I was amazed. I forgot about the camera and picked up a mouse, stuck my right arm out the door, and made a grenade-type throw, lobbing the mouse onto the roof of the cage. Instantly, the visiting red-tailed hawk grabbed it with its talons and then put it to its mouth and swallowed it whole. I had three more mice, so I backed out of the cage, latched the door, and pitched a second and third mouse onto the cage top. Each were eaten as the first one was. I threw the fourth one on the ground at my feet, and it was on it, tearing it to pieces in an instant.

I had no mice left, so I went inside the house and to the garage and brought four more mice back outside with me. I also brought my raptor gloves. The bird was still standing on the patio where I had left it. I took one mouse between the thumb and index finger of my gloved hand and extended it in the direction of the visitor. It instantly flew to my fist and began ripping at the mouse. I held onto the mouse firmly and carried the bird on my glove through my house to my heated garage, where I set the bird on a temporary perch. It was not tethered, and it sat and ate a total of eight ounces of mice until no more could fit into its crop. A normal daily diet for a red-tailed hawk would be about four ounces or four of these mice. I put my gloved hand out toward the bird's talons, and it stepped onto it without hesitation. I set it back down and left it to digest its massive brunch.

This wild raptor, under the right conditions, took only five minutes to train to willingly fly to and sit on my arm. It took eighteen months to acquire even less results with Thunder. The red-tailed hawk was less than half its normal weight, and I would guess that its flight onto my glove would probably have been its last one. It was so close to starvation. Technically, the bird would not have starved to death but more likely frozen while lying in the snow, too weak to be able to fly, let alone hunt.

After a few days at my place, getting it stabilized, it was taken to the center, where it spent two weeks in an ICU cage. After its weight was near normal, it was put into a flight cage. By this time, its belly was full, and there was meat on its keel (breastbone like on a chicken breast). Strange—when I visited him, he had no feeling at all for the guy who saved his life.

Amazing how that works. I bet that if I had withheld food from it for a week or so, it would have acted quite differently. And the fact that Thunder had not ever really missed a meal was likely the reason we were just where we were. She might not like me because her wild instincts told her not to, but there was a sense of trust developing between the two of us. This would last longer than the time it took to digest a pound of fish or mouse meat.

Sometimes it seemed I was a relatively slow learner. Thunder and I had spent over a year and a half together, and it had finally dawned on me that our problem wasn't training; as I always mention, it was trust. Plain and simple, she didn't trust me, and I didn't trust her. I would feed her tiny trout hearts with my bare hand, and she would take the offering, but I think we would both hold our breaths as we went about it. I still wore both my gloves when I jessed her, and I hadn't touched her with bare hands except when necessary for a physical exam. Then she had her head covered and was relatively restrained. I wouldn't call that trust. She had never done anything to me that would be enough for me not to trust her, and she might likely say the same, but she was still wild and formidable to say the least. I value my safety, and I was certain she felt the same way about her safety. So how do we each overcome this mistrust?

Trust is a very basic concept that I think even tiny infants possess. Some people sort of exude trust to infants. It is likely the ones who don't even trust themselves picking up a baby make the baby feel equally insecure with the situation. This is likely an oversimplification of the relationship Thunder and I shared, but I think that trust for survival's sake was a basic and deeply held promise. While I did trust that Thunder would not just attack me without just reason, I was not sure I could trust myself to be able to identify what "just reason" for Thunder would constitute. So if you are getting the idea that I'm putting all this on me, well, you are almost correct. I am more in control of Thunder's destiny than she is of mine or, for that matter, her own.

It was late summer now, and my new course of curriculum had changed from training to "growing trust." I would continue my routine of daily activities with gradual introductions of new stimuli and alternating patterns. My definitions of these words were likely not clinically correct, but I was going to use them as follows. For example, a stimulus might be bringing a small stick into her cage for the first time. Alternating patterns would be what I might do with the stick this time versus the next time. A more simplistic example might be me entering her cage. I always have to do it through the door, but I could swing the door open with my left hand instead of my right hand and enter the cage backward. I could also stand on the other side of her pool when I emptied and cleaned it each day, doing the same trusted activities but doing it in a different language. The more variations I could expose each of us to, the more one's confidence in the other's trust would grow. I'd already concluded this would take a while.

I think as often as I told myself how much I trusted her, well, I don't think I really believed it myself. She had a menacing presence about her. For example, each day, I went to her cage for my usual routines, and on the way there, I was studying her demeanor to see if there were any characteristics I could identify that might lead me to understand the mood she was in at that time. After I got in the cage or very close to it, I could tell by her physical behavior whether or not we were going to have "a good hair day" or "a bad hair day" (I don't know what description I would have used if Thunder had been a male).

As a comparison, we could look at the expressions on a human face and define joy, happiness, sorrow, fear, disgust, or even confusion. I just got one look from her, and it was always the same. I always make a joke about her expression that's pretty much depicted on this one T-shirt someone gave me ages ago. On it is a full frontal view of the head of an adult bald eagle—it has that look. Under the picture of the bird is the caption "I am smiling." That about sums it up. If any of you have ever had the privilege of seeing her in person, well, you know exactly what I mean. Otherwise, you're just going to have to trust me.

Our daily work and routines continued. The days got shorter, and daylight-savings time had come and gone. That's a man-made thing, and to Thunder, it was dark when it was dark, and daylight was twenty minutes before the sun came up—nothing fancy—but of course, my routine as well as hers changed accordingly. She adjusted much easier than I did though.

Now I had an hour less of daylight to work with her in the evenings, an opportunity to introduce another pattern variation. Now we spent a bit more time working in the morning as well. By "working," I simply mean cultivating our trust. We let fate dictate the new stimuli or pattern alternation as they happened. We continued our routine of putting her jesses on her, hooking up her leash, and getting her on my arm. We would do multiple repetitions of "ups" and "downs" to get her used to getting on and off my arm on command—again, more trust growing.

One day, a very pretty fall day, we were basking in the cool air and warm sun doing lazy "ups" and "downs." She, being left-footed, would always step onto my right arm with her left leg, placing her talon on my arm just below the elbow. Her right leg would then rest near my right wrist. I wore my heavy long-cuffed glove on my right hand and my elk-hide gauntlet, which started at my wrist and went to my shoulder. The area from my wrist to about halfway to my elbow actually had two layers of heavy protection.

As we did the "ups" and "downs," we were both very relaxed. Thunder was having a good hair day. We had done many of these reps, and each time I would give her the "up" command, I would position my forearm perpendicular to her body to facilitate her ease of stepping up onto it. This went on for a while—too long, in fact, so long that neither of us were paying attention any longer. Now she was hopping onto my arm instead of stepping.

Then one time I got out of sync with the arm presentation on the "up" command. It was already in place, but when I gave the "up" command, I moved my arm away as I would if I had just given the "down" command. She didn't notice until she hopped, putting both feet off the ground for an instant. She reached for my arm with the left foot and realized it was not there and that she was about to fall. She, out of desperation and reflex, reached out with her right talon in an effort to secure a perch on my arm. This happened very suddenly and lasted only a fraction of a moment. Her right foot, in an attempt to keep from falling, landed on my wrist. At this time, she had fallen below my arm and grabbed with enough force to assure a proper position on the perch: my arm.

In doing so, she applied so much force to the bones on either side of the wrist where the hand was attached that I thought she was going to crush it. Honestly, it felt as though someone had placed my wrist in a steel vice, snugged it up against those two protruding wrist bones, and then gave one hard quick twist to tighten the vice and just as quickly released the pressure. That really sent spears of pain through my body. I gave a "down" command and lowered my aching arm. The pain had shot up my arm to my shoulder. I removed the glove and gauntlet to examine my wrist. It looked fine, but even with the two layers of leather, she still managed to leave an imprint of her toes, which wrapped around my wrist. There were no punctures made, and all this pressure had been accomplished solely with the wrapped flat surface of the toes.

I could not believe the pain, and later that night, I could not raise my right arm at all. The next morning, my forearm was a dark shade of purple. I thought that purple must stand for pain, a simple conclusion to reach since they both start with *p* and I was in possession of both of them. This was my first real threatening encounter with Thunder's physical capabilities, and this was not an intentional thing she did to me. She did it to keep from falling off the tree branch—just that simple. I will tell you one thing, and you can believe it or not, but if she tried to duplicate that application of pressure while standing with one foot on each of the shoulders of an adult like myself, she would, without a doubt, crush the bones in the shoulder, including the collarbone. My arm took three weeks to get back to where I could use it completely.

I believe this incident was by no means intentional. What she did was quite natural under the conditions given. So when I refer to trusting and not fully trusting her, this is the reason. I don't know enough about her or bald eagles to drop my guard. That's what we both did. While there are a lot of written words about bald eagles, I don't believe there are as many facts as there are speculations and suppositions about them as a species. I don't think their behavior is understood, and I sure haven't found any references in all my searching that would have helped prevent this accident.

One thing I will say is I have all the respect in the world for wild animals and a big extra dose for Thunder. Most bald eagles that are used as we intend to use Thunder come by way of imprinting. If it's not imprinted and you really, really want to control it, you better starve it. Bald eagles, especially the larger females, have a spirit I have not remotely seen in any other raptor I have handled over the past forty-plus years. They aren't mean, but they are certainly spirited and potentially dangerous. You have to respect that.

Some days we would take short walks also in an attempt to get her more accustomed to moving around while standing on my arm. This would be necessary at future education programs. She would do fairly well, but once again, I was not certain I could trust her behavior at venues that might present stimuli we had not yet addressed. It was sort of like public speaking; you can practice all you want, but the real facts and issues don't appear until you step in front of that live audience for the first time.

The one issue I was still presented with each time we went for our walks was her jesses. It normally took me about twenty minutes to get them on her. We did have certain rules though; if, while I was trying to jess her, she happened to go to the ground, I would wait for her to return to her perch on her own. I would not chase her around in her cage. This could take ten to fifteen minutes at times. Again, this was the patience I would have to display to discourage her from using this avoidance technique. If she went to the ground, I would not leave the cage without jessing her up.

Another problem was the process of actually attaching the jesses to her ankles. The jesses, as I have mentioned before, are soft, supple, yet strong leather straps that were about a foot or so long and had tapered ends with one-inch slits cut in them. When putting the jesses on, I would have her stand still long enough that I could put a jess around each leg and slip one of the tapered ends into the slit on the opposite end. Then I pulled them snug around the ankle, making sure the jesses were positioned on the foot sides of the bands. It was made even more difficult while wearing heavy gloves that protected my fingers. After I had the jesses secured, I would reach into my left pocket, where I kept the leash that attached to the jesses. Remember, the leash has a swiveled snap hook on either end. One end, I attached to the two jesses, and the other was kept in my left hand, with my little finger hooked through the human end of the leash. I would carry the leash in my pocket but keep the swivel hanging out of it a bit. This made it easier to access with the gloves on. If I was wearing a coat or jacket, I would keep it in that pocket.

She was okay after I finally got the jesses on but balked a good bit when I pulled the leash from my pocket. The leash meant work, work she didn't particularly like. We had been doing this for a few months now, and her dislike for the leash had not lessened in the least. I really needed a plan to get her more comfortable with it. Her cage was a great place to think. Spending time with her was not overtaxing my brain (note the reference to my superior intelligence?), so I continued to address the leash-avoidance behavior.

Then out of the clear blue, it came to me. I had always read and/or heard that any new habit can be formed or an old habit eliminated in twenty-one consecutive days. This would be the answer to my dilemma and might also solve many of the world's problems as well. So here it was. I would drape the three-foot-long leash around my neck, allowing it to move freely and be in plain sight for the next twenty-one days. I would not try to jess or leash her during this time. I would let the leash just hang there, swinging harmlessly as I moved about the cage.

What a plan, I thought. *Why didn't I think of it sooner?*

Day one began, and my first appearance with the dangling leash received some concerned eye contact, but she wasn't entirely distressed by this new bling I was wearing either. I continued this for the full twenty-one days and only did "ups" and "downs" on a daily basis but without jesses.

It was now late November, and the twenty-one days had passed. It was now time for me to bathe in the success of my genius. I headed to her cage at around five o'clock on a cool and overcast evening. I had fed her earlier that day, and I brought nothing to the cage but myself and the bling I was wearing. I got into her cage and removed the leash from around my neck. As soon as I did that, she started hopping from perch to perch calmly but in an attempt to avoid me and the leash. When she moved from one of the perches to one that was perpendicular to the one she was on, she slipped and dropped four feet to the ground. It was really starting to get dark fast, and I hadn't figured on her falling from a perch. I assessed the time and decided we would have to wait until tomorrow and call the game because of darkness. It would be pitch dark by the time I waited for her to return to her perch. So I left, slightly disappointed that I didn't get to prove my superiority that night.

So the next evening, I tried again, but now I had her food as well. When I approached the cage, she was calmly sitting on a back perch. As I approached the door, she looked right at me and then took one step back, left her wings folded, and dropped to the ground. Again, it was getting late and dark as well. I decided I would leave her dinner and try the leash trick tomorrow. I was confused; why did she step off the perch? I left her cage, and she remained on the ground until I got about a hundred feet away. Then she flew onto her perch, where I had left the fish, and began eating. I could have gone back then but really didn't want to interrupt her dinner.

We'll get it tomorrow, I said very convincingly to myself.

The third night, I made it a point to get out there earlier in the evening. I did indeed, and I approached her cage as she sat, calmly and directly facing me. I was about twenty inches from her cage, and she gave me a confident look as she once again took one step back off the perch and, without opening her wings, landed on the ground. I would almost swear that she made a gesture in my direction as she was dropping to the ground. At that point, I admitted that I had been bested again by a bald eagle. Since the first evening, when she very unintentional fell to the ground and I left her cage directly afterward, I guess she figured if this worked once, she would keep trying it; after all, she was working with an intellectually superior being.

My feelings were hurt, so just to show her that I would not go down in flames, I calmly waited for her to return to her perch. I reentered her cage, and we finished what I had started twenty-four days ago.

After looking back at that evening, I would say that there was an improvement in her behavior, but the more I rehash the entire course of events, the more it is likely she just felt sorry for me and let me believe my plan had some merit.

Chapter 20

Our Third Christmas Together—Already

Time continued to pass, and now it was the third anniversary of Thunder's shooting. It was still hard to believe that she could have been shot, but as I said earlier, we don't believe that all these bald eagles were being shot as bald eagles but just as big brown birds—not that that, in any way, justifies the shootings. As I stood there thinking of this, it came to me that at three years of age, if literature was correct, she should have a considerable amount of white on her head and tail by now. That would seem logical if she was going to be sexually mature as an adult at age four. She was soon to be four years old, but where were the white feathers? Pictures I had seen of three-year-olds showed considerable white streaking on the head and tail as well. I knew how old Thunder was; she was banded as a nestling. Did the folks identifying the ages of those photographed really know, for sure, how old the birds were? I think this could be part of the reason we shoot these big brown birds; it's not like anyone really knows that much about our national emblem. We hope to start eliminating this ignorance gap very soon.

Rethinking these past years made me even more impatient about getting her ready for the education circuit. She was not as great an asset in her present state as she would be when we could use her as an ambassador for the sake of all other living creatures. I hoped to have each of us ready by this coming spring, 1995. Contemplating these future events made my mind go into planning mode. I'd given thought to this previously but only in passing.

But now it was time to consider how she would be transported to various venues. I needed something to carry her in and something to carry that in, a cage large enough to accommodate her that I could still lift and carry as necessary. Also, a vehicle large enough to transport the cage would be another necessity. We already had columnar cages constructed for other birds like the red-tailed hawks, screech owls, and great horned owls. This cage would need to be much larger. The red-tailed hawks and great horned owls were both in the three-to-four-pound range, measuring twenty-four to thirty inches long with four-foot wingspans. Thunder was a bit larger, weighing a healthy twelve pounds, measuring from tip of tail to top of head about forty inches, and sporting a six-and-a-half-foot wingspan. That was with the one-foot wrist of her left wing missing. With both wings complete, she had almost a seven-and-a-half-foot wingspan.

All our cages were pretty much the same, with major variations being the scale of everything, from height to diameter, door size, perch sizes, and even the size of the rope that wrapped the perches. All of them had removable perches on the top that the birds could feel safe on while being displayed. They were removable to reduce the height during transport. So after I considered everything, I decided Thunder's cage needed to be thirty-nine inches high with thirty-eight inches of inside space for her head and tail, remember that the forty-inch length of Thunder was measured at about a thirty-degree angle. That's about what you get drawing a line from head to tail on most raptors. Owls stand a bit straight up and down. So the thirty-eight inches would provide a few inches for both head and tail.

I wanted to make the diameter as large as practical. One limit was the standard thirty-six-inch door we would be passing through at many of our programs. I calculated a thirty-one-and-a-half-inch diameter would fit through all doors we would encounter. Most thirty-six inches would yield a net of about thirty-two inches from jam to jam. So the cage would be thirty-one and a half inches wide and thirty-nine inches high. All perches would be fabricated with four-inch thin-walled PVC pipe and wrapped with half-inch hemp rope. This would make her perches just over five inches in diameter.

This girl had some big feet (talons). There would be a cross perch inside that went from side to side and helped provide support for the entire cage. There would be another detachable perch that would be threaded onto the top for easy removal and strong enough to hold her weight. It too would be made of thin-walled PVC. A six-inch piece would connect to a PVC T-connector. The entire perch was only high enough to keep her tail from touching the outside top of the cage and just about ten inches wide.

The bars of the cage, forty-seven of them, would be very thin-walled tubing. It was very light and, at three fourths of an inch in diameter, plenty strong. Most of our cages were constructed with wooden dowel rods. The weight of one of the wooden ones of the same length would weigh just a bit more than six of the aluminum tubing rods. The circumference of the cage would be about ninety-four inches, and with one bar per two inches, I'd need about forty-seven bars. Eight of the wooden dowel rods would weigh the same as the forty-seven aluminum ones. That would make my life much easier loading and unloading the cage with Thunder in it.

The base and top would be half-inch plywood. That was the strongest and lightest material I could work with. I fastened the top and bottom pieces together, marked my forty-seven holes, and drilled a tiny pilot hole representing the center of the rods. I drilled through both boards and marked the outside edges of each piece so I could get them in the same place when I drilled the recess holes that would contain a quarter inch of the end of each tubing bar. Now the inside board making up the bottom of the cage (the floor) and inside of the top board making up the ceiling had recesses drilled in them that lined up perfectly with one another. I used four quarter-inch all-thread rods to bolt the bars as they were placed between the top and bottom. Two of them represented about one third of the circumference, which would represent the door hinge and the post that the door would fasten to. There were only two more bolts equally spaced that would hold the cage together. There was no more metal in the cage at all. The door and latch were also constructed so metal hardware would not need to be used.

Construction was complete, and now I had to dress it up to be fit for our national symbol. The last two years of working with Thunder had been difficult at best, with seemingly minimum accomplishments. Constructing her cage was a way to instill a bit of enthusiasm and hope into the effort. Now to put the finishing touches on the transportation for what I hoped would be the most worthy ambassador for all living creatures.

Since overheating would be more of an issue than the cold, I went with basic white for the entire cage. The bars were aluminum, but I sprayed their insides to eliminate their reflectivity. I splashed a bit of patriotic red and blue to the perches to go with the white. I was finished, and it looked suitable to transport our proud national emblem in. The drape used to cover the cage was a white sheet. Covers are necessary to keep the birds calm. Sound/noise doesn't affect birds' behavior, but motion sure does, hence the drape.

We were almost ready to travel. The only things lacking now were a bird that would travel in the cage and a vehicle to transport the caged bird. Thunder wasn't yet ready for public appearances, so I figured I had some time to locate a vehicle. I didn't want a cargo-type van, but most other types I considered were not capable of carrying something thirty-two inches wide and thirty-eight inches tall, at least not standing up. After visiting many different dealerships, I finally decided on the Chrysler-produced minivans. We were now set for travel as soon as we finished our training.

At this time, I began to realize the enormity of this entire situation. The question I was now asking myself was, will I be ready to take her out in public? I was actually feeling a bit apprehensive and a touch of doubt when considering the variations of venues we might have to visit. I had done hundreds and hundreds of these types of educational programs, and I knew what to expect from those planning the event as well as the audiences. Our audiences varied greatly in age. One program in particular, I remember, was at a large church. The seating capacity was something over three hundred, and it was full. The ages of the attendees ranged from four to ninety-four. I just had a red-tailed hawk with me that evening, and she was a very easy bird. Nonetheless, I struggled with that large audience largely because of the age difference. Speaking to a large audience of a similar age group is not that difficult, but when you add all possible age ranges, it becomes necessary to pay close attention to the audience to make sure you aren't talking over their heads or insulting them with elementary-school vocabulary. If either mark is missed, that segment of the audience will quickly be put to sleep.

Thunder was doing fine in this venue, but how do we prepare for the absolute unknown like the one just described? The size and temperament of the bird was going to be the X factor. Annie, the red-tailed hawk, was imprinted, very experienced, familiar with large groups of people, and weighed only three pounds. If she bated at any part of the program, I didn't even miss a beat; she was that easy to handle. Thunder, on the other hand, was a wild bird, not used to strange venues, a female bald eagle that lived up to the reputation of female bald eagles, and she was very large. I kept asking myself, how do I handle the crowd when she decides to bate? At twelve pounds and instantly at a speed of ten miles per hour, I would be on the dumb end of a three-foot leash that now had a force of about 120 pounds pulling against me. I thought it would be difficult to concentrate on my subject matter while contemplating the worst possible scenario involving maintaining control of Thunder.

That was enough worrying for today, and I decided that we had gotten this far and there was no logical reason to believe we couldn't accomplish our remaining goals. Tomorrow was another day, and we would continue with the training plan as scripted in my head. *I'll be back tomorrow, Thunder.*

We continued through the winter, same routines but with hope that the repetition of our basics—jessing, attaching to the leash, doing ups and downs, and generally walking around—would help prepare for that first program. It was February 1995, and I knew it was just a matter of time until there would be a specific request for Thunder at one of our programs. We had not been advertising her, but she was definitely getting to be the talk of the town, so to speak. We weren't trying to keep her a secret, but by the same token, I didn't think we were ready for the stage just yet. Many of our other volunteers thought differently though. They were talking her up as though she was already a veteran ambassador—far from the truth. That made me more tense, nervous, and almost frightened of the prospect. I kept those emotions to myself, but the knowledge of the eventual first program kept ringing in my head.

As we continued working on our basics, ups and downs and the like, I began to notice that when we would walk, she would extend her wings as though to keep her balance. I understood that, but once we would stop, at times, she would still keep them extended. This would be a problem that I recognized we might have to address down the road. Then I began to apply that thought to getting her into her travel cage. No way would she go through that door—or any door, for that matter—with those seven-foot wings, even partly extended. I was glad I thought of this, but now I was wondering how many more things like this I didn't even know enough to realize they would or could be a problem.

Keep in mind that Thunder and I had little physical interactions. In fact, I was still jessing her with both my hands gloved, not much touchy-feely interaction going on between us. The next time she had her wings extended and we weren't walking, I reached up to her left wing and touched the end of it with my left hand. When I did it, I gave her the command "Fold 'em." Surprise, surprise—she did it. The next time they were extended, I did the same thing and gave the same command. Again, she folded them to her side. The next time she extended them, I told her to "fold 'em," and I didn't touch her. Yep, you guessed it; she put them into her body.

Great, now I can get her into her travel cage. I extended that thought to another "what if"—we needed to go through a doorway. That was easy. The next time we were out walking about, I decided to go to my office building and see if we could get through it. As we approached the door, which was closed, I guessed that I could open it with my left hand and have her "fold 'em," and we would walk in. I was sure this would be a no-brainer. She had folded them on numerous trial commands, so she should do as well here.

As we approached the building, I was preparing to open the door when a strong and unexpected gust of wind caught us both by surprise. I tried to correct for the sideways push, and Thunder tried to correct for both me and the wind. It was simple—she threw her wings out as though you would do with your arms had someone shoved you. They went out quickly, and she retracted them quickly. But I didn't respond to her response quickly enough, and before I could raise my arm higher to allow the wing to retract and clear my head, well, I didn't, and she did, and that powerful contraction motion permitted that partially amputated wing to come crashing down on the center of my skull with the end of the amputated bone.

It hit me so hard, unintentionally, that I almost went to the ground. For an instant, I actually saw a white flash followed by a blackout. My knees buckled, but I caught myself by grabbing the doorknob that I had been reaching for. That was close. I seemed all right after a few seconds, and then my head began to hurt, followed by a strange feeling that something was on my face. I put my hand to my left cheek and felt something wet. When I looked at my hand, it was covered with blood. I continued to bleed as I opened the door and began to walk through it.

As I advanced, Thunder showed a tiny bit of reluctance and began to open her wings. I instructed her to fold 'em, and she did. We walked inside. I turned the light on in the garage area, and I immediately bent down and gave her a down command. She hopped to the floor. I dropped the leash and began looking for paper towels to press onto my bleeding scalp. I got the bleeding stopped and my face and neck cleaned off, at least mostly. This was an accident, nothing intentional, but the mere impact of her closing her wing felt like someone hit me on the head with a piece of two-by-two-inch lumber, not as heavy as a baseball bat but definitely a big stick. I would live. Another point for Thunder.

I thought it time to return her to her flight cage. I had other things planned, but I wasn't feeling very well. I knelt down on the floor, extended my arm, and gave Thunder the up command. She seemed a bit confused for an instant. I was not sure why; I was the one knocked almost unconscious. As she obeyed her command, I had my arm at a bad angle, which confused her, and she turned and got on my arm, facing the wrong direction. She was on my arm backward, and I knew we could not leave the room with her in that position. I would have absolutely no control, and she would be facing away from my body.

This was a no-no, and I wasn't feeling very well, so I reached up with my left hand, pushed her tail to my left gently, and said, "Turn." She did it. I was so pleased, my head quit hurting for a brief moment. She was on my arm correctly, and we then proceeded out the door with a "fold 'em" command that she obeyed. I turned, closed the door, and headed back to her cage.

As we walked and I bled, I realized that we now had four commands that I could count on her to respond to. They were "up" and "down," and today we learned "fold 'em" and "turn"—quite the day. If I were British, I likely would have said, "And quite the bloody day, mate," but I'm not, so I didn't. Thunder was now safe in her flight cage, and I was staggering back to my cage. I was later told that I should have had stitches, but I healed, and I was forced to give Thunder yet another measure of respect.

Chapter 21

Preparing for Our First Offsite Presentation

April 22, 1995, will forever represent the beginning of Thunder's travels as an educational ambassador for the benefit of all living things. We had received our first official invitation to do a public presentation that we were prepared to seriously consider. Honestly, I was not sure I would have done this program, but since this was on Earth Day, well, maybe this was an omen of sorts, the firing of the starter gun or the Kentucky Derby call "And they're off!" At any rate, the commitment was made, and we needed to plan accordingly.

I honestly don't remember a time in my life that I was this nervous, not when I had to speak to the entire student body in fourth grade, dressed in a pale green suit as the king of the court, or in the eighth grade, when I had to recite the entire Gettysburg Address before the class. I had been working up to this happening for years now, and that was likely the cause of all the angst. The public speaking was not a consideration but public speaking when I wasn't confident that, as they say, "all's well that ends well." I'm not exactly certain what is meant by that, but it too could be telling me to not be worried about this one; things will smooth out, and in the end, well, all's well that ends well. At this point, I had done hundreds and hundreds of public presentations, but none of them had so much interference thrown into the mix. I wasn't certain I could concentrate on Thunder (trying to anticipate what she might do in front of a large audience and what I might have to do in response and if I would be able to do it) while I was also at least trying to make a presentation that, in some fashion, was worth listening to.

I still had most of March and three weeks in April to formulate a plan. *Formulate a plan,* I thought. There really hadn't been a good formal plan from the start on December 22, 1992, when I took responsibility for Thunder. *A plan? Who am I kidding?* I have talked about my plans from the start of this book, but there never were any that amounted to anything. The most I had even been hopeful to plan for was generally less than a day or a single event, and I don't remember getting any of those right. Remember the plan to get Thunder used to the leash? Well, that didn't go very well; that's for certain.

As I tormented myself more and more, I began to realize that she and I had worked hard, and while there were no formal plans, since neither of us really knew each other well enough to develop a strategy in the beginning, I at least had a long-term goal. That was to prepare her to be able to make public presentations/appearances while maintaining her health and looking out for her overall welfare as well as the welfare of the audiences. So I guess that was the plan. Remember how I talked about all my previous plans and how none of them worked? We will see.

As we prepared for the big day, I went over the strategies I had made for the entire event, and anything that I thought could go wrong was addressed. We went over the handling, transportation, and ultimate unveiling. She had not yet even been in her travel cage, and I decided not to do that, just in case, until the day of. That might seem a bit foolish, considering all that could possibly go wrong. For one, she might refuse to get into the travel cage. That would be bad, but I thought positively in a double-negative fashion. What if we struggled this time when we were merely practicing and she hated it, and then when I really needed to get her into the cage, she refused to go? I was not sure I could force her to do anything unless she was sedated. If this happened, then the next time I really needed her to do it, she would refuse. Remember that she is a "once, and it's learned" girl. I chose to wait until that day.

April 22, 1995, came and we were to visit a local mall. The program was to be held at a raised stage at center court. I made a trip there the week earlier to make sure there would not be too many surprises. The mall floor came to a center area from four directions that dropped four steps into a parapet-like area on the floor around the bottom of the raised stage. That level was about thirty inches below the main floor level and nearly four and a half feet below the stage floor. One area had a bridge to access the stage. It was a slight incline.

So I knew exactly where we were going, but while I was there, I realized I would need a way to carry her cage from the mall's parking lot. The cage wasn't very heavy but its size—thirty-one and a half inches wide and thirty-nine and a half inches high, made in a circle—was a bit bulky to carry, especially with a twelve-pound eagle inside. I was glad I made the visit. I decided I needed a portable cart to transport her on. My answer stood before me—Sears. It was just a stone's throw away, so I headed inside and back to the tool department. There it set, a dolly-like cart combo (I could use it as a two0wheeled dolly or change the handle and use it as a four-wheeled cart). It was lightweight and fire-engine red—perfect, a bit more red to help her get over that color red hysteria. I paid the thirty-six dollars for it and wheeled it out with receipt in hand. Now we were ready for sure. I distinctly remember telling myself that.

We were scheduled for a two-o'clock presentation. The drive and setup and getting Thunder to the stage should be done easily in one hour. I was going to give myself forty minutes from when I entered her flight cage until we got loaded. I had the travel cage already in the minivan. There were wing windows that opened on each side in the rear of the van. The inside of them had a bar that the windows pivoted on when they opened. I tied some light nylon rope to each window part and cut each to the length needed to secure the cage from two sides. This would keep it from moving forward or from side to side. The back gate secured it from behind. I gathered all my gloves, the jesses, and the leash and placed them into the back of the van to the left of the cage.

It was high noon, and I pulled my van out into the driveway closer to Thunder's flight cage. I got out of the car, gathered my gear, and began feeling like I was headed for the OK Corral for a giant shootout. I knew that was just what could happen too. The back gate was raised, and the oversized door on the travel cage was opened as far as it could go. I began that twenty-five-yard walk to her cage with a feeling in my stomach like none other I could recall. I began talking to her as I approached and tried to act calm. I entered the cage and began messing with the water in the pool, trying not to show my tremendous anxiety.

Finally, I moved slowly, the way I always did, toward her, all the while asking her to be gentle. I was surprised that jessing her took much less than normal time.

I hooked up her leash, presented my arm and said, "Up."

Up she went. I praised her—like she cared—and then told her, "Down."

We did a couple more ups and downs, and I decided it was time to load. She was on the perch, and I laid her leash down as I went to the door. I opened it as wide as it would go and quickly returned to secure the leash.

I said, "Up," and she was on my arm. I turned and headed for the door.

As I neared it, I turned so I could back out. I started doing this long ago as a means to provide something to block her bating to get out the door. This worked well, and we were soon out in the lawn, heading for the van.

As we approached the van, a first time for her, she bated. I wasn't sure if it was because of the van or just because she could. She did two pretty good loops and was back on my arm. She was breathing a bit, but then so was I. I continued walking with her perched on my arm. We were now near the van.

I stood as close to the cage door, which sat inside the back of the van, as possible, lowered my arm near the big perch inside, and said, "Down." She did it. We did it.

I swiftly shut the cage door and secured it. She didn't budge. Then I pulled the cover over the front of the cage. The rest of the cage was already covered with the intent of giving her a more secure feeling and place to perch. This was what I did when she was placed in the original cage in my garage, but this time, she was completely covered with a white sheet. She wasn't in the dark, but she couldn't see me anymore, and I guess that was a good thing. I secured the rear hatch of the van by lowering it.

I got behind the wheel, and just as I started to accelerate, I wondered how her balance was and how she would ride. I slowly went the last 150 yards out my driveway.

As the vehicle moved forward, she seemed to stumble briefly and then regain her footing. The driveway had a slight slope to the main road. I had to stop before turning right on the highway. As I carefully came to a stop, she shuffled only briefly. When I accelerated again, there wasn't a peep out of her. I didn't drive like a Sunday driver, but I did not brake or speed up, and I took the turns gently. I did not tailgate at all.

We arrived there and thus far without incident. We were more than thirty minutes early, so I didn't rush. I removed the new cart from the van and placed it near the rear gate. As it turned out, this would be the first of hundreds of times I would repeat this routine.

I raised the rear gate of the van and found Thunder calm and quiet. I untied the ropes used as cage tie-downs. I slightly raised the cover and peeked inside. She was fine. She looked at me as if to ask, "What?"

I dropped the drape and grabbed her cage by both sides and lifted as I slid the cage partway out of the van. It was then that I realized how much more her twelve pounds really weighed. When I put the cage in the van, it was empty. I grabbed the top ledge of the cage with both hands and, with one smooth motion, plucked the cage out of the van and placed it on the cart. I positioned it so she would be situated facing the direction of travel. I'm over six feet and two inches tall and weigh about 210 pounds. A shorter and less physically developed person would have had a very difficult time removing the caged bird by themselves. It wasn't the weight so much as the height of the cage and the angle by which it had to be lifted. Even I couldn't get close enough to the cage to use either my legs or my back. It was all arms.

I loaded my gloves, armguard, and leash on top of her cage and screwed the short perch to the center of the top. I had hoped this would be where she would stand for the entire presentation. When we got to the door, we were met by one of the mall representatives and the person who set up the twenty-fifth Earth Day anniversary celebration. They did the natural greetings and then asked if they could take a peek at Thunder. I didn't really speak but looked at them as if to say, "Born at night? Yes. Last night? No."

We kept walking, and they began offering assistance wherever they thought they could. The Earth Day representative finally specifically asked if there was anything I would like for her to do. I stopped the cart, looked at both of them, and announced that this would be the first program for Thunder and me.

With a straight face, I looked directly at her and said, "If you really want to help, it would be nice if, after you introduce me and as I start my presentation, you would kindly remove Thunder from her cage and set her on the perch atop the cage."

She gleefully replied, "Really?"

I smiled and told her that I was joking but appreciated the sincere offer. I went on to explain that I had absolutely no clue what was going to happen when I opened that cage. The looks on their faces were priceless, and then the lady said, "You are kidding, right?"

I smiled again and, this time, responded that I most certainly was not kidding. "For this reason, I would like the parapet area below the stage roped off so no one can come down the stairs. I would also like to have some security there to make certain the barriers are respected as well."

The mall manager got on his radio—cell phones were not yet the thing—and made the arrangements for security and rope.

We got to the ramp, and up we went onto the stage. I placed the cart where I hoped it would stay for the next forty-five to sixty minutes. I had done a scouting mission earlier in the week but now realized that I hadn't been very observant as I scanned the people already waiting, the children holding balloons on *long* strings, the blinking colored neon lights, the reflecting window glass, the red blinking 50% Off sale signs, and the hordes of moving humans. The noise was terrible, but that was not a concern. Thunder just cared about what she could see. Right now, I was very glad she was covered and really, genuinely, for the first time, wondered if this was not going to be a visual overload for her. And I thought she was ready? Silly me. The audience was likely 20 percent or more dressed in some fashion of red. How would I handle this? *Improvise*, I thought, and I've always been good at that.

It was five minutes and counting. I asked the lady to do whatever introduction she wanted to do and leave the rest to Thunder and me. I looked at them both, smiled, and said, "Don't worry. What could possibly go wrong?"

The mall manager ensured that the security was adequate and left the stage, possibly the entire building. Then the MC began her introduction with the fact that I would be here with an unspecified special guest that was going to help us all celebrate the twenty-fifth anniversary of Earth Day. Then she handed me the mic as the growing audience applauded. I thought that might be a bit premature considering the circumstances.

I now recognized the first problem that I had not considered. How was I going to hold Thunder and the microphone? Panic set into a once fairly calm guy. I decided I would have to make my first on-the-fly course correction.

I took the mic, thanked the master of ceremonies, and greeted the crowd. The first thing I said after the niceties was "Have you heard the one about the bull in the china shop? Well, folks, that's just what we might have here in this cage behind me. You see, I have this large raptor, and this is her first public appearance. Just so you know, some of her likes and dislikes, I will name a few for you. First, all you folks wearing noticeable amounts of red, you all know how bulls react to red, right? Okay, then would you possible targets for the bull try to hide as much of it as you can? Stand behind someone else, put on a jacket, or if you are fearful and feel the urge, now would be a good time to leave. She also doesn't like the moving colored balloons on those long strings, so, parents, please tie them off down low and make sure they don't go drifting off into the bull's space. She also doesn't like the blinking lights, neon signs, or reflective glass everywhere around us. She would be grateful if you stood fairly still and definitely do not approach the stage.

"Now as for the things she likes, let me think. That's right. Thus far, I have come up with none. Now I ask one more thing of you, and that is to be patient with us. We have a logistical issue here, and I need to correct it before we can continue. The problem is the handheld microphone. I will need both my hands, so I am going to try to stuff the left glove and hold it up into my shirt with the cuff up. Then I'll stuff the long glove into my shirt, all the way, and then insert the mic into the open end of the glove."

I stuck the mic into the glove, and it stayed fairly stable. I told them that I was going to try it this way, and if necessary, I could possibly reposition it from time to time. I then asked that they all remain as still as possible while I got Thunder out of the cage. We were surrounded—360 degrees of human bodies—and as I talked, the audience got larger and larger. I was only going to face one direction, so a lot of folks were going to have rear views of Thunder and me. With the public-address system, they would still be able to hear and at least see Thunder.

I approached her still-covered cage, slowly lifted the drape from just the door area, put my gloves and right armguard on, and slowly opened the door. She didn't really appear too agitated. I reached inside and got the ends of her two jesses. Fortunately, the other ends were still attached to her legs. I had the swivel in the left hand, and I reached inside the cage and hooked the jesses to the leash.

Now for the fun part—the big welcome. I turned slightly to the left to better position my arm in front of her. I gave the command "Up," and she immediately stepped up onto my right arm. I backed away from the cage, keeping myself between her and the audience as I stood up. I placed her on her perch, but as soon as I told her, "Down," she got down but then immediately got back on my arm. I was sweating bullets, waiting for Thunder to bate.

She held fast as I introduced her to the audience, who were doing a lot of *oooh*ing and *aaah*ing. I began by asking if anyone other than those there from the raptor center knew what this big brown bird was. No one came close. No one even guessed a golden eagle—lots of hawks and buzzards. I explained that she was a three-year-old American bald eagle. The audience was amazed and even more so when I explained the absence of the white head and tail. They were also very sorry to hear how she had been shot.

Thunder did well. She stayed on my arm the entire time as I perspiring profusely and tried to maintain a rational train of thought while concentrating on her situation. That was difficult to do. I hardly ever use a script when doing public speaking, so the words come easy for me and even with one of our other birds on my arm, which are small enough, up to three or four pounds, to handle without much thought. They all have a lot of public-presentation experience as well. Thunder was not small, and she required all the attention she got. I did not feel as though I could drop my guard a bit. I continued my presentation, and Thunder held fast. I wasn't certain if she was calm or so frightened that she literally could not move. She never left my arm.

Now that our time was running out, I felt the verbal part of the presentation was just barely okay. I was really distracted, and this did not, by any means, represent multitasking. In retrospect, I would have liked to have known what my vital signs were during this forty-five minutes, like how my internal reaction responded to the kid's balloon that went floating to the ceiling about midway through the program or the purple neon sign right in front of us at a perfect eye level when it began flashing off and on. Somehow she stayed on my arm the entire time and hardly flinched. I was so glad she stayed put, but about twenty minutes in, my entire right arm began to fall totally asleep. I wanted to clinch my fist to try to get some blood circulating, but do you think I did? No way.

Later—much later since I'm a slow learner—I realized that like a lot of children, Thunder was much better behaved among strangers than at home. Sounds funny to make this comparison, but it is true. Strange people to a bird or a child yield the same results. They both feel more comfortable with what they are most familiar with. Mom, you sometimes might think that your daughter hates you, but put her in a "this or that" situational choice and see where their loyalties or trust lies. At the end of this program, I had not yet made that correlation regarding behavior. I felt a bit like I would imagine a person working on a bomb squad would, not that I know that, but I felt I was working with a small ticking bomb, not having a hint as to what the timer read while I waited for the end. Really, it was that trying. I have survived numerous more dangerous things in my life up till now, but I was never so ill prepared as I felt right then.

Now it was time to see if we could end this drama and test whether or not she would go into her cage a second time. I don't remember how I ended this talk, but once I made that commitment, the first thing I did was to ask the audience to help me witness this second historic moment of the day by standing perfectly still for just a moment longer while I returned her to her cage for the first time in public. Everyone was so nice and obliging.

Now I needed to unlatch her cage door and then open it all the way. She was already on my arm, which was very much asleep. I raised her and brought her to the front of the cage, where I now squatted down to place her on the inside perch. As I got down to the perch level, she automatically hopped onto her perch; no command was given. I quickly unsnapped the jesses from the leash and closed the door. I pulled the cover over the front of her cage and breathed a huge sigh of relief.

As I began to stand, I placed my hand on the top of her cage and looked up. I could not believe what I saw. The ceiling was made of one-foot square pieces of mirrors connected at angles as they covered the concave side of the domed ceiling. All that I saw in those mirrors were people; all the people around us on the floor moving around were doing the same thing up above. No wonder Thunder didn't move the entire time and would not get off my arm. She was totally surrounded. I'm not sure how much she trusted me, but it was obvious from her good behavior that she at least trusted me more than anyone else there. My first really big win and an observation I used during all our future programs: she doesn't like me, but she dislikes everyone else even more.

After the program was over, our director of operations came and praised me for the fine training I had done with Thunder. He said it appeared that any of the education volunteers would be able to handle her. I thanked him and then revealed the truth. I explained to him that she was simply too frightened to leave my arm, and even though she appeared to like me, I was simply the lesser of two evils. She never did like me; she just disliked everyone else a lot more. I agreed that I was in favor of others handling her at programs, but I would strongly advise that we start with baby steps. These baby steps would take place at my place, not at a public venue.

Our first public presentation was over, and Thunder and I were the only ones who thought it was a borderline disaster. Everyone there thought she was beautiful, so regal and well behaved. I loaded her into the van, drove home carefully, and returned Thunder to her flight cage. I removed her jesses and went back to the house, and I then returned with her fish. When I got back to her cage, she was in the water bathing, an obvious attempt to clean the human stench from her feathers. From that day on, she always bathed after our programs, rain or shine and winter or summer—something about the human odor, I guess. Now Thunder and I were both happy and planned to relax for the rest of the day. She ate her fish after her bath.

I went back to the house and unloaded the cage and other gear before heading upstairs. As I was fixing myself a snack and something to drink, I couldn't help reflecting on this major event. I managed a somewhat selfish smile over the fact that we pulled this off without incident. The corners of the smile soon went south as I relived the most disorganized presentation I had ever done dating back to my fourth grade. I relived the "sweating bullets" uneasiness I felt for the entire program and the relative ineffectiveness of the broken-up presentation. Really, it was broken up by me trying to talk while concentrating 100 percent on the presence and well-being of Thunder. I felt as distracted as if I had been speaking to a large crowd while, at the same time, trying to extinguish flames on my pants legs. Honestly, I have never even come close to this mind-splitting experience. I wondered if it would ever get better.

After the brief pity party I had just attended alone, I got a grip of myself and began to realize that all was not bad about the entire story of today. After all, this had been the culmination of two and a half years of work by myself and Thunder. All in all, I was very proud and pleased with how things went and assured myself that it would likely only get better. I knew she would continue to be a distraction and sometimes her behavior would not be as good as it was today. Bad hair days would have to appear from time to time, and I could almost guarantee that I hadn't even begun to scratch the surface when it came to really knowing Thunder. I was convinced that more hurdles would appear without warning but confident we would both grow and learn together as we overcame each one. We have the same issues with many of our other education birds, but they go unchallenged and unnoticed, the difference being size. Thunder is a monster at twelve pounds, while the next size closest to her would be less than one third her size. This makes a big difference when controlling these birds.

During the next few months, we continued to do an increasing number of programs, but it was always just Thunder and me. I had no trouble loading or unloading her, driving, or, for the most part, having her behave during the presentations. If, for some known or unknown reason, she didn't like the venue and seemed stressed, I would put her back in her travel cage. She felt secure there. This was quickly identified by me as a safe zone for her. From the first time I placed her in the cage, she never refused to enter it. In fact, she was usually very eager to go there. I didn't understand this for a while but gradually began to realize that in here, she was safe, and to a certain extent, safe did not necessarily include me. If you picture the covered cage with the door open and only that part of the drape raised, you would understand she viewed it as a safe place because she could not see anything in the surrounding area, either moving or not. As soon as she stepped on her perch, I would close the door and cover her completely. She was fine, and I made sure that this was her private space and would not allow anyone to raise the drape or even "take a peek."

Without knowing, I had created a very positive situation for her, and once I realized this, I made certain that her privacy was never violated. I later explained to audiences that while covered, she felt totally safe. If she could not see you, then you didn't exist, at least as a threat. All raptors are sight orientated, and even though we know they can hear, they don't seem to be startled or even concerned by sound. One example of this, which I explained to audiences, is that while Thunder was covered, I could fire a revolver a foot from Thunder's cage, and she would not flinch, but if I uncovered her cage, where she could see me and I merely cocked the hammer to the revolver, she would go ballistic. This has been true with every raptor we have dealt with. It's all about what they see, and since Thunder was my responsibility and I was charged with her safety and general well-being, I made certain that no one ever did anything to her, least of all when she was in her travel cage. Owls are, to some extent, an exception to this observation. They use sound to help locate food, and over the years, they seem a bit more sensitive and reactive to abstract sounds.

Chapter 22

Presentation Variables and Substitutes

We were asked to bring Thunder to a nongame wildlife weekend hosted by the DNR. I would not be able to attend, so our director of operations volunteered to take Thunder and do a couple of programs. Remember Dave from our first program? He thought Thunder was an absolute angle. It was good to have a positive attitude when working with Thunder, but a bit of on-hand experience would also be helpful. I told Dave that he might want to work with her a bit before making that commitment. He was pretty sure that she was well trained enough that he most certainly could handle her. I consented and told him he would have to use my vehicle since she did not fit in any others.

The Friday afternoon that he and Thunder were supposed to arrive at the event, Dave came by around noon to load her in the van and head to the program. It was a very humid mid-June day, and there was a light rain to make it even stickier. It took about twenty minutes before Dave was about to throw in the towel and cancel the program. He was having extreme difficulty keeping her on his arm, let alone loading her in the carrying cage. She was severely beating him with her huge wings as she would bate. Remember that it required a great deal of special arm strength to keep her up and away from your head when she was flapping her weaponry in the form of wings. Dave was being severely abused. He was going to have to deal with her at the program, so it was necessary that he be aware of what would be required of him during a presentation.

Well, to shorten a long story, they got there and back, all in one piece. Thunder was taken out of her carrying cage once. He got her back in, and she stayed there for the remainder of the event. Dave brought her home and got her back in her flight cage and never handled her again. I asked how it went, and without uttering a word, he just shook his head and walked away.

After that presentation, Thunder's reputation definitely preceded her. Although almost all the volunteers wanted to work with her, they knew that it was not likely to happen. I would not object, but if you wanted to work with her, then you would have to do lots of training plus muscle development. She was a big strong bird. Honestly, the wings did more damage to anyone holding her than anything. Most folks had arms so short that the slightest open-and-close wing action would put knots on the holder's head. The wingbeats were usually just her arranging her wing feathers, nothing more. Most settled for pictures, holding her while the arm holding Thunder was resting on the cage perch. I would hold the leash just in case. Over the years, only one other person ever did or attempted to do a presentation with her. She exercised her arms and back and got into shape, but even then, Thunder's strong wings proved too invasive to protect her. She did manage to handle her for two programs, and she did well, but I did the talking so she could concentrate on handling her. She was the last to make an attempt in public.

The dozens of programs we attended in the early months were definitely learning experiences for me. While seated audiences were the norm, the venues were quite varied. Sometimes I would be on a stage in a school or in front of a seated audience in the basement of a church. One of my programs was scheduled for an evening at a public library. When I got there, I had no place nearby to park, and there were twelve steps leading to the front door. I would always arrive early to allow adequate time to get set up, but I'd never yet or would ever again park almost a block away and traverse so many stairs. These two items went on my set list of things to ask before I agreed to present a program.

Back to the library—I had to leave Thunder in the van while I went to get some help and hopefully a better parking spot. I definitely needed help carrying the cart and cage up the steps. I vowed that this would be the last staircase we would have to negotiate. It was a warm summer evening, and the sun was still out, so I left the engine running with the air conditioner on to keep Thunder from overheating. I still had to lock the car, but minivans had a safety thing on them that would not allow you to lock the door with the front-door lock button while the car was running and the driver's door was open. I guess you couldn't lock yourself out of a running car.

The librarian was glad to see us and allowed us to use a staff spot next to the building to park. She and a gentleman helped with the stairs. I was responsible for Thunder, so I had to make sure that those helping to carry her would not trip and drop her.

We got her up the steps and into the first set of doors leading into the air lock. When we tried to go through the other set of doors, her cage would not fit. I had designed the maximum width of her cage to be thirty-one and a half inches wide, which would accommodate any thirty-six-inch door that has a thirty-three-and-a-half-inch actual opening. This cage was way too wide for this door. What now? The librarian suggested we use the loading dock at the back of the building. So down the stairs we went and rolled the cart and Thunder around the building—and what did we have? It was a loading dock, about four feet off the ground. The libraries have this saying: "Reading is fun," and it is, but getting Thunder into the library most certainly was not.

We got set up, and there was a really nice crowd there, lots of parents with their children. I like to see this mix in an audience. It's nice when the parents participate in the children's education and provide them with as many diverse opportunities as possible.

This qualified as a diverse opportunity. There weren't many places that you could go and see a wild bald eagle stretching its wings in a public library.

While I had the audience I had hoped for, now I was already worn out from trying to get into the building. When I did have her set up, the audience was fine, but all the other people moving about the library provided quite the distraction for both Thunder and me. I had noticed that most of the programs I had done to date were less than effective as I had difficulty concentrating on both the audience and Thunder. This one was particularly bad. There were times—most of the time—that I had to concentrate on anticipating what Thunder was about to do to the point that I could hardly keep a train of thought. My thoughts were, in reality, more of a train wreck. It was bad. Most folks in the audience didn't really notice or even care as long as they had this huge bird to watch as its antics and bates were much more interesting than what I was trying to say.

We finally finished, and once Thunder was back in her cage, I could speak effectively to milling-around audience members. As I drove home that evening, I began to have severe doubts about this entire endeavor of traveling around with Thunder and trying to speak as well. The speaking part wasn't at all difficult for me. I had been doing it quite easily for many years while handling red-tailed hawks and other similar species. This was different. I was discouraged, genuinely so, for the first time since I started working with Thunder three years ago. I sought suggestions from others in the raptor center, hoping for that magic pill to appear. It wasn't there, but after a quiet few weeks, we thought that if I could more effectively control the setup, the rest might fall into place.

Summer was almost over, and I was doing more and more mini programs at my house where I kept Thunder. These went well, and I learned a few things since my search for sanity after the library debacle. At home, when I would take Thunder out to work with her or to show her off, I noticed that the time of day made a big difference in her behavior. I already knew this but was so distracted by the requests for her presence, I allowed myself to forget the basics of her security. These were things like the following:

- She didn't like sunny days, when everything must have been so vivid.
- Windy days had too many moving parts to keep track of, especially when she was on my arm and concerned for her own welfare.
- Being out in the wide-open spaces was a ticket to Panicsville, USA.
- Having moving people or things surround her was a masochistic move on my part as well.
- Heat and hot humid weather, she despised, especially if there were mosquitos buzzing around.
- She didn't like bicycles and tricycles, strollers, wheelchairs, large television shoulder mounted cameras and handheld SLR cameras with big lenses. If it moved toward her, she did not like it and immediately called for a recess and was on her way to the playground. In other words, she just flew off my arm.

I already knew all this, and sometimes I had decent—if not good—setups, but I still had difficulty concentrating on my unscripted presentation. I figured, at this point, that as long as I had total control of her setup, I would learn to relax more with time. I thought that was a satisfactory compromise. As some of the other volunteers doing education programs and I discussed, these needs, we also put on paper. Now I had a list of requirements that the host would have to agree to if I was going to do a presentation with Thunder. I jokingly told our other volunteers that in addition to this list, I was also going to ask for fresh fruit for me and fresh fish for Thunder to be waiting for us in the "green room." We laughed and joked about what it was like to have to work with such a prima donna. She was not a prima donna, but she was special, and even in her juvenile plumage, she commanded respect.

Chapter 23

Who Is Thunder?

We had now made enough public and private presentations that the audiences had numbered into the thousands. It was time to realize just what this bird represented. Every time I took her from her travel cage and she sat either on my arm or on the perch, I would ask the audience what kind of bird she was. Believe it or not, no one ever said she was a bald eagle, a few golden eagles but no bald eagles. Think about it—our national emblem, and no one could identify her. It was 1995, and in those years, bald eagles were scarce, and you had to be in the right place to see them.

Additionally, with the full impact of the pesticide DDT still in effect (it was banned on December 31, 1972, and still persists in living organisms), more than an entire generation of humans came and went with hardly any juvenile bald eagles ever hatching in most of the lower forty-eight states. Is it any wonder then that big brown birds, including Thunder, have been shot by the dozens (very, very illegally, I might add) based almost entirely on ignorance and much less so on intent? If you shot a big bird with a white head and tail, you knew what it was without question. You knew this because you see the symbol of our country's freedom and strength on almost everything, from money and motorcycles to billboards and books. From that moment of eliminating our ignorance concerning this matter, we immediately revised the intent of our educational program to include this information about what can happen purely and innocently based on ignorance. We vowed to change that, one person at a time if necessary.

For many years after that, I would go into schools and, each time, ask if they had a library. If they did—and fortunately, most did—I would offer them a thousand-dollar donation to their library if anyone could find a photo of an immature bald eagle that was not in any way associated with a nest or the parents. To date, there have been none found. Why would that be?

Another amazing example of juvenile bald eagles getting no respect was in a documentary done by National Geographic on bald eagles in Alaska. During the hour-long film, there were no juveniles in focus except when associated with the nest. Once they hit the ground, they could be seen feeding with groups of adults, but the youngsters were never in focus, always in the background. To make my point, if you had a camera and a juvenile was on one branch and the adult on another, the adult would have nearly all the photos taken of it. When you had enough, you would likely snap off a few of the juvenile.

Why not? It's the adults that are being represented on the U.S. national emblem and anywhere else they appeared. Be it in advertisements, commercials, or artwork, the much more spectacular bird with the white head and tail against that dark body is what everyone associates the bald eagle with, even though and likely because it is our national emblem, chosen on June 20, 1782, because of its long life, great strength, and majestic looks and because it was believed to exist only on the North American continent. The juveniles do not possess this majestic look and thus have been cast to back stage and pretty much still remain there today. Even more than a century later, it is more likely than not that the larger majority of our population could not tell a juvenile bald eagle from a golden eagle or even a vulture. This is in part how certain situations develop in nature, from ideas and beliefs passed down from generation to generation. This is the real reason that snakes are so feared today.

It was now the summer of 1996, and Thunder had nearly completed her fourth feather molt. While she should be an adult, by most books referenced, she was still a long way from having a white head and tail. In fact, she barely had a few tiny white feathers on her head, and a few of the brown tail feathers had a couple of dirty white streaks through them. I have kept and catalogued all her feathers as she molted year after year, and it wasn't until her sixth molt at age six years and five months that she donned the characteristically white head and tail. Even then, it wasn't pure white.

I'm not certain how many places have collected the feathers of a bald eagle of known age for twenty-one consecutive molts. We did just that and catalogued them as well. And while our Thunder was only one specimen, we haven't been able to find any other collections to match these. Again, she is just one bird, and she might not be characteristic of the overall population, maybe not, but the more recognized bird books of the sixties, seventies, and eighties indicate that sexual maturity and adulthood was attained at four years. This would mean that the age of four would be attained in the spring, but the fourth molt would not start until around June heading into the fifth year. According to this, Thunder was at least two years behind what some say "she should be." My point here is not to discredit anyone but to point out that some of the "facts" in print don't make a lot of sense at times. Please read on for my attempt to explain the point that I'm trying to make.

Chapter 24

Feather Development and Aging

The bald eagle became the national symbol in 1782. The population at that time in the United States, Canada, and Northern Mexico was estimated to be about a hundred thousand nesting pairs. Who made this count/estimate anyway? Our explorers like Lewis and Clark didn't begin their treks west until after the Louisiana Purchase of 1803. But let's say there is some validity to this and we based our future counts and estimates on this number. My science background and math tell me that if you start with bad numbers and extrapolate from those, then what you get will be even worse numbers.

Anyway, we knew there were some out there in the early days, but by 1940, it was fairly obvious that our industrial machine was devastating habitats for most living things, including bald eagles. The population of the bald eagles in 1940 was so low as to be classified as heading toward potential extinction. And since the bald eagle was our national symbol, there was a concern that the shooting of these birds and the habitat loss as well as the loss of their prey species (mostly fish) was being adversely impacted, causing a genuine concern for the long-term survival of the bald eagle. It was then that a bald eagle protection act was put into place with the federal government. With the implementation of this new law, it was quite likely that the population would benefit positively.

World War II ended in the mid-forties, and our industrial complex continued to grow. One of the best and worst things to arrive on the scene in 1950 was the chemical pesticide dichlorodiphenyltrichloroethane, more commonly referred to as DDT. It was a miracle chemical that all but eliminated the malaria-carrying mosquitos that ravished our Southern states. It was also a one-stop pesticide used in agriculture that greatly increased our food production.

In 1962, a scientist by the name of Rachel Carson published the book *Silent Spring*. This was the beginning of our serious awareness of our environment and the negative impact some of our life practices had on it and would ultimately have on us as a species. One major point was the adverse impact that DDT was having on the overall health of the planet. Depending on the soil type and other factors, the DDT would remain viable as an effective pesticide for anywhere from two to fifteen years. It has also been determined that it will accumulate in an organism that consumes it via the foods that are eaten and will persist in the human body for forty years or more. It also had a very negative impact on species of birds of prey, including the bald eagle. The consequences of between two and twenty-five parts per million was enough to reduce the thickness of the eagle's egg shells to the point that the incubating parents would crush the eggs in the nests. As a result of this fact and many other similar effects of the chemical, it was finally banned from use in this country in 1972, but the effects live on. The bald eagle population was already in jeopardy from our ignorant and somewhat selfish practices.

DDT had been used for over twenty years, all the while reducing the reproduction of a species that was already in serious danger of becoming extinct. The fact was that there were few bald eagles being hatched, while the existing population continued to age and ultimately die. This population continued to decline, and in 1967 the Endangered Species Act was passed, and the bald eagle was one of the first species to be placed on it. As time went on, the population would slowly climb to where there were, as I had mentioned earlier in the book, an estimated three thousand pairs living east of the Rocky Mountains as late as 1992. This is a long way from the projected/estimated population of over a hundred thousand nesting pairs in 1782. In a bit over two hundred years, we had destroyed approximately 97 percent of a species that was not only our national symbol but also a species that had been around for millions of years. What have we almost done?

Okay, now for a summary and recap concerning research done on bald eagles. In the 1940s, the population was supposedly heading toward extinction. In 1950, we began further decimating the population with DDT. Again, we were on the brink of seeing our national symbol become extinct. We passed protection laws in the 1960s to protect them, but the DDT would remain in their systems for years to come, again eliminating juvenile birds from the population almost entirely. So from the forties, fifties, sixties, seventies, and eighties to early 1990, there were very few birds to actually study. In fact, the estimated population of nesting pairs east of the Rocky Mountains in 1992 was three thousand pairs. That's only 3 percent of what was estimated to be the total population way back in 1782.

So if what I am saying is at all reasonable, when did the research take place that describes a three-year-old versus a five-or six-year-old? I don't think there were enough immature bald eagles that someone could have researched for ten to twenty years. And to get an accurate assessment of the aging process, you would need to start with hatchlings to be certain that they were known aged birds.

Another question is, where did the money come from to do this research? There sure isn't much of it, even today. If you want to conduct research on an animal other than humans, then you'll need to pick a game species. Why a game species? Because there is money for this research, and it comes from the sportsman. These research funds come directly from hunters' and fishermen's license fees and self-imposed federal taxes. By now, it is likely that every state has some sort of nongame wildlife program. It too is more than likely that all these organizations lack funds to do all the research they would like to see conducted. Some states likely struggle to maintain a state-employed staff to work with nongame resources within those states. A coalition of states back in the late 1980s tried to muster support for the nongame programs nationally by instituting a use tax on things like birdseed, birding books, binoculars, and the like. They just wanted an across-the-board 5 percent tax that would be collected by the federal government and then doled out to the individual states. Each state's cut of the action would be loosely determined by the size and population of the state. Likely, California would have received the largest share. This failed miserably because the birdwatchers, hikers, and general nature lovers would not support their own interests. I bet Rachel Carson turned over in her grave.

Now the hunters and fishermen/women felt differently about supporting their sport. In 1937, a U.S. senator and congressman by the names of Pittman and Robertson, respectively, coauthored a bill called the Pittman-Robertson Federal Aid in Wildlife Restoration Act. This was mainly to bring back the low populations of game animals like ducks, turkey, and white-tailed deer but also to benefit all game species. The Dingell-Johnson Federal Aid in Sport Fish Restoration Act was passed in 1950 to do the same thing for fresh-and saltwater fish sought for recreational or commercial uses. Each act, while modified over the years, will collect a federal excise tax ranging from 10 to 15 percent on fishing and hunting equipment, respectively.

All the hunters and fisherman supported these laws. Since their inception, there have been billions of dollars from these funds used to directly benefit both fish and wildlife and to also benefit the sportsman and the national economy as well. The majority of these funds go to research and habitat improvement projects. Now I'm not selfish or anything, but wouldn't it be nice if nongame wildlife received the same consideration? None of this money goes directly to nongame, but for every acre of habitat improved for white-tailed deer, there are likely hundreds of other animals, both game and nongame, that directly benefit as well. So why do nongame enthusiasts and users not financially support their sport/hobby as well? I guess they want to sit at the table and eat but believe someone else should buy their food.

The WVRRC has survived since 1983 with no paid staff. They do and have done this because they think this is their part in providing help to raptors while state and federal agencies do next to nothing to help the orphaned, sick, or injured. Both agencies provide legal support (laws) protecting them but little education to make the laws less necessary. We use these nonreleasable birds for educational purposes. While the few that we are able to release, about 50 percent, make little difference to the overall population, the humans we educate will help millions and millions of not just raptors but also living things. While our raptor care is the most urgent of our missions, the education effort is by far our most important.

Chapter 25

Thunder Goes to the Beach

As Thunder and I continued our education efforts during the summer of 1996, we received a thirdhand sort of sideways request for our most unique educational request yet. See, I have a friend by way of my marriage. They have a daughter, and she had just recently married. The friend asked me if the daughter and new husband could get a visit with Thunder. Had there not been this connection, I would have still welcomed them to visit. That was what Thunder was here for.

We set up a time, and Ray and Tressa appeared as scheduled. Out of curiosity, I asked Ray what he did. You know how you sometimes ask those questions but aren't positive that the answer would make any difference one way or another? Well, I did that, but I usually had a reason. I tried to unscientifically put a profession to their reaction to Thunder and what she stood for. He said they were living in Texas—I already knew that—and that he worked for a telecommunications company. So he was a computer-engineer type, I surmised. They stayed for about an hour. We did some photos and had a great visit/educational program. They both loved Thunder, but the more we discussed her and all we had gone through to get to this point, the more they were both impressed by her. Ray was so enamored by her presence as well as her behavior. They left, and that was that—so I thought.

The next week, Ray called me. He thanked me for the visit with Thunder and said he was showing off the photos of her and trying to repeat the stories about her at his workplace when the vice president of the company asked him if I would bring her to their conference in September to do some educational programs. They would sponsor the trip and make a nice donation to the raptor center. I told him that we were flattered, but Texas was a bit out of our range. He laughed and said they wouldn't ask me to bring her to Texas but wondered if we would be willing to travel about ten hours to Hilton Head, South Carolina. He said it would be about four days with travel the weekend following Labor Day. I told him we would consider it but to please send me the details.

He said that a lady by the name of Noreen would be contacting me. "She handles events, and she just wanted to see if I could sell you on the idea first."

I spoke with her the following day. She was a very nice lady and seemed far more than just competent. She asked me many of the right questions regarding Thunder's needs and asked if I had additional specific needs. She had the plan; now I had to plan what would be needed for Thunder's first overnight trip. She was going to the beach.

It was early September 1996. Hurricane Fran was smashing the South Atlantic coast. We were scheduled to leave for Hilton Head early on September 7, but as the storm raced north, it was questionable whether we would have any place to go if we did leave. So we waited and watched. Tekelec, a telecommunications company from Texas with a division located in North Carolina, was to be our host. They were making a sizable donation to the WVRRC plus paying for all the expenses. We were to attend a national telecommunications trade show where Thunder and I would provide environmental education programs for two days of the show. But the big question that loomed was whether or not we would be going. It was Friday morning, and a decision had to be made soon. Mother Nature was not cooperating, and there was nothing we could do but wait.

Later that day, Noreen Jurek, my contact with Tekelec, called to report that although Hilton Head Island had been missed by the hurricane, extensive damage had been done inland. She would let me decide if we wanted to risk the trip. The trade show was going on as planned even though some attendees would probably cancel because of the weather.

I really wanted to go. Thunder and I had worked very hard for the past four years getting her ready for major public appearances and lengthy journeys. This seemed to be the right time for such a test. I felt we were ready even though I could only speculate what obstacles we would encounter. Traveling and living with a frisky, independent bald eagle is not nearly as glamorous as most people seem to think it is. And while she and I had made great strides during the past twenty-nine months of doing public presentations, she was still a wild creature that was being asked to accept or adapt to new people, places, and definitely things on a regular basis.

It sounded like a lot of fun, going to Hilton Head, lying around the beach, living it up in an expensive room, and being the center of attention to an absolutely captivated audience. *Wrong.* After the trip was over, I was asked about the experience. The best way I could describe it was to equate it to a single parent making this trip with six-month-old triplets. I've never done that, but it's probably about the same.

On Friday evening, I decided to go. It was time to pack. I had a checklist, and I started at the top. *Thunder—do not forget the bird. I'll load her last thing before we leave in the morning. She would appreciate that, I'm sure.*

I was driving a Dodge Grand Caravan that had a lot of room. She had traveled in it many times before and really didn't seem to mind. She felt safe in her cage, and since she had her own air and heat controls, I didn't worry about her comfort in that regard. All but the two front seats were removed. I started loading. Her bathtub/pool was a must, as well as ten gallons of water for her tub, five five-gallon buckets to raise her cage to a comfortable height for me and others to carry cleaning supplies, and a box of rags, towels, tarps, and drop cloths. I bought two packs of ten very thin plastic ten-by-twelve-foot drop cloths. I also bought a couple of rolls of special painter's masking tape so I could tape the plastic to the walls without pulling the paint or wallpaper off when I removed it.

Her portable perch was fashioned from a twenty-seven-inch bicycle tire and rim that I poured solid with concrete so it wouldn't tip. I could use this on hardwood stages and other valuable areas where we didn't want to cause damages. This was a regular front tire from a bicycle. It had a tire mounted on the rim, and the modifications included a threaded bolt attached through the center hole in the rim. That would be used to screw a thirty-inch high T-shaped perch made from four-inch PVC thin-walled pipe. The tire was then laid flat on a piece of plywood. I then mixed some concrete and filled the entire area inside the rim solid with the concrete. This would make the perch for a very large bird very bottom heavy so it wouldn't tip over when Thunder landed on it. The rubber tire soon became deflated, but it still worked to roll the rubber along the floor, not having to worry about damaging any of the floor surfaces. Granted, it was heavy but not too bad when it was rolling.

Her carrying cart was most certainly included, as well as all her handling equipment, with spare jesses and material for additional leashes and extra fifty-foot lengths of rope for who knows what. Another box for educational and display materials was loaded. We were running short of space, and we still needed to include her travel cage, of course, and two coolers for ice and a four-day supply of food (thus far, I haven't had too many offers for her to eat in restaurants). That was it. There was barely room for my suitcase.

On Saturday at 6:00 a.m., I got Thunder out of her flight cage to let her stretch a bit. After a few minutes of vigorous flapping, she was ready to load. It was pouring rain. I checked the weather channel earlier, and they were still tracking the storm. The eye was now dead center over West Virginia, although it was no longer a hurricane but a significant source of rain. I was concerned about projected flooding but figured we could turn back if necessary.

We were off, and I was more than a bit apprehensive. We were beginning a journey that I only hoped we were prepared to make. A million what-ifs ran through my head as we headed south through the wind-driven rain. All my concerns were about Thunder. Over the years, I had become extremely protective of her safety and well-being. I had to monitor her stress level very closely and assure that she would not be put in situations that would endanger her in any way. This was my concern. Sure, I had made certain that all the necessary arrangements for her comfort and consideration would be arranged upon our arrival, but I was forced to take the word of strangers who really had little understanding of this bird's needs. Even though they said they understood, how could I expect these people, no matter how good their intentions, to comprehend the complex needs of a wild animal of this type? This was a real fear that I was forced to deal with mile after mile, even though I had to believe that my judgment concerning the situation was correct. As I had these concerns racing through my head, I decided to stop in the pouring rain, get out, and climb into the side door, where I could get to Thunder's cage and lift the drape between us so I could watch in the mirror for her reactions to different things we might encounter during the long drive. This would be the longest drive and first overnight trip to date.

About an hour later, the rain was reduced to a light drizzle, and not long after, it had stopped completely. Suddenly, within a matter of only a few minutes, the sun was shining, and nearly every cloud had vanished. This was good. I was relatively sure Thunder didn't care one way or the other, but I certainly felt a lot better about continuing. And continue, we did.

As I drove, I glanced in the mirror from time to time to check on Thunder. For the most part, she faced our direction of travel, but some of the time, she would turn to face the rear. She was likely tired of looking at me.

We were on the Interstate at one point, about two hours into the drive, when a very loud dirt bike was approaching us from the rear. I likely would not have paid much attention, but I heard Thunder turn to face the rear. She was a large bird, and her turning was an event. After the fact, I then recalled hearing the motorcycle from behind us, but had Thunder not turned to face the direction it was approaching from and then turn again to face the front as the motorcycle passed us, I would have likely not even noticed it. It was going twenty miles per hour faster than I was going, so the entire process took only ten seconds or so. I assumed that it running without a muffler, like dirt bikes do, was the reason Thunder noticed it. I had never had her around sounds like that, and I began to wonder what other surprises lay over the horizon. We soon began to find out.

As we continued through Southern West Virginia, we had to go through two tunnels. The first one was on the border of West Virginia and Virginia. Traffic was light, but when we approached the tunnel, everyone seemed to slow to below the speed limit. I was in the left lane, and the right lane was open. As we got into the dimly lit tunnel, I glanced back at Thunder since it was a slightly louder and different sound than usual. She was sitting calmly.

Then from behind us in the right lane came an empty auto-carrier tractor and trailer. He was downshifting to slow, and every piece of metal on the trailer was making so much very loud noise. It pulled directly alongside of me and could not pass, so it stayed beside us for the duration of the tunnel. I cringed, wondering what Thunder's reaction might have been after the motorbike response. This was a much louder noise than the bike but very different as well. When I looked back to observe her reaction, well, there was none, absolutely none at all. I was relieved but very curious. Her response to the motorbike out in the open was quite obvious as she even turned to follow it. The sound in the tunnel was so confined and continued to bounce off the side walls and never lessened—no response. That would be recorded as a curious observation.

We got through that tunnel, and the next one was only about ten miles farther south. Just minutes after we cleared the last tunnel, Thunder shifted her feet, rearranged her stance, and sort of straightened her body and leaned and looked forward as though she was watching something in the road in front of us. This section of the Interstate was hilly with numerous curves. As we continued winding, she continued looking more intently.

Finally, after about ten miles of this, we began to catch up with a car in the right lane. She continued to look ahead, and as we eventually passed the car, her eyes remained to the front, more intent than ever. Eventually, we got on a straight piece of highway, and the only thing I could see ahead of us at this point was a large touring-type motorcycle.

Several more minutes went by, and as I got into the left lane to pass, I noticed how absolutely quiet it was. It was not a chain drive but had a regular transmission and a good muffler system. It was as quiet as a car. As the motorcycle was now beside my passenger door, I glanced in the mirror at Thunder, and her head was turning to the right as we passed the cycle. Once it lined up with Thunder, she actually turned completely around in the direction of the bike. If she had been watching it out of the front window, she was no longer able to see it through her cage cover. Once it was entirely behind us, she continued looking in that direction for several more minutes. Eventually, she turned back around to face the front.

In summary, the dirt bike got her attention. An even louder tractor and trailer was next to her in an echo chamber of a tunnel, and she didn't even flinch. Then she stared down a motorcycle that was no louder than a quiet automobile. I had always known that she could hear, but there was never a response to any sound or noise she had ever been exposed to. Vision was the only thing to get her attention—until today.

During our entire trip, she had similar responses to every motorcycle we encountered. She never seemed frightened while in her cage and protected, but on a couple of occasions at rest stops, we would encounter parked motorcycles. If they left while we were there and she was out of the vehicle when they started their engines, Thunder became very irritated and would try to leave the area. She had always responded negatively to bicycles, strollers, kids in wagons, or similar moving objects, so it would not be a surprise that she would react to motorcycles the same way. It was obvious, however, that there was a pitch or frequency that all sizes, makes, and models of motorcycles made that definitely commanded her attention. To date, there have not been any other types of engine-powered vehicles, including jet-and propeller-driven aircraft, that elicit such a negative response from her. Lawn mowers, both large and small, only bother her if they are moving in a direction toward her—more questions with no more answers.

We had driven nearly five hours, and both Thunder and I were in need of a break. I needed gas as well. We had just left Virginia and crossed into North Carolina on I-77, where the temperature on my car read ninety degrees. I saw a welcome center/rest stop just ahead. I pulled in and was pleasantly surprised to find a large multisectioned rest area that was heavily shaded. I drove around until I found a relatively secluded spot near the end of the rest area. All rest areas that I had been in had one-way traffic patterns and diagonal parking. Since I didn't want to attract attention, I maneuvered my van so I could back into my parking space. This was rather difficult, and I sort of stood out, but I wanted a bit of privacy while unloading Thunder. Being at the end of the rest area also eliminated people entering from seeing us until they were leaving. Most folks wouldn't stop again since they too had destinations in mind.

I took Thunder out and put her on her portable perch. I got her tub and filled it with water. She was pretty well out of sight from vehicles leaving the rest area and seemed to be enjoying the chance to flap her wings and stretch. Then Murphy's law struck.

Here came a North Carolina highway patrol car cruising through the rest area. When this guy spotted my van backed into a diagonal parking spot headed the wrong direction, he must have figured he had a real nutcase. He made a sudden turn and whipped the cruiser into a spot three spaces down from us. I think Thunder was laughing at me. He exited his vehicle, but once he saw Thunder sitting on her perch, stretching, his attitude changed from "what's going on here" to complete amazement. Almost as soon as he saw her, his radio started squawking. He immediately reached down and turned the volume down. He was a nice guy, and he stayed around for the duration of our forty-minute break. He did comment that this was a first for him. I didn't doubt that. We had several visitors who did spot us and stopped over for some photos. Thunder did well. I was proud of her behavior to this point in the journey. We packed up, and we were headed South again.

Three hours later, we made one more stop at a rest area in South Carolina. This wasn't nearly as nice an area, and it was really hot. Gnats and mosquitos were everywhere, and all Thunder wanted to do was get back into the van with the air-conditioning turned on high. The bugs were a bother, but she really didn't like the steamy heat, even though we were in the shade. She wanted gone from this place, so we went on. Next stop: the Hyatt on Hilton Head Island.

After ten hours, we had arrived at our destination. I got out and almost dropped from the smothering heat and humidity. I left the van running, locked it, and went inside to get our room. This was a pretty swanky place, but Thunder was going to share a room with me (or vice versa). It took three luggage carts to get the essentials to the room. The people were great and had been thoroughly briefed by Noreen as to what we might need. It was as if I were traveling with a dignitary. Little did I know at the time that I was.

Once in the room, I put Thunder on her perch outside on our ninth-floor balcony. Yes, she was tethered. I put her pool out there with her and went back inside to get the room Thunder proofed. It wasn't long though before she had left her perch and moved as close to the open sliding door as her leash would allow. She wanted out of this heat. I hurried to get things ready. I used the ten-by-twelve-foot plastic paint drop cloths to cover the wall four and a half feet up and let the remainder extend from the intersection of the wall and floor out across the room. This was where her cage would be located, and the plastic would protect the wall and floor. Thunder's cage would be positioned to one side of a corner across the room from my bed.

Once I finished eagle-proofing her cage area, I brought her inside, placed her on the perch on top of the cage, and removed her jesses. She flapped her wings, stretched, and indicated that she was content. I had a knock on the door and, when I cracked it open, saw that it was a member of the hotel staff. He wanted to know if there was anything they could do for us. I asked him to come in, and as he did, he saw this monster bird sitting on top of her cage. He paused, and I assured him that he was okay, and I asked him to not make sudden moves. He and Thunder were both safe, and over the years, this was the way I would introduce her to new situations, somewhat boldly but with a great measure of caution.

I responded to his question by replying that we needed a place for her to bathe. I had checked the shower area, and it would not work. I told him I had a small pool that she normally used, and I pointed it out to him. I told him that I would like to put down some plastic, place the pool in the center, and then place towels around the outside of the plastic to catch the water she splashed. He said that would be fine, and he would bring me more towels. The room was really big, so there was lots of room for another drop cloth to be added to the floor. I finished securing the drop cloths on the wall and then taped down the edges of the one that now had a filled pool sitting in the middle of it. By the time I had finished my tasks, the hotel staff was at the door with a laundry bin filled with forty towels. He said to use as many as I needed and, if I needed more, to just call the front desk. I covered the entire plastic with one layer of towels and then put a second layer adjacent to the pool itself. If only I could have had a photographer traveling with me.

The rest of the evening went by without incident. I didn't even have her tethered, but she showed no signs of wanting to move from the familiar perch. We had a very large room, at least twice the size of a normal one. After I finally was settled, I decided to try a little television. I watched her closely. She did react but only in a curious way. Her curious look was nothing more than her looking, and as she did, she would cock her head from one side to the other. If she was really trying to get something in focus, she would almost turn her head completely upside down but not quite. She wasn't alarmed, but she did respond to brightly colored commercials more than normal programming. For instance, she showed no interest in baseball or normal programming. She was a bit perked up for the fast action of cartoons and absolutely was glued to the extreme snowboarding used for the Mountain Dew commercial. Television was not her thing.

It was late, and I was sure Thunder was as tired as I was. We had a big day planned for Sunday, so I thought it was time for bed. I hadn't done it before, but I was going to try to sleep with Thunder unleashed and perched about fifteen feet from my bed. I slept well, and from all indications, I assumed she did too.

We were up early. I wanted to take Thunder to the beach before most people were up and about. I was curious as to whether or not she would react noticeably to what I guessed would possibly be her first experience of the sights and sounds of the ocean and breezy beach. When we got down there, the beach was all but empty. Only a few shell hunters and walkers were distantly scattered. When I took her out of her cage, I turned her into the strong ocean breeze, and she immediately spread her wings and began to sail. She didn't let go of my arm, which was immediately lifted to full extension.

We walked down to the water in this position, and I gave her the command "Down." She released her grip on my arm and sailed briefly until she settled to the sand. I had her on a very long lead so she could move about more freely. She liked the early morning sun and the wind but seemed less impressed by the surf, gulls, and pelicans. The fun was quickly over.

After only ten minutes, it seemed as though the entire hotel had spotted us. Those that weren't walking toward us were watching from their balconies. I still couldn't figure where they all came from so quickly. As the hordes of curious observers drew closer, Thunder became more uneasy. In situations as this, all I needed to do was extend my arm, and she would launch herself to what she felt was safety. We stayed around for about half an hour, but my arm could take no more. See how long you can hold twelve pounds on your extended arm with your palm down.

On our way back to the room, we stopped by the beach shower. I needed to rest my arm before continuing. This was where you showered the saltwater from your body or the sand from your feet with that little three-and-a-half-foot-high showerhead. I put Thunder down again, and fortunately, the crowd didn't see us stop. Thunder walked over toward the wall where the showers were mounted. I thought she might want a shower, so I turned the standard shower on, but most of the water missed her. I tried the foot shower—perfect. Thunder splashed and flapped her wings the entire time the water was running. When she finished, she looked like a dog that had just had a bath—not her most regal look. We hung around for another twenty minutes as she began to dry off. Too late—we had been found. I got her loaded up and made a joke to the crowd about them watching a lady shower, and we were on our way to the room.

It was breakfast time for both of us, but Thunder didn't like to be watched eating; in fact, it was a rare occasion when she ate in front of even me. I gave her about a half pound of trout and left her alone as I met with our hosts for breakfast. On my way out, I put the Do Not Disturb sign on the door. Even though all the staff had been instructed to only enter my room between 10:00 a.m. and noon, I wanted to make sure no one walked in on her while I was gone. This would be the first time she had been untethered and not in my vehicle or at my home. I was nervous. Thunder would not hurt someone intentionally, but I was worried more about her bating and flying into something and hurting herself.

Noreen had not yet seen Thunder, but all Ray could do was talk about her. She was excited, and I told her Thunder was eating and she would get an up-close-and-personal look when we came down for the first programs. After we finished breakfast, we made a trip to where we would be set up to do our programs. Noreen was a perfectionist and wanted to make sure this yet-to-be-seen creature had all she needed to feel comfortable. Earlier, I had described to her the size and type of setup she would feel most relaxed in.

When we got to the site, it was huge. They had an area adjoining us where they had set up their display. Remember, this was a telecommunications trade show, and we were there as guests of the event but sponsored by Tekelec. Since they were paying, they got to have their display next to ours. That only seemed fair, and I felt very good about the entire surroundings. I was only guessing this based on our previous programs and reflecting on my list of likes and no-nos as far as setups were concerned. As far as I could tell, the layout seemed perfect. We also went over the schedule for displaying her and the planned presentation times as well. The workload would not be too tiring for either of us, but Noreen said that this was an outline, and I most certainly was to do only what I felt Thunder was comfortable with. I never had anyone make that offer before. It was a bit after eight o'clock, and we had until ten to be set up. Noreen said she would send someone to give me a hand at about nine forty. I wondered, *Why not nine forty-two?* Noreen was a perfectionist, and precise details mattered to her. That was fine with me, one less little thing I had to be concerned with.

I went back to the room and began cleaning up the scraps of fish that had been gently tossed aside. When Thunder was eating, if she came to an undesirable part of the banquet—such as the lower gastrointestinal tract, the brown parts—she merely took it in her beak without stopping, flicked her head, and sent the undesirable parts flying. Fortunately, her floor drop cloths were adequate in covering the battle zone. Not only did I have to clean up all this to limit the "raw fish had just been cleaned and eaten in this room" smell, but also, there was the not-so-small issue of her personal waste.

At this point, I hope you are remembering my description of traveling with Thunder and likening it to doing so with six-month-old triplets. Well, her personal waste, both liquid and solid, is excreted from a single opening and thus is more of a nonhomogenous semisolid waste. This anatomical variation is just another of the reasons birds can fly. The most obvious reasons, most could guess, are their hollow bones and feathers. Collectively, they don't weigh much, usually together only about the same as the rest of the bird. They are designed in ways that will eliminate extra parts, like a bladder. As a side note, the ostrich is the only bird that has a bladder, and it can't fly. There are other large nonflying species that do not have bladders. I do not want you to get the idea that if you can't fly, it's because you have a bladder. Think about it though—what would be the advantage for a bird to store waste in a sack? When it's full, it might weigh enough to prohibit or limit flight. Also, waste excrement occurs often, and the more the species has to eat and the larger the bird, the more, it stands to reason, there would be waste, not unlike triplets producing more waste than just a single baby.

Nature has, over the millions of years of existence, honed each species to not only fill a niche but also be designed to be as effective in their role in nature as possible. This is the only way they can survive. There is no welfare or health care for birds and other wild animals. If they can't do what it takes to survive, they will obviously not be able to reproduce and thus not pass along those debilitating genes. A medical condition in humans can be treated on a daily basis, and life goes on. A good example of this might be diabetics. We once had a bird that was diabetic—imagine that. It was a red-tailed hawk, and a change of diet would not fix the problem. Tiny shots of insulin did work though. To have this bird survive in the wild, we would have to have it come in for a daily shot. Unfortunately, that was not a solution in this case. So nature is a wondrous thing but seemingly cruel at times as well.

Now back to cleaning up Thunder's body waste. Since she is a large bird, there will be more waste. Since they have very large nests, nature has given them the ability to project their waste from the nest while incubating eggs. They merely raise their back ends and literally let it fly. This may not be the sort of discussion most want me to dwell on, but I think it is necessary for you to see just what makes her, a single twelve-pound bird, equivalent to triplets in function. Here's why, and let me be as graphic as necessary. Not long after she had consumed a large meal, maybe two to three hours ago, some extra waste would be passed through the digestive system. In her case, when fully loaded and standing on her three-foot-high portable perch, she would lean forward slightly, and out it came in a high arc, a perfectly confined stream about a half inch in diameter. It left in an arch, and when it finally reached the ground, it hit terra firma from the starting point. As I said, it is semisolid and sort of oily, which allows it to not hit and stick but rather hit and run.

While we are on this subject, let me leap forward to an incident that we will use to help close this topic. A couple of years down the road, we were invited to speak at a balloon festival. Our program was set for noon, and we would be part of the agenda that set the balloons off into the air. As we arrived, my van was in a long line to pay to get into the show. We would not be charged, but this was our only in.

As I got to the front of the line, a young man was there collecting money for the entry fee. It was a perfect October day, no clouds in the sky and the temperature near seventy-five degrees. He was wearing shorts and sneakers with a short-sleeved shirt. When I told him who I was and that I had the bald eagle, he was really excited. He said they had told him to look for us, and he said he really hoped he could get a look at her. I told him that we could do that, but we should be quick about it since the line was so long.

I shut the engine off and went back to open the rear hatch. There was a car that had pulled up a bit close, and I couldn't raise the hatch. The driver saw this and backed up enough to give the gate clearance. I motioned a thank-you and put the gate up. The young man came around the other side, and I asked him to stand still as I uncovered her for him to see. He agreed, and as the curtain went up, Thunder was facing front, but she began to turn around. Her first move, unfortunately for the young man, was to lean forward and let a big load fly. The timing and placement could not have been better—or worse, depending on your point of view.

As Thunder came into the view of the folks in the car behind us and the young man, her waste stream flew perfectly between the bars and hit the gentleman squarely just above the knee. He was a bit over four feet from the cage, and as it hit his bare flesh, that oily mixture ran completely down his leg and into his sockless sneakers. I felt really bad for him, but everyone, including the folks in the car behind us, broke into hysterical laughter. I left Thunder's cover up and handed him a bunch of paper towels from a roll I learned to always have handy. He cleaned up, and I took the paper towel and stowed it in one of the Ziploc bags I kept for such events. The young man thanked us, as did the family in the trailing vehicle.

After the fish parts were collected and the poop was all cleaned up, I took a little break before we had to leave for the first shows. During the duration of our stay, we did about seven hours of educational programs that were scheduled at the booth sponsored by Tekelec. Another four hours of a more spontaneous nature occurred during the three days. I was extremely pleased at the reception and consideration we received from everyone but especially by the wonderful folks from Tekelec. They might not had ever had to organize their participation in a trade show around a bald eagle before, but we had never been better received or more considerately so from a standpoint of Thunder's needs. The thousands of attendees and participants were the perfect audience. Thunder was the perfect educational bird, and the trip could not have been any more successful. While I was extremely pleased with the way things went with Thunder, I was even more pleased and hopeful knowing that executives from a telecommunications company understood the necessity of a healthy ecosystem and realized that man is a part of nature, not apart from nature.

At about 6:00 a.m. on September 10, 1996, I crawled out of bed, not quite rested from the late-evening activities hosted by Tekelec. After dinner, we did a summary of our visit, and Noreen wanted any suggestions that would have improved the experience that Thunder and I shared. I went over a whole list of the details her fellow employees and the hotel staff provided in such a professional and giving fashion. I had no negative comments, and Thunder seemed to suffer from no stress during the entire stay. She, like myself, did tire a bit by day's end.

I was glad we made the trip, but now it was time to plan an exit strategy. I got everything but the diva packed up and loaded into the van. The last thing I did was to place Thunder in her travel cage and finish cleaning up the plastic wall and floor coverings. After that was done, it all went into a garbage bag, and we were on our way to the elevator for a ride nine floors to the lobby. We headed out the door at about six forty and thanked all the staff we saw for all their great help and special attention. They all wanted a last peek at Thunder before we left the lobby; we graciously obliged.

I didn't know if Thunder would ever be coming back to this particular beach or not, so I opted for one more trip down to the ocean side. I parked her cart at the end of the concrete and got Thunder on my arm. We walked to the beach, attracting crowds already. The tide was about between high and low, so we had lots of room to move around. Thunder had her wings stretched out, facing the nice steady breeze. Some of the first beach walkers had seen us there before and actually took the initiative to keep the crowds a nice distance away from us. We talked to them for several minutes and then politely excused ourselves since we had a ten-hour drive ahead of us.

It sure was nice sometimes, traveling with a bald eagle. People were really respectful and genuinely caring. While I was the mouthpiece and the mode of transportation, Thunder was the reason, the only reason, these people ever had a word to say to me. And you know, that didn't bother me in the least because I was one of very, very few people on this planet who traveled with wild bald eagles, sometimes just on my arm, an honor and a privilege as well as a great responsibility.

As I carried Thunder back to her travel cage and loaded her into the van, it finally started to dawn on me as to just how significant and loved this bird was to the people who had seen her since our first program almost eighteen months ago. The trials and tribulations of the first eighteen months I had her, not forgotten by any means, seemed to be much less intolerable and definitely well worth the grueling thousands of hours spent working with her. I was not sure about Thunder, but I was beginning to see us as a team.

It was almost 9:00 a.m., and we finally said our last goodbyes and were on the road. We hoped we could make the return trip in not more than ten hours. It was a Saturday when we drove down, plus there was some bad weather that could have delayed us a bit. Hopefully, we would make good time since it was a beautiful Tuesday.

We got home at 6:00 p.m. and still had about an hour and a half before sunset. That gave me plenty of time to get Thunder back into her cage, put her pool back, fill it, and get her some dinner. I no more than walked away from filling her pool than she hopped into it and began bathing. She had to wash the road dirt off her one and only outfit. I brought her some fish a few minutes later, and she just ignored me as she continued her bath. I placed her fish near her pool and left. I spent the next two hours unpacking and stowing our gear and cleaning the van. I took the rest of the evening off. We both deserved a break.

After the Hilton Head trip, I felt a lot more confident about traveling with Thunder as well as our future hotel stays. I had learned a lot on this trip. Maybe that is overstating it a bit. I might not have learned that much but more of had my notions of what might happen in any given circumstance confirmed. Most of the learning was regarding the traveling part of the trip. This was her first long drive. While she still had an edge about her, there was a bit more overall calmness and sense of security that greatly reduced her stress level. Yes, there were still situations that disturbed her, but for the most part they had diminished a lot from the first program we did in the spring of 1995. A large portion of it was her, but I was also becoming more relaxed and felt more positive about the presentations I was giving. I still had to pay close attention to her every twitch as well as all the external stimuli. She had greatly improved overall and as a team member, and I felt much more comfortable regarding the impression we projected to the audiences.

I always tried to make learning fun, but if I was so stiff that I couldn't laugh and make light of some of our trials and tribulations, then I believed the audiences were being shortchanged. On the other hand, if they had never heard me speak before, they would not know what was missing from my performance anyway. After a bit of consideration, I didn't think it really mattered that much though; as long as I had Thunder on my arm and she flapped her wings every few minutes, that was more than most had hoped for. I knew there was more potential though, and I did these environmental education trips because I felt our message was very important. In the long run, they were even more important than Thunder. But when it was all boiled down, it was obvious that we needed to be a team to be the most effective, and we were heading in that direction.

We had made lots of progress so far, but I believed that the future measure of progress would be like dividing something by half. Even if you keep dividing it in half, you will never reach zero. So we can strive for perfection yet realize we will never really attain it. For now, I would settle for the rate of progress we have been making. We would divide it by two again, and while the amount of progress seemed less significant, we were still getting closer to perfection. We would work with that for now.

I'll be very candid. I had a plan to work with and train Thunder, but by no means have I been able to stick to it. We have gotten from point A to point B but by no means in any semblance of a straight line. I guess it's only the results that matter. It has been difficult working with a very large wild bald eagle. When I start feeling too badly about our progress, I would be reminded that there are no more than a handful of others in the country who may have done what we have done. I honestly believe that a handful is also more than likely an exaggeration. In fact, we know of no other birds like Thunder, wild and not imprinted, anywhere in the country, and we have been searching.

Thunder and I still had more teamwork strategies to perfect, and we were given plenty of opportunities. It was now early fall in 1996, and schools were in session. The majority of the WVRRC's programs were to schools, and now that the word was out that there was a bald eagle available, well, you guessed it. The early programs we did for schools were usually assembly-type programs done from a stage. It was still too soon to take her into a cramped classroom, and I didn't know if we ever would be able to do that. We did, however, conduct fifteen more programs before the end of the year. January and February were usually less busy months, mainly because of the potential for foul weather.

CHAPTER 26

Feathers and the Molt

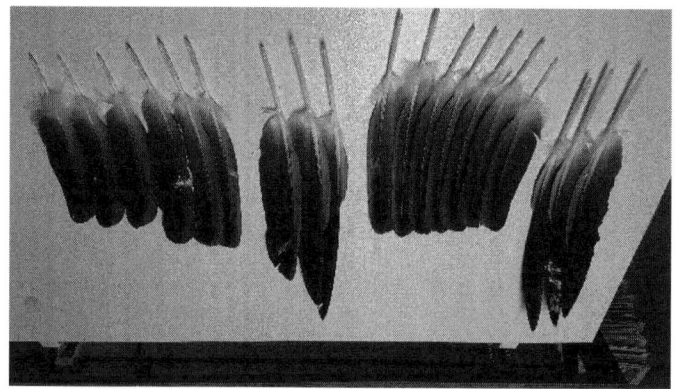

As the spring of 1997 rolled in, Thunder turned five years old. She hadn't molted this year yet, so it was possible there could be some significant white feathers appearing on her head and tail by late summer. We would have to wait and see, but according to literature and bird books, she was already at least a year behind in maturing. The first-year bald eagles are labeled as juveniles. The second and third years are referred to as second-and third-year birds, and the fourth year, they are adults. This information is published in a very common and prominent birding book used by a significant population of amateur bird-watchers. It has been updated since the publishing date and remains a reputable reference for birding. Most people I have met over the recent years not only are unaware that bald eagle maturation requires more than five years but more likely assume that there is no such period at all. Right now, with Thunder at age five, most amateur birders would not be able to identify her as a bald eagle. As I said earlier, she was by no means an adult in appearance or behavior. Could it be because she has been in captivity? My guess is no, and that is just a guess on my part because I don't think I have enough information to say yes or no for certain. There isn't a large-enough sample size to be able to make that claim either. It had now been five years, and Thunder was already at least one year late. This book, *Raising Thunder*, was supposed to be about raising a wild bald eagle until it reached maturity at four years of age. Now what?

At five years and one month, she had begun her fifth molt. It began in June each year. It would always start with a tail feather or, less often, with a primary, and each molt began between June 2 and June 18. The date of the first feather to molt changed from year to year. The twelve tail feathers would not be completely replaced until September, sometimes early and sometimes late in the month, but she would molt all of them every year. Between mid-to late June, she would start replacing breast feathers, secondaries, and maybe a primary or two. Remember, she only had one set of ten primaries as her left wing tip containing the primary feathers on that wing was amputated by a gunshot. July and August were always the heaviest months for molting, and all ten of her primary feathers would be molted by early to mid-September. She also molted each of these feathers every year, along with all her secondaries, from both wings.

I did not keep as accurate a count of her remaining 2,650 feathers (approximate). Many were much too small, and no doubt, many of the small ones might have been cast to the wind. The bottom of her cage would have feathers of all sizes and types scattered about. Some days there would be significantly more than others. These were likely nights that she preened more diligently. Her head feather molting was reserved for last. The largest number of these was replaced by mid-to late November. While the head feathers on most birds are small, those on Thunder were approximately two inches (about five centimeters) long and about three eighths of an inch (about half a centimeter) wide. That's larger than the longest primary feather on a hummingbird, which might reach 4.7 centimeters.

All her feather types were specially designed and likely grew or were replaced in some order for a specific reason. As each of the replacement feathers began to grow, they would force the old feathers out. It was a lot like a kid replacing its baby teeth with permanent adult teeth, but with this bird, it happened every year.

If at any time during growth these feathers were broken, they would bleed. They wouldn't bleed enough to cause death, but a few drops would be lost. On Thunder's left wing, her wrist was amputated by a bullet. None of her ten left-wing primaries were present, but there remained a small amount of tissue, nerves, and blood vessels. There wasn't much there, but at least three times each year, Thunder would attempt to grow that tenth primary. It would grow to where about three inches of it had pushed out of the sheath. It would then die at the base and fall out. On a few occasions, she would bump it into something and break it off at the base while it was still growing, causing it to bleed. I had her at our state capitol one time, and during the course of the program, she did a self-adjusting wing flap. I was not prepared for it, and the tip of the wing just lightly brushed across the side of my face. I noticed immediately that her wing was bleeding and set her down. I tended to her and then cleaned the blood from my face. In an instance like that, a little blood goes a long way. This would have made a great training site for doing forensics on blood-splatter patterns. I doubt that this has ever been documented before. There were hundreds of very tiny blood splats covering a fairly large area of the white marble wall we were standing in front of. We cleaned the wall before we left.

For you to get an idea of how powerful her wingbeats are when splattering blood or not, let me give you an example of the potential wind-generation capabilities of that pair of gigantic wings. The place where we were set up for this program was with our backs against a circular wall in the capitol rotunda. Many displays were set up along this same wall. The entire circumference of the rotunda might have been about three hundred feet, but usable wall space would only account for less than a third of that. The other was open, allowing foot traffic to enter the area from all parts of the building on that floor. To increase the display area in the rotunda, a second and complete circle of displays were set up about fifteen feet inside of those of us on the outside of the circle. With this setup, there was a fifteen-foot walkway with displays on both left and right of the people walking through and viewing the displays. Our display was set up behind banquet tables. The front of our table was about fifteen feet from the front of the table across from us. Thunder and I were behind the table, so our distance was closer to twenty feet from the table across from us. Their table, as did most of the other displays, had paper handouts, business cards, and cardboard stands used as display boards. They were set up when we arrived.

After we had our three tables set up and all our displays and literature secured with weights, I took Thunder out of her cage. Anytime I removed her, she perched herself on the top cage perch with one nice flap of her wings. As soon as I lifted her halfway up to the top of her cage and gave her the command "Down," she did as expected. Since we had never shared an area like this before, I gave the flapping no consideration. That was viewed as a mistake by us and the folks across the room from us. Thunder's one easy flap turned all the eight-and-a-half-by-eleven-inch papers into airborne confetti. Posters went flying like you would expect a billboard to be tossed by a tornado. The table covering was even partially ripped from its taped edges. In less than a second, Thunder made her presence not only known but also a reputation. Everyone was so amazed by the wind effect. No one was upset, although that display was moved to a less windswept location.

The following years, we set up in the exact same spot, but strangely enough, there was never another display anywhere near us. It was a sort of catch-22. Everyone wanted to be near Thunder for her crowd-drawing ability, but just because there was a crowd around Thunder didn't mean that you would receive any of the attention. Thunder always had the most press and the largest crowds no matter the competition. In this same building, we were later asked by the governor to please attend a birthday celebration for our elder U.S. senator. He was a big fan of bald eagles, his favorite bird, and we were asked to stand to the right of the podium. All the major cable networks were there and some people I know were watching; one of them said that Thunder had the cameras panning to her during the whole event. It seemed that every time she would put those feathers into motion, the camera operators could not resist the potential, hopeful, no doubt, that she may take off for some unknown destination.

The thing that made the molted feathers from Thunder so much more unique than feathers from most other species was simply their size. If it had been a robin flapping its wings at the senator's birthday party, it was likely no one would have even noticed. Even the tiniest eagle feathers could be studied with the naked eye. The tiny down feathers on Thunder that were shaped similar to the seed head of a dandelion were still as large as dimes. They were plumaceous and had many noninterlocking barbs, lacking the barbules and hooklets common to flight feathers. That was how they managed to trap air next to the skin, which acted as an insulating layer.

There are also special types of feathers called powder down feathers. A keratin powder is formed when the barbs of the down disintegrate. The keratin powder is then spread over the feathers while preening. This provides waterproofing for the feathers and helps clean them as well. All feathers are made of keratin, just like your hair, but only the smallest feathers will be broken down and used for maintenance purposes. When a large bird like Thunder has been doing significant preening and they roust (that's when they fluff up their feathers to get air under them and then shake, similar to a wet dog shaking), this dust/powder is quite visible to the naked eye. It settles on things like dust on a table or dandruff on your shoulders.

Two more very unique types of feathers are semiplume and filoplume. Somewhat like the tiny down feathers, these are equally fragile looking. The semiplume came from the breast of Thunder and was at least four inches long. When she molted, this year-old feather still looked like new. The tip of it covered about the same area as half a dime. It had single branches that ran to the base. The filoplume is similar but has no definite tip. Both are so frail in appearance, and these make you wonder how much care they must have been given for them to be in such good condition after a year's use in the wild.

The timing of the molt didn't seem to fit into any special timing slot that I could recognize. It would seem that since this was definitely nesting season, maybe it would be better to wait to get new feathers until after nest building, maintenance, and incubation had occurred. But the period after that might seem more important from a flying standpoint. There would be lots of flying from June till the end of summer, with hungry and large mouths to feed.

Another way to speculate might be that since the old feathers could be more worn and possibly damaged from the previous year's use, it might be more effective to have a few missing feathers at any one time than potentially a lot of less effective feathers that were worn and broken. Something else to consider as well was that Thunder was a Northern girl and maybe didn't molt the same way that Southern ones did.

There are differences that we do now know. Almost all species of both birds and mammals are larger the further north you go in their home range. Thunder weighed in at her top weight at thirteen pounds (5,900 grams). Granted, that weight is on the upper end of the scale, but a Florida female of the larger variety might weigh in the neighborhood of nine pounds (4,086 grams). Thunder hatched in New York in the last week of April. Bald eagles nesting in Southern Florida would hatch broods in mid-January. That's about a three-month difference. There are practical reasons for this, I'm sure. For instance, lakes and rivers may still be at least partially frozen that early in the year this far North. Other possible prey species such as rabbits would still have a winter population count since their early offspring aren't yet on the market. That doesn't hold quite the same standards in Florida since the water doesn't freeze and other prey species are far more abundant throughout the traditional winter months. In both areas, I would imagine that the birds that take up housekeeping the earliest would be more likely to get the prime spots. This is like shopping on Black Friday—the earlier you go, the better the selection of parking spots and products.

CHAPTER 27

Roadkill and More

It was April 1997, and Thunder had just turned five years old. I thought I would give her something special to celebrate her hatch day. There was a four-mile-long road that connected the one I lived on with another more prominent road. I traveled it often. Last year, I started noticing how many rabbits and squirrels were killed by vehicles. It wasn't one a week or anything like that; it was more of a daily happening. Some days there might be three or four. It wasn't a road where vehicles traveled at high speeds but a rather narrow one with vegetation growing to the road's edge. This was likely the main cause; they would just jump out in front of a car going twenty-five to thirty miles per hour, and the drivers had no chance of stopping or swerving.

Last year I started collecting quality "roadkill" as a diet diversification as well as a treat. Thunder *loved* rabbits, likely her meal of choice. I didn't find one on her special day, but I had a reserve in the fridge that I was thawing out just for this occasion. When I took it to her, she immediately recognized it through the gallon Ziploc bag. She started drooling and extending her neck toward me in a fashion not unlike a hungry infant stretching their head toward the bottle—both recognized a good thing when they saw it. Thunder sure did, and this was the only food she ever took from me in any sort of aggressive fashion. She still only used her beak though, never the talons.

As she began removing the soft fur from the rabbit, I recalled the first rabbit I had given her. A bald eagle eating a rabbit—or anything, for that matter—might conjure up an unbearable image to some, but I assure you, it is anything but the gory mess you are likely visualizing. When I gave her the first rabbit she probably ever had, she was cautious and very skeptical. Even though this was obviously something new, she seemed certain that she wanted it. Back then, I just placed the food near her; she wasn't yet taking it from my hand, and she proceeded from there. It was only the back half of the rabbit, and she wasted no time snatching it with her huge talons. Her first nip at it was to remove the fur. She got a bit in her beak and tried to get it off by slowly tossing her head from side to side. The fur was persistent and didn't have any intention of leaving her beak with that technique. She struggled for a bit longer, and then just as though your child almost instantly knows how to ride a bicycle for the first time, just that quickly, she flipped her head with a sharp snap, and the fur began to fly. (That's likely where that saying originated.) It was no time at all, and most of the one hind leg was bare of any signs of fur. She took that first bite, and we both instantly knew this would be a favorite.

From that day on, she always knew when a rabbit or part of one was being presented to her. Although Thunder normally only ate a bit over a pound a day, if and when I gave her an entire two-to three-pound rabbit, she would eat every bit of it. And when she finished her fresh roadkill rabbit, she would enjoy a bit of dessert as well. If the rabbit was fresh and not previously frozen, she would take the femur from both hind legs—only after there was no more meat left on them—and place one of them with the knee end to the outside of her talon that she was standing on. She would then use that sharp beak as a bottle opener of sorts and snap the knuckle-type cap off the end of the knee. She would then insert the very sharp end of that giant beak into the marrow of the bone, pull out a tiny bit of the marrow, and manage to get it on her tongue and into her mouth. She appeared to savor each tiny morsel of treasure she was extracting from the end of the bone. Once she could not reach any more, she would slide the femur to her right, exposing the empty end of the bone. She would place her beak round about a half inch of the bone, and with no apparent effort, she would shear it off with the ease of a massive paper cutter. Then she would dig more marrow from the bone until there was no more marrow or bone. She would spend over thirty minutes mining for the marrow in both bones.

Her other roadkill was squirrel. She did love squirrel but not to the extent she did rabbits. Squirrels had tough hides, and she would spend a great deal of time just getting herself a starting place. Once she did, though, it was all over for the squirrel. She wasn't messy with the squirrels either. Her squirrel-eating technique reminds me of how afraid of birds some people are, mainly concerned that the bird would peck out their eyes. I always tell them that there is no real nutritional value in the eyes and that the only reason these predators go to the eyes is simply to provide easy access to the brain, which they do like very much.

Thunder's squirrel-harvesting technique would start with her removing some of the fur from the eyebrow. After she was done with that, she would stick that powerful beak into the area between the eye and the brow—the occipital lobe—bite down, and snap a huge chunk of the bone away from the skull, which she would then swallow. This would expose part of the brain. She continued breaking off pieces of the skull. She would eat the bone and then the brain. This was a sort of mashed-potato-and-gravy combination. Once the brain was gone, she would continue down the body, peeling the hide away from the meat like she was peeling a banana and with about as little effort. She would actually eat the squirrel from the inside and remove all four legs as she came to them. It was not messy or gory; in fact, I never recall anyone, even the most squeamish, who would not marvel at how impressive her technique was. Her eating techniques did improve as she grew older and experienced new and challenging culinary delights.

While fish remained her staple, mainly trout, she had some interesting experiences with her fish diet. First, let me explain that while she obtained her food from a variety of sources, it was, nonetheless, closely monitored. Since she ate a lot of fish and as time had passed, there were lots of fishermen and women who wanted to donate their catch to her. If I knew and trusted them, I gladly accepted the gift on Thunder's behalf. If I did know the donor but determined that they were really caught by someone else whom I didn't personally know, I would graciously accept the fish and then dispose of it. I would not feed her any food that originated from third parties or other unknown sources.

The same held true with fresh roadkill. If I didn't know you, I would not even take it, and rabbits and squirrels were the only species I would accept. All the roadkill contributors—and there were just a few—knew that we didn't want them severely damaged or had the obvious appearance of early decay, just the best for Thunder. Those who hunted usually restricted their activities to that one road that today is still referred to as Roadkill Alley. This name is known and referred to by many of the residents living in that area.

A midway reference point for the road was indicated by a small but steep hill, the kind that made your stomach jump when you went over it too quickly. It too had a name that it got one day while I was driving my young grandchildren over the road and we crossed over this hill, causing all of them to break into laughter. The youngest one, about five at the time, was still laughing as he explained that the hill almost made him puke. He continued to laugh, as did his elder brother and sister, and I announced that from then on, that hill would be called Pukes Peak. And so it still is today. So as the roadkill patrol returned with some food for Thunder, we would always mention whether it came from this side or the other side of Pukes Peak. The roadkill patrol was given gallon Ziploc bags to stow their bounty in. Most of them had pickup trucks, and they just tossed them in the back bed. Before they were stowed in my refrigerator or freezer, they would be placed in bags. Thunder's food did not mix with mine. She had her own large chest freezer and a small refrigerator freezer where I kept a three-day supply of food thawing or thawed.

I used the Ziplocs in my vehicle. Snatching up fresh roadkill was developing into an art. Well, maybe we were the only ones who considered it an art. My technique went something like this. After I spotted the roadkill trophy, I would quickly assess its merit as Thunder food. Several things determined this. One was the time of year. If it was ninety degrees or so, I would start looking for swarming insects, mainly flies. I would pass on these and leave them to the crows. Next would be the location they were lying in the road. If they were along the center line or the edge and were not flat, I could nearly always assume that they were fresh. If it was near the center of the road, I would reach behind my seat, which had a little pouch to keep magazines or similar items for use by the backseat passengers. Instead of magazines, I had mine filled with neatly placed Ziploc bags. The zipper was always on top, so when I grabbed one, it would slide out easily and quickly. All the Ziploc zippers were opened before I stowed them. I would grab the center edge of the bag and give it a sharp flick (I learned that from watching Thunder flick rabbit fur off her beak) to open the top. I would slide my left hand to the bottom of the bag, where I pinched the center of it, flicked it again, and then had the bag inside out. Without taking my right hand off the wheel, I would set the bag against the wheel for a second while I moved my hand from the outside bottom of the bag to the inside of the bag.

Now I was wearing the bag on my left hand like an inside-out mitten. If I had good front and back visibility with no other vehicles in sight, I would line up my van so the front wheel would just be to the right of the trophy. As I approached, I would slow to about five miles per hour, open my door slightly, and reach out and down toward the pavement. Since the plastic bag did not afford much protection, it was always best to hover just above the rough pavement. At the present speed, I would have about three seconds from the time the roadkill left my line of sight until it reappeared under the opened door. If all went as planned, I would scoop it, flip the bag to the right-side-out position again, pinch the right side of the bag with my right hand as I held the wheel, and then zip the seal shut. As I reached over to close the door, I would drop the bagged trophy meal on the floor between my feet. Then we were off again and likely in possession of two additional days of high-quality food for Thunder.

Roadkill placements in the center of the lane or along the right or left edge of the other lane provided additional challenges. Multiple passes when the roadkill was positioned in a curve were always required, and sometimes I just had to leave it for the scavengers. When the Chrysler minivans started coming with "stow and go" second-and third-row seating, I initially had great difficulty scooping the roadkill. To make room for the seats to fold into the floor, it was necessary to raise the chassis four additional inches. This so adversely affected my scoop style, I was forced to remove my seat belt at the last minute, and actually hold myself in the vehicle by the steering wheel. This might have been foolish and dangerous as well, but I always made certain that traffic was clear and I had no minors in the van for which to set a bad example.

So this was one of the bizarre things I did in obtaining some of Thunder's food, and here are a few of her unique eating styles and abilities that actually trumped my efforts. First of all, Thunder could actually swallow a ten-inch trout whole. Maybe she could have done larger ones, but she at least did one this large. She also swallowed whole a seven-inch rainbow trout, followed by a seven-inch golden trout and then followed by another seven-inch rainbow trout. The three of these fish equaled just a bit over one pound. She ate these three fish whole and one right after the other as fast as she could grab them from the perch. I was working in her cage for a few minutes after that, and all at once, she started moving her head and neck from side to side and up and down. It was like she was trying to reposition the three fish. I had seen her do this to a certain degree but not nearly to this extent. I wasn't surprised. I kept watching to make sure she wasn't choking.

She continued this off and on for several more minutes until, at the fifteen-minute mark, she picked her head up and pointed the beak to the sky, opened her mouth very wide, lowered her head to below her perch, and spat up the golden trout. This was the second one she ate. Not knowing if that was her intention or if she just felt uncomfortable with the three-fish arrangement, I picked up the fish that had come from her crop. It was still perfectly formed but had turned to a stiff Jell-O consistency and smelled like nothing I had ever smelled before. The digestive juices really worked fast in the crop, and the resulting odor was the most pungent thing I had ever smelled. It literally almost took your breath away. The reason I think she was selecting the golden trout to regurgitate was because she didn't like the taste of it. Given either choice with any fish, she never took the golden trout. She did eat some from time to time but only because there was no alternative short of not eating at all.

Her next fishing episode involved a sixteen-inch channel catfish. A friend of mine had caught it, and I was curious as to whether or not she would even eat it. The sharp sticklike dorsal and lateral fins contained a toxin to help protect them. Their skin was also smooth and did not have scales as most fish exhibit. Their skin was also considered nonedible. I can remember when I was younger that the catfish we would catch had to be skinned before they were cooked. I wasn't sure if Thunder would even attempt to eat it, but I wanted to see. I placed it next to her on the perch with its belly down. The dorsal fin was about two inches long, very hard and sharp, and standing vertical. The two lateral fins were just as hard and sharp.

I wondered if this was a good idea after I set it there. It was quite possible that if she grabbed one of the hard fins, she could puncture her foot. This would be a severe injury, as were any injuries to the bottom of the foot. They easily became infected, and since a bird never sat down, it would always be standing on them. If it chose to stand on the good foot only, it would be just a matter of time till that would no longer be possible. Now it would have one infected foot and one tired foot and leg. In time, the hunting success would lessen till the bird would likely starve to death.

Considering these possibilities, I still chose to leave it. Thunder definitely seemed to be studying it. Now cautiously but with a purpose, she placed her huge right foot on the head in front of the lateral fins. She reached down with her beak and took each of the stiff, sharp fins in her mouth and snapped them off one at a time like she was biting through a toothpick. She did it in a very matter-of-fact fashion and with a purpose. Then she loosened her grip on the head, and with her beak, she turned it over, exposing its white belly. Faster than I could describe what she was doing, she made a long slit below the head as though she were cutting its throat. She repositioned the fish to where the head was now facing front. With her beak, she grabbed the skin at the incision, secured her grip of the head, and straightened up, pulling the entire skin off the fish to the tail. She dropped the skin from her mouth, and it now hung from the tail, where it was still attached. This was a completely and perfectly skinned catfish, and it took less time than if you were to remove a shoe and a sock. I couldn't believe it. Of all the food species she ate during these years, rabbit came in first place and catfish finished a close second. I would never tire of watching her eat.

Chapter 28

Tennessee Trout

My sister lives in Maryville, Tennessee, and after she had a few encounters with Thunder, she wanted to help supply fish. She didn't live too far from the little tourist village of Gatlinburg in the foothills of the Great Smoky Mountains. The west fork of the Little Pigeon River ran right through the center of the town. Anyone could buy a one-day fishing permit and catch and keep five trout. So she, her husband, and her son would go there occasionally and catch their collective fifteen-fish daily limit. Most of the fish were the same size, between twelve and fourteen inches and weighing a pound, a perfect daily portion for Thunder. They would not clean them but rather freeze them whole as per my request.

One time I visited, and we went trout fishing. It was a beautiful small stream, and it literally ran right through the center of town. I found it a bit too civilized, trout fishing with a McDonald's about a hundred yards from where I was fishing and a local policeman about half that distance from me directing traffic at a busy Gatlinburg intersection. Other people were fishing, and I noticed some, no, actually, many of those fishing were using canned corn as bait. They would put it on their hooks to try to imitate real fish eggs. It was cheaper than the salmon eggs that were sold for the same purpose but for several times the price. I also noticed that the kernels of canned corn stayed on the hooks very nicely. The same couldn't be said about the store-bought cheese eggs. And lots of people were pulling fish to the bank using this technique. When we finished, the four of us had caught twenty rainbow trout. I inspected each of the twenty to make sure there were no fishing lines extending from their mouths. We put the fish in the cooler with three in each gallon Ziploc bag. When I finished my visit, I left with forty-five frozen rainbow trout that would feed Thunder for about as many days.

I left a couple of the bags of fish unfrozen so Thunder could have a few when I got home. She appreciated the texture of really fresh fish. It was a bit more difficult to tear apart; plus, it helped to keep her beak sharp and worn down as it would be in nature. Not only did she like it, but also, it allowed me the luxury of not needing to take a Dremel tool to her beak because it was getting too long. I had visited many other raptor centers in the East, and every one of them, at that time, routinely trimmed the talons and the beaks as well. If they had conditions and food that mimicked their natural environment, neither of these practices would have been necessary. Even if Thunder's beak would have required trimming, I'm not sure how it would be done without her being anesthetized. And as for her pedicure needs, well, the large rope-wrapped perches made that unnecessary.

When I got home, I took one of the unfrozen trout out to her. I grabbed it by the head, belly side up, and handed it to her. She grabbed it with her beak, placed it on the perch, and secured it with her left talon. Her first move on fresh fish always went this way. She would take that tiny area that connected the ventral side of each gill, snap her head to the side, and tear the gills loose. The gills were bright red and rich with something she liked because in an instant, they were both gone. Her next move pulled the esophagus from the back of the mouth, followed by her then pulling the stomach and all its attachments most of the way from the body before finishing by swallowing the entire conglomeration. After only a moment of having the stomach and associated parts in her mouth, she raised her head away from the fish.

I watched in amazement as she held her head perfectly still while slightly opening her mouth and flicking pieces of corn with her tongue in my general direction. At first, four corn kernels came flying—one, two, three, and four—but when the fifth was expelled, it hit the stones on the ground and did not harmlessly come to rest; it kept bouncing and making a metallic sound. *Corn with a lot of iron*, I jokingly mused.

But I was concerned, and with luck being with me, I quickly spotted the gold-colored fishhook that Thunder had just expelled from the stomach along with all the corn. So now did I need to worry that she might not find one of these tiny hooks and it ultimately could harm or even kill her? I just had a forty-five-day supply of fresh trout given to us—should I pitch it? I decided not to and that the hook and corn expulsions were not flukes, and as big and bad as she was, I was amazed at her oral sensitivity. None of the trout that she had previously eaten could not have these items in their stomach since they were hatchery fish that had died.

I continued feeding her these trout, and it got to be so comical to watch how quickly she was learning. The next day, she got another of the fresh fish handed to her in the same manner. Her technique remained the same—remove and eat the gills, tear the esophagus loose from the back of the mouth—but wait, she wasn't ripping the stomach and associated parts from the abdomen. Instead of pulling the stomach loose, she left it attached, took the upper and lower mandibles, and began gently feeling the stomach. Apparently, she thought it felt like corn. She put the mandibles on the top and bottom of the stomach walls, applied light pressure, and slid her partially open beak toward the open end of the throat. Kernels of corn came shooting out of the opening like machine-gun fire. And I was worried about her. Another example of her intelligence.

Three weeks later, I took her another of these fish and handed it to her in the usual manner. It was now commonplace for her to expel the corn from every fish she had been given, and there was corn in all of them. As she sprayed the corn all around me, it was basically old hat by now. I would only respond if one of them hit me squarely. As I was cleaning her cage floor, a sparkling item caught my attention. It was a spinner bait, complete with metal shaft, gold spinner, feathers, and treble hooks to bring up the rear. I found this a bit more alarming since it was over two inches long, and the hook set was tied, so it could bend and flex. I imagined that would likely have a greater potential of snagging something in her mouth. It didn't, and again, I was amazed at how sensitive her mouth area and tongue really were. As she continued eating these fish, I continued to check the throat and stomach with my fingers. I never found any other fishing equipment from this lot of fish, but as an afterthought, I planned to use a metal detector on any more of these fish that didn't come directly from the fish hatchery.

Chapter 29

Thunder Flies to New Orleans

In late April 1997, Ray Shaw, a personal friend and employee for Tekelec working in Texas, called me. He said that Tekelec would be participating in the world's largest telecommunications trade show in New Orleans, and he wanted to see if Thunder would be willing to represent the WVRRC as their environmental education guest. He informed me that there would be approximately six hundred companies represented, and the attendance expected to exceed forty thousand. He assured me that not only would Tekelec cover all expenses and make all arrangements, but also, there would be a considerable donation made to the WVRRC as well.

My only concern was transportation. The program schedule would be for two programs on June 3 and 4 and one program the morning of the fifth. If we were to drive, it would take two days to get there and the same to return. We would do programs for three days, making the whole trip seven full days. That would be an exhausting trip for Thunder. When she rode, she sat on her perch. Even the most considerate driving would require her to continually grip the perch, which would not allow her to relax or rest. I found this to be the case when we drove to Hilton Head the year before. After a ten-hour drive, which included three rest stops, she was exhausted. I felt that four days of driving in a seven-day period plus an exhausting education schedule would be too much. After considering these factors, I decided that driving would not be an acceptable option.

After considering all this, I called Ray and told him of my decision. We agreed that I should call Noreen Jurek in their North Carolina office. Noreen handled situations like this and was the organizer for the trip to Hilton Head last year. She did an excellent job, and I figured that if this could be done, she would be the one with the answers.

When I called Noreen and explained the situation to her, she said they would arrange for air transportation if I thought that would be acceptable for Thunder. I figured we could look into it and decide after we had more details. Well, we learned more, probably more than I wanted to know. As it turned out, US Airways was the only nonstop commercial carrier to New Orleans from Pittsburgh. The plane was a 727. The cargo bay door that was used for loading was three by three feet. There was lots of room once inside, but the objects loaded must fit through the door. Thunder's cage was thirty-nine inches high, so it would have to be tipped on its side to be loaded. This was not good. Plus Thunder would have to be left alone for at least five hours. I didn't mind her being left alone for that period as long as she was left alone. I didn't think I could trust that curiosity wouldn't get the best of at least one of the handlers. If this happened and Thunder was sufficiently frightened, she could very easily injure herself—too much to risk. Commercial air transportation was out. At this point, I figured the trip was pretty much a wash, but Noreen then suggested the possibility of a private charter. My first thought was, *Boy, these folks really want this bird in New Orleans. Okay, let's see if we can do it that way.* I was given the approval to start checking from my end.

I mentioned our need for a charter at a rotary meeting, and it took about thirty seconds to come up with a name and phone number—Elaine Heston with Heston Aviation from Pittsburgh. I called, the arrangements were made, and the trip was on. It was almost that simple. Elaine was briefed as to the special needs for transporting a bald eagle. This was no problem. She would simply remove seats to make room for the cage, which would sit next to me. Provisions would also be made so the cage could be secured with a safety belt of sorts. We were to leave on June 2. Elaine said it would be no problem to stop in Clarksburg to pick us up. That would save us the drive to Pittsburgh, and we were heading South anyway.

All the preparations were made, and departure day had arrived. We got to the airport, and we were met by the local TV station (WBOY) that did a nice piece about an eagle making her first flight *again*. We got loaded and were on our way. Thunder didn't mind the noise or the vibrations associated with takeoff. I watched her closely, which wasn't difficult since she was only three feet from me. I uncovered her cage to see if she was interested in looking out the windows. She was a perfect height for this and didn't miss a thing. She would look intensely in one direction, and I would try to follow her focus. After staring in that general direction for a while, I would usually spot the glimmer of another aircraft in the far distance. Thunder definitely had eyes like an eagle. But confirming her sightings of other aircraft only meant they were close enough for me to see.

The only really new observation I made on the flight occurred between 5,500 and 6,000 feet in elevation when she would open her mouth as though she were trying to equalize the pressure in her ears. She would do it at about the same time I did it. She did this each of the four times we took off but during none of the landings. I did it during the landings as well. I wondered why but quickly assumed there would be a very good reason. I can't say for sure, but it seems like they might feel the same altitude pressure changes we do when we significantly increase or decrease elevations. I thought that while a bird like Thunder was ascending, it would be done while she was flying at a fairly slow speed. It would seem likely that ascending at speeds at about twenty miles per hour would not prohibit them from opening their mouths to regulate the internal pressure.

Okay, that was a plausible explanation, but why would pressure equalization not be required while descending? I'm not certain of this either, but it would make sense in birds to have automatic pressure regulation during diving flights. It would not be in the best interest of an aerial predator to be diving at speeds in excess of a hundred miles per hour and find it necessary to open their mouths to adjust air pressure. That would definitely serve as an unwanted air brake. As for the altitude, eagles and many other species would often fly at altitudes well over six thousand feet. It is possible there is a mechanical part/valve that would perform this function automatically, or it is even possible that descending altitude does not cause this pressure difference. All birds have as few parts as possible to get any task done to help ensure they weigh as little as possible to assist with flight. Since humans neither ascend or descend at a high rate of speed outside of another vehicle, there is no need for this automatic pressure adjustment valve. We do it manually.

Thunder spent almost the entire flight searching the skies for anything that moved. This must have brought back memories of seeing things from this perspective, one she had not had for over three years now. It was sometimes difficult to spot what she was looking at, but as the plane continued its directional travel, her gaze would be altered if there was something she was focusing on. From observing this and the time between changes of direction, I would ultimately be able to find a tiny glint in the sun at a really great distance.

Only on one occasion that I looked, I couldn't locate anything. This time she had a steady gaze in a single direction for a very long time, almost twenty minutes. Since she wasn't really shifting the direction she was looking, I assumed it was a great distance away and moving the same direction we were traveling. I was curious now whether or not she actually was focused on an object. I knew how to find out. I walked up to the cockpit and asked the very nice pilots if there was anything on their radar, like another plane. They quickly glanced at the screen and told me there was nothing there. I was puzzled and still believed she was looking at something traveling in almost the same direction and speed that we were but at a slightly higher altitude. Then I asked them how far the radar could see. They said it was at about twenty miles. I asked if they could possibly look farther and explained my theory. They flipped a couple of switches and reported that there was indeed a commercial flight about ten thousand feet higher than we were flying, traveling roughly in the same direction, and it was about forty miles away. There was nothing else on the radar screen. I was amazed and equally certain that Thunder was watching that plane—no actual proof she was, but by the same theory, no actual proof she was not.

After about two hours, the pilot as me if it would be okay if we made a short stop in Birmingham. Who was I to object? I thought that maybe we needed fuel. We started our descent, and again, I opened my mouth to adjust for air pressure, but Thunder did not. Shortly afterward, we made our touchdown and began taxiing toward the private side of the hangars. As we got closer, there was a building outside the fence, and a pretty large crowd was hanging onto the fence while watching us approach. We pulled up close to the fence, and the pilot turned off the engines.

The pilot came back and said she had been talking to some friends there and told them about Thunder. She asked if Thunder needed a little stretch and, if so, if I would mind taking her off the plane so her few friends could see and photograph her. Her few friends had quickly turned into well over a hundred. I said I would, and I took Thunder out of her cage while in the plane. The pilot was very surprised that I removed her from the cage while on the plane, and I told her we would give her friends a real treat. She asked what I was going to do with a bit of worry mixed in with the question. I told the pilots to get off first, go stand near the fence, and tell the friends to get their cameras ready. They did, and after they were clear of the plane near the fence, I backed through the door, blocking Thunder from view with my body. Once down the steps, I turned quickly and let Thunder bate to the end of her leash. When she was way out there, heading toward the crowd, I turned her to return to my arm. At the highest point in her arc, she was easily twelve feet off the ground. As she settled down on my arm, she was one impressive bird. Everyone there agreed.

We stayed another ten or so minutes, boarded and caged Thunder, and were airborne again. Once we reached that magic altitude, Thunder and I simultaneously equalized our ear pressure. The pilots were really pleased with the performance by Thunder, and they said the folks on the ground were still chattering on the radio about the size and magnificence of Thunder. It was good to have happy pilots.

As we were on our long approach, the pilot told me that the New Orleans airport had lots of traffic, and it would be a nice gesture on Thunder's part if she would keep a sharp eye out for fast-moving bogies. I responded positively for Thunder, telling them that she was on it.

It wasn't much longer, and we were taxiing to another private terminal. This one was considerably bigger than the one we had left, where we had made the brief stop. Here, there was a much larger crowd and television crews as well as a number of photographers waiting for us to exit the aircraft. We were met there by Ray, driving our eagle limo. They even had a green carpet rolled out for her. It would have been red, I was told, had Thunder not had an aversion to the color red. The van was just like the one she normally traveled in. That was nice because everything fit, and it was already customized for her stuff. Again, I was asked to take Thunder out to stretch and to show off a bit for this audience and the local press as well. Everyone enjoyed her brief appearance, but now it was time to head for the hotel. We were staying in the French Quarter, at the Hotel De La Poste.

The employees were expecting us, but I was not too sure if they knew what to expect from Thunder. This was a first for them. I was certain they had had some special guests in the past but probably not quite like Thunder. I would be sharing a room with Thunder. It took us about an hour to get the place eagle proofed and all the furniture rearranged. We were ready to settle in for the evening. It was nice that we had this time so she could rest a bit and view the busy little street in the middle of the French Quarter from her third-floor window perch.

After she was settled, I got my things unpacked and hers organized, which included setting up her pool like we did at Hilton Head. One extra bed was also taken apart by the staff, and the mattress, box springs, and headboard were all neatly stacked against the wall out of our way. When finished, the bellboy told me that when I was settled and had a few minutes the hotel manager would like for me to come to the front desk. I told him I would go now if I could be assured that no one would enter the room while I was gone. He assured me that with the Do Not Disturb sign on the door, she would not be bothered. He also told me that the entire staff had been briefed on dealing with our room because of the untethered bald eagle perched inside.

When I got to the front desk, the manager was waiting for me, very nice and equally professional. He gave me a bit of a briefing about the history of the hotel and the amenities they offered plus attractions located nearby. He then took me on a short tour inside the hotel before we went outside to walk around the pool and garden area. Naturally, there were plenty of wrought-iron fences and gates securing the entire grounds outside. New Orleans is noted for a lot of things, and the wrought-iron work certainly is one of them. Very impressive, it was as plentiful and pleasant as sand at a beach. As we walked through the eight-foot-high gate, he began describing the statuary and small detailed gardens that decorated the entire area. Obviously, the pool was sort of the main attraction, but the gardens and the thirty-foot-wide stairway that accessed an elevated seating area were impressive as well.

Before I could ask, he told me that if Thunder needed any outside time, he would be glad to post a guard at the gates leading to the pool to ensure a secure area for her to do whatever bald eagles did. He even pointed out a large magnolia tree with a six-inch-diameter branch about seven feet above and hanging over the pool deck, which she could use as a perch to eat and rest. He said they had been briefed about her basic needs and food preferences as well. He asked what would be a good time to secure the area for Thunder. After a bit of thought, I suggested 6:30 a.m. I told him our work day began at about 9:00 a.m. each day, and that would likely work best for us. He added that not many guests would be visiting the pool at that time of the morning, and if they did, they would be rewarded with a very special treat. He assured me that no one would enter the pool area as long as we were there. I then asked if she could eat while in the pool/garden area, and he was quick to inform me that she could sit on the magnolia branch at the pool's edge and get her fill of the fresh fish that they planned to provide for her daily. I studied the branch and its proximity to the pool and told him that I figured the perch would work well but cautioned him that when eating, pieces of less desirable parts would be strewn about the pool deck. I also asked if, in his briefing, he had been made aware of the quantity of the excrement of bodily waste she projected, especially after a fine fish dinner. He told me they would put a nice clear floor covering (not *red*) over that entire section of the pool deck to make it easier for the staff to put the area back in order for human use. I was impressed with not only his knowledge but also the sponsoring group for being so thorough regarding Thunder's needs. Noreen and Ray and the rest of the Tekelec staff had done a great job in making this as pleasant as possible for Thunder. That, of course, carried over to making it pleasant for me as well.

Not far from the magnolia tree was a well-camouflaged garden hose on a nice reel tucked into the landscape. I asked if it would be okay if I used it from time to time to mist Thunder while she was perched on the magnolia branch. He didn't have any objections, and as soon as he gave his approval, I remembered to tell him about the possibility of Thunder molting a few feathers. I told him to tell his staff that if they found any feathers, no matter how small, that I had not found and picked up before we left, they were not to keep them. They should put them in a bag or something and then turn them over to me. I then explained the severe legal ramifications for any nonpermitted person to be caught with any part of this bird, including her feathers.

With that disclaimer now out of the way and our playground tour completed, I suggested I return to the room to check on Thunder, and then we both could get some rest after our all-day trip. Tomorrow would come early for us. As we parted, he again welcomed us and expressed his gratitude for his hotel being selected to provide a place for such a magnificent bird to be staying. He really was honored and proud that he could be part of this new adventure for the hotel.

The next morning, we were up at six, and Thunder seemed in good sorts and appeared well rested, as was I. No time was wasted. I called the front desk and asked if we could go to the garden a bit early just in case we needed extra time to become familiar with the new surroundings. I was given a thumbs-up and told someone would meet me in the lobby. I told them that it would be about five minutes before we got there. I officially said good morning to Thunder as I was putting her jesses on her respective legs, hooked her up to the leash, and got her on my right arm. I let her stretch a bit before I placed her on her perch inside her travel cage. She had spent the night on the screw-on perch mounted outside and on top of her cage. I dropped the white drape over the entire cage, and we were now ready to head to the lobby. I made sure her perch was centered on the travel cart, and we were out the door, into the elevator (which Thunder never seemed to mind), down three stories, and out into the lobby.

We were met immediately by our security guard, who was carrying a small cooler. He led us out to the garden area and opened the gate for us. After we got inside, he set the cooler down and then went back out where he closed it and took his very formal-looking post outside the gate. He told me there was a fresh fish in the cooler for Thunder's breakfast.

The sun was up, barely, and the temperature was already eighty degrees. Thunder was a Northern girl, and from our experience in Hilton Head, she didn't much care for extreme heat. The temperature was okay now, but later in the day, it was supposed to be in the mid-nineties. By then, we would be back in an air-conditioned environment. I raised her cage cover and turned the cage ninety degrees so the inside perch faced me as I stood on the side of the cart. When pulling the cart, I always made sure she faced the direction of travel the same way she would ride in the vehicle. The cart was just a slower moving vehicle.

I opened her cage door and offered her my arm while giving the "up" command. She obediently stepped onto my right arm, and I removed her from the cage. The next instruction as I brought her up and toward her top perch was "down." Now she was on a very familiar perch off my arm but with me nearby. I was going to take her to the magnolia tree, but I believed in playing fair. She was used to the routine of coming out of her cage and then flying onto her top perch. She was familiar with this, and it made her comfortable. This was no different than a person waking up in a new place and taking a while to get their bearings. Remember, Thunder had been covered from before we left the room till I took her out of her cage here at the pool. She had not seen anything in between, and there would be no reason she would feel comfortable sitting on the branch of the magnolia.

I gave her about thirty seconds and then gave her the "up" command as I again presented my arm to her. Now that she was a bit adjusted, I walked her around the garden area and briefly put her down on the ground—back up quickly though. She liked being on the ground but on her terms. Here, not being on her terms, with unfamiliar surrounds, she would prefer to be up higher, where she felt much safer. This was my way of gradually introducing her to the tree branch. Yes, it was higher, and in theory, she should feel safer, but that wasn't always the way it worked. Being up high equated to safety, but in a case like this, in a strange setting with a stranger standing about twenty feet away, along with a small group of early risers who were watching the show as well, she would normally feel much safer sitting on my arm. This was one of those times. While she didn't necessarily like me, she did like me better than the strangers or even the tree branch that she still saw as less secure than I was. From the very beginning of working with Thunder, I had to constantly remind myself to take baby steps and break every activity down into the least complex scenario. What seemed logical to me and other humans did not necessarily square with Thunder. She had been difficult enough the past few years, so I could see no reason to aggravate her when I could avoid it.

The spectators were increasing in numbers, but they were safely behind the fence, so Thunder was beginning to feel more comfortable. In fact, as I moved in the direction of the horizontal branch, she was actually eyeing it, I thought, as a place she wanted to be. As I got closer, she was certainly ready for the perch. Noticing this, I told the folks outside the fence to get their cameras ready, and I turned to put my body between her and the tree branch to block her view. When I was close enough that I knew Thunder could make an impressive short flight to the branch, I simply stepped aside, and she launched. A spectacular bird now perched above my head but still in reach not far from the edge of the pool. There was also an increase in the discussions taking place outside the fence. I told them that if they wanted to watch her eat, which proved to be a treat for most, they should stick around. At that, I reached up and unfastened the leash from the jesses and then removed the jesses from her ankles. I assured the audience that she would stay put while I retrieved the cooler holding her breakfast.

I opened it up, and a fish of an unknown species to me, weighing about two pounds, was resting on a bed of melting ice. Now that I knew where Thunder would be sitting and where any mess would likely hit the ground, I took the plastic tarp and spread it over the ten-by-twelve-foot area. I was given four bricks to secure the corners. I told the spectators, which were rapidly growing in number, to get ready as I was about to present Thunder with her first Louisiana fish.

I reached into the cooler, stuck a finger into the gills and another into the mouth of the fish, and lifted it into view of Thunder and everyone else. Thunder was hungry and anxious for what she judged to be a fine specimen that I was about to offer her. Without hesitation, I raised my right hand and placed the fish on the magnolia branch beside her right talon. Without hesitation, she bent down and grabbed the fish at the throat with her giant beak and transferred it to her left talon, which she used to pin the head, securing the fish to the branch. With the next motion, the fresh threadlike protein structures comprising the gills were, in one swift and smooth motion, ripped from the throat of the fish and swallowed. The next bite extracted the throat and internal organs, leaving them hanging as she plucked the heart from the mess. From this point on, it was devoured in large chunks as the beak pierced the flesh and then ripped it from the body with a quick snap of the head. Pictures were being taken, but no one was saying a word. They were amazed by the exhibition they were witnessing. It was later described by some of the audience as fast, powerful, smooth, and not at all messy as would be expected. The fish was completely consumed in less than fifteen minutes, and Thunder's "crop" had a large noticeable bulge in it. This was where food that won't fit in the stomach would be partially digested with the acids of nature. The bulge would be gone well before we began our program in about three hours.

When breakfast was over at about six forty-five, Thunder began to clean her talons with her beak and her beak on the perch first and then, for the final cleaning, rubbed it on the front edge of her wing. I asked our security if it would be okay to use the hose. He said yes, so I turned on a light spray and directed it toward Thunder. She loved water and would position herself as though she were showering. After a couple of minutes, I shut the water off and allowed her to finish her cleaning. When she finally finished, it was almost seven thirty, and we had a really big crowd now. It was funny listening to the first groups there briefing the latecomers on the action they had missed. I will say that the effectiveness of Thunder as an educational tool is beyond amazing. These folks were reciting almost word for word what I had told them later. The amazing part of it was the enthusiasm and confidence with which they were briefing. I was impressed; Thunder was indifferent.

I began to clean up a bit when the security told me to please leave it and that someone would take care of that for us. I did as instructed, put the jesses back on Thunder, hooked up the leash, and got the big bird on my arm. I told the audience if they would stand fairly still, I would bring Thunder to them to get a close-up and some more pictures. They were thrilled, Thunder was relaxed, and I got to answer about a million more questions. That was what we had made the trip for—really nice folks, locals and travelers alike. I loaded Thunder back in her cage and dropped the drape, and we headed back to the room to get really ready for work. Again, we had a security escort, but now we had an entourage as well.

The first program wasn't until 10:00 a.m., so Thunder had a while to rest before we had to leave. While she rested on top of her cage, I went to the restaurant and had my own breakfast. I too had fish.

The shows were being held in the Ernest N. Morial Convention Center, a rather large place. Ray picked us up at nine o'clock, and we were on our way. We got there and had plenty of time to get set up. We actually drove the van into the place, the very center. They told me that gasoline vehicles never drove in here; they used electric vehicles and equipment, but they made an exception for Thunder. They said they had never had a bald eagle in there before.

When we began unloading the van, excluding Thunder, I noticed several gentlemen nicely dressed in dark suits. They were, I later found out, our security detail. They would make sure the audience stayed an acceptable distance from us (really Thunder; she was the concern). I had also told Noreen about Thunder's adverse reaction to the color red. I didn't know what caused it, but I knew that it existed. I was not alone; everyone who had been around Thunder when someone approached wearing red, as little as a scarf, had seen her extreme reaction as well. The security detail also told me of the memo put out by Noreen asking that all those attending should refrain from wearing red. I could see how she could control the Tekelec employees, but I wasn't sure how they would control the tens of thousands of people who they were expecting to attend. It was obvious that the plan for this event had been well thought through.

Thunder and the things representing the WVRRC were set up in the center of Tekelec's forty-by-forty-foot display area. Noreen had even rented live trees to make Thunder feel more relaxed. It worked, but I really didn't think Thunder cared if they were live or not, but they did provide her a degree of privacy, blocking her view of possibly scary things going on elsewhere. That might not seem like much, but again, consider that Thunder was visual and her main concern dealt with the number of moving objects that she could see, out of sight, out of mind—at least in her case anyway.

The setup was first class all the way, and most importantly, Thunder was very relaxed. The audiences were large, attentive, and polite. In addition to our display, we were also asked to do a program for the entire audience. The place was packed;

they said over forty thousand. I didn't count, but I did know that those in the upper reaches of the seating looked about two inches tall from my vantage point. We had a stage set up in the center of the floor. They had a fabulous sound system, and I was only speaking for about twenty minutes. After about five minutes, three of the security team started up into the audience, racing to the top. When at the top, they went around the upper concourse and approached a lady wearing a long flowing bright red dress who was walking toward them. After they spoke, she was ushered to an exit, and she disappeared.

The program ended without further incident, and some of the audience came to the floor to talk, ask questions, and get pictures of Thunder. Toward the end, a lady wearing a khaki-colored jumpsuit walked up to us and immediately started apologizing. I was confused and didn't know what she was referring to until I heard her blurt out, "I was the woman in the red dress." I laughed and told her that I—and likely Thunder as well—saw her but at that distance, Thunder didn't perceive her as any kind of threat. She said after they asked her to leave, she asked if, if she changed clothes, she could come back. So here she was, and she was genuinely sincere. I let her have a real close-up picture, just her and Thunder. I just backed away but didn't let go of the big bird. She probably still has that picture in a frame hanging in her home. Thunder had that effect on most everyone.

The remaining four programs (two hours each) went just as smoothly. There were highlights for Tekelec as well as for us. Tekelec was presented with the award for having the best overall display. That, I was told, was a really big honor, especially considering that all the biggies in the telecommunications market were there. And we received an award as well. Mr. Allan Toomer, president of Tekelec, presented Thunder with a check for five thousand dollars for the WVRRC.

In addition to that generous donation, they also paid for all expenses related to the trip, which I'm sure were substantial.

I want to sincerely thank Tekelec and all the wonderful employees who made this trip so successful. I am very pleased that a California-based telecommunications company with a division located in North Carolina shows such an interest in our environmental efforts. A round of applause for all of you—you should be proud.

We finished our presentations Wednesday morning, packed up all our stuff (really mostly Thunder's stuff), cleaned the room by removing the drop cloths, and made sure there were no feathers left behind. I didn't want any of the great hotel staff getting in a legal jam for being caught with one of her feathers. On our way out to the van, we stopped in the lobby to give the staff a quick peek of Thunder. Everywhere we went, the staff did such a great job taking care of us. We had a wonderful trip and met many great and generous people, and I have no doubt that Thunder left a lasting and positive impression on all those who met her in the Big Easy. Before loading into the van, we paused outside the garden and gave a big salute to the magnificent magnolia tree that Thunder spent so much quality time perched on. Then it was off to the airport.

As the right engine on the plane was all warmed up, we said our goodbyes and boarded the plane. We got all strapped in as the second engine fired up, and in no time, we were taxiing for takeoff. It was wheels up, and we were heading back across Lake Pontchartrain in a now northerly direction. Before we crossed the huge lake, about 630 square miles, Thunder and I were once again adjusting the air pressure in our ears. That meant we were between five thousand and six thousand feet high. I asked Elaine, and she confirmed we were at 5,300 feet. While I had her attention, I asked if it would be out of the way to stop at the Knoxville, Tennessee, airport. I thought she might be agreeable since we stopped in Birmingham on the way down to visit her friends. I told her that I would like to have my mother and sister see Thunder on her first plane ride. She said okay, and I gave her the contact information. About a half hour later, she came back and told me that all the arrangements were made, and my sister agreed to meet at the designated time and hangar.

During the next hour and a half, Thunder kept her eyes fixed on the sky, intently looking and watching for I'm not sure what. As we began our descent, there were more aircraft for her to watch, but as we passed the ear-pressure altitude, her aerial observation was not interrupted by the pressure changes. She just kept looking until we touched down. After a rather long taxi, we pulled up to the gate on the private side. My seventy-six-year-old mother and younger sister, who was recovering from multiple heart-valve replacement surgery, were all smiles as Thunder and I got off the plane. That was a nice surprise for them and nice for me as well. Thunder was definitely indifferent but agreed to pose for some pictures with all of us. The pilot-turned-photographer did a great job of that as well. Back aboard, after some guarded hugs and kisses, Thunder was still on my right arm, making it a bit more trying than usual.

The flight ended with a perfect landing, just like the rest of the trip. Thunder stayed on board, while I got our van and parked much closer to the plane. We got unloaded and loaded into the van but not before both pilot and copilot had their pictures taken with Thunder while standing in front of the aircraft. We had many thank-yous for Elaine Heston, our pilot, but Thunder said it best by admitting Elaine's flying abilities would rival her own. I guess you realize that Thunder really didn't say that, right?

We returned from New Orleans. I gave Thunder a few days off to get herself back into a normal eating-and-personal-maintenance routine. You know how it is—no bed or pillow sleeps as well as the one you are used to. The same went for Thunder; she liked her flight cage and her own little bathtub. In fact, she hadn't been back but for a few minutes when I put her pool back into its place and filled it with fresh clean water. Before I got to the faucet and turned the hose off, she was already splashing in her pool. If you had watched her, you would agree that she thought she had lots of road dirt to clean off her feathers. Right now, that was more important than eating. It was late afternoon, and there was still lots of sunshine for her to get dried before dark. Either way, she likely would not have waited till the following day.

There weren't any programs scheduled for the rest of this week or the following week. We were averaging about a program a week for the entire year. During bad weather in the winter, there would be long periods where we or no one else wanted to travel or schedule these programs. When spring rolled around, there weren't enough days in the week to fill all the requests. We had several other birds to use for education programs, and everyone loved the owls, but given a choice, Thunder would be the first pick with few exceptions.

In the mid-nineties, bald eagles, while making a big comeback, were still about as scarce as hen's teeth, especially in West Virginia, where we had only two confirmed nests. Both were along the south branch of the Potomac River, which is located in our eastern panhandle. This was an expansion of the Chesapeake Bay bald-eagle population. When the young became mature, they would return to the general area where they were hatched. If their parents or any other adults were nesting in that area, the young, having no seniority, would be chased away. Since they ate more fish than anything else, it would only be natural to head upstream until they found suitable habitat, food, and nesting trees that weren't already spoken for by more mature adults. There would be times that aerial battles would take place between two pairs competing for the same site. Sometimes there would be injuries and possibly deaths as well. The deaths probably occurred accidentally. Fighting to the death for real estate was not a common practice. Defending a nest from other predators was an entirely different story. Sometimes the losing predator would not only lose but also be killed and eaten by the chicks. I'm not certain what is or isn't fair in nature, and I'm equally unsure that nature doesn't keep track, but successful reproduction by a species could be one such indicator.

Thunder was quickly becoming a youthful veteran of the raptor-education circuit. She had two long and overnight trips under her belt, and she was still a good ways from adulthood in either looks or reproductive behavior. She traveled well and sometimes seemed to really enjoy it. The days she didn't, I referred to as "bad hair days." When I made that reference, the ladies always laughed. I'm not sure they believed me.

This summer officially began after our return from New Orleans, and she was working on suiting up in her sixth set of feathers, which would be her fifth molt. She was over five years and three months old, and she had a few dirty white head feathers and similar markings on her tail. She was banded while a nestling, so her accurate age was known at the time. According to lots of literature, she should be a full-fledged adult, but this one wasn't even close. Her molt normally started with tail feathers in very late May or early June. I kept track of all major feathers and dates of molts. As I said before, this bird didn't coincide with literature sightings or most of the aging information found in popular birding books used by professionals and armatures alike. I just wanted to state, again, how she was not part of the pack. Another thought I had had was that maybe she was just like the rest of the pack, but we were printing some less-than-precise information. One day we will know for sure.

It was the summer of 1997, and believe it or not, another July 4 came and went—and not a single request for an Independence Day program. My feelings were actually kind of hurt, and I was wondering why no one even considered having a nonwhite-head-and-tail bald eagle represent our country's Independence Day celebration. Well, this was another year, and we stood by the mailbox with flip phone in hand, but alas—no requests for Thunder's presence again this year. We would survive.

We spent the balance of July and August attending church summer day camps—4-H and Scout camps, both day and sleepover types—and any number of other local fairs and celebrations for both youth and adult groups. The venues varied greatly, from very nice indoor accommodations to wide-open spaces in the middle of a field. Those were the worst types for Thunder. I quickly learned that the big girl needed a corner to stand in, ideally having a partition behind her and one on her right side. I was the security for the left side. She also was unmanageable in windy situations. It seemed at times that I would be beaten, nearly to death, with those flapping wings as she attempted to maintain her balance. Facing into the wind definitely helped, but no wind at all was a better solution. It was all on me as I let others put us in these situations. These types of setups only happened once. I made sure of that.

Many of the programs requested included the other raptor ambassadors as well. So many of them were booth style or used a round-robin-type of display, where the small groups would stop for a ten-to-fifteen-minute presentation. There were sometimes as many as eight or ten stations. This was not for Thunder either, plus mixing in with three to four smaller raptors required such a large space. Ultimately, we decided that if they wanted a booth style set up for a certain number of hours we would require, if Thunder was to be present at all, she would appear at a set time to do a solo on-stage type of performance. This worked out well, and the diva, as most of our volunteers affectionately referred to Thunder, would come, do her show, and depart, leaving the rest of the birds and volunteers to finish the day.

Chapter 30

A Favorite Hotel

The summer of 1997 was a great learning season for me. My presentations were pretty good now that Thunder was more accustomed to travel, varying venues, and, of course, the people whom I was responsible for controlling. If the audience—including strollers, wheelchairs, bicycles, and photographers rushing in our direction—were not there, the setups were not as crucial. I did, however, learn that the people didn't matter that much as long as the setup was right. In other words, a bad setup was okay if it was just us, but if people were present, a great setup was terribly necessary. It was simple—she needed to feel secure no matter what we were doing or where we were doing it. This summer's programs prepared me for future programs, and with school back in session, there were more and more requests for Thunder's presence. The word was finally getting out, and we were ready for most anything—at least we thought we were. Thunder was doing so much better, improving with each presentation, and even though she was full grown, she was still a pup by comparison.

School was back in session now, and the calls were still coming in. One of the earliest from this school year came from a group representing Washington County's school system in Ohio. I was passed the message to get back in touch with them. Our director of education for the WVRRC learned long ago not to schedule programs for Thunder; that was left to me to decide if we could or would fulfill the requests. After a couple of major oopses, she thought that it should definitely be left up to me to speak on behalf of Thunder's needs. Don't misunderstand; everyone admired Thunder and wanted photos of them holding her, but no one wanted to even attempt to present her at a program. In hindsight, I'm certain that was a good decision for both of us.

I returned the call and spoke with Paul, who, with his wife, Dion, put on an environmental day for all the seventh graders in the Washington County school system. It was a two-day camp where half of the students would come each morning, and they wanted Thunder to be part of the program. I guess I was invited as a necessary extra. I asked, and they explained the venue and schedule, and I asked why it would take two days. He explained that the number of students precluded having an effective program with all the kids in one day. I could understand that. He continued to tell me that there would be seven stations for each day, and the students would spend about forty minutes at each. I politely stopped him there and told him that there wasn't a way we could survive that many programs merely from a physical standpoint—way too much work for both of us—plus the extreme stress placed on Thunder would not be tolerable. I said we would have to decline the invitation. He was determined that we participate, so he asked if there was any way they could work it out so that all the students would be able to see and hear about Thunder.

While I was considering his most sincere request, I was trying to come up with a scenario from past programs that might work here. I told him that I couldn't come up with anything other than doing each day's group of students with one presentation. He was very pleased with the idea and quickly suggested that we do it first thing in the morning each of the two days. That meant we would do it on the first day at eight thirty and then hang out until the following day at eight thirty.

I proposed the following compromise. "On the first day, we do the entire group as a whole at the last station at the end of the rotation, and the following day we do the first station with the entire group for that day. Now is there a place where we can get everyone together, and could I have electricity for a portable public-address system as well?"

He said that we had a deal, and he was excited. He stressed his interest in bald eagles and excitement now that there was a nest along the Muskingum River. He said he would set aside one hour for each of the programs, and I could use as much or as little of it as Thunder could stand. He also told me he would make reservations for me at the Lafayette Hotel in Marietta for the first night, and our food and lodging would be covered. A sizable donation would also be made to the WVRRC. While we were negotiating, I explained that when we traveled, Thunder stayed in the room with me. We covered and protected everything, but she did not stay in the vehicle. I told him that this could cause a problem with the hotel.

Paul got back to me two days later and told me that Thunder and I definitely had a room scheduled for the designated night. He would pay for my meals as well but didn't know what to do about Thunder's rations. Jokingly, I told him she was brought fresh fish from the local market every morning while we were in New Orleans. I let him off the hook and assured him that we would take care of her food.

This trip worked out as well as any we had done. We left home around lunchtime and drove the 110 miles west through North Central West Virginia and then into Ohio, where we changed to a more northwesterly heading. We arrived, our first time passing the sign that read Hervita 4-H Camp. It was part of the Ohio State University College of Food, Agriculture, and Environmental Sciences and was run by the Washington County extension agency. When we pulled in, they knew it was us and immediately hustled over to meet us. I was given directions as to the location of the program, which would begin in less than an hour. They parked me as close as possible and then made a tour of the site where we would be. It would be held in a large barn-type building, very nice though with bleachers to accommodate hundreds. It had electricity as well.

It was warm inside the building, but large doors opened at either end to allow good ventilation. It was a hot day and sunny, with temperatures in the mid-eighties. Thunder was locked in the running van with the air conditioning on. She was comfortable and would stay there, safe and sound, until a few minutes before the program began. I got out the portable speaker system I would use. It had a clip-on microphone so I would have both hands free to handle Thunder. It took two hands, and a third would have been nice. Afterward, I looked around the camp and visited some of the staff, who gave me some background information on the camp and the program we were presenting for—very nice folks, and believe me, that is important. Some places we went had rude and insensitive people doing something they hated and were usually not suited for. This group was not one of the bad ones.

A loud bell sounded, and seventh graders came flying toward the building from all directions. The bell represented the shift change and, in this case, a chance to get a close-up of a really large bald eagle. Once they got near the building, an adult arm was raised, and the hordes descending upon us suddenly slowed to a quiet walk—so nice to see such polite and respectful behavior. They filed in like they had done it hundreds of times before; each reached a seat and sat quietly.

I had brought Thunder inside while still inside her covered cage a few minutes ahead of the students. Paul introduced me, and the program began as usual. Thunder's cage stayed covered, but I raised the back section covering her door. As I raised it, she was aware to position herself for the grand exit.

As I slipped on my armguard and glove and opened the door so I could attach the leash to the jesses, I announced, "I would like for all of you to meet Thunder, an American bald eagle."

By now, she was on my arm, and I was removing her from the cage, still out of sight. Right on cue, at the words *bald eagle*, she launched herself, giant wings spread wide, as she rose from behind the cage and positioned herself on the perch attached to the cage top. She sat there, gripping the perch, and beat her wings several more times in an effort to stretch after the long ride.

Once she stopped flapping, I presented my protected arm in front of her and said, "Up," at which time she obediently came to rest on my arm. There were *oooh*s and *ahhh*s from the entire audience, and all of them were sporting king-size smiles, a first for all of them as Thunder made her grand entry. This was not done with the intent to impress the audience, but it had worked out this way. When she first got up on my arm, it was to get out of the cage to stretch, and when she flew to the top, it was merely a continuation of that desire to stretch. A few seconds later, she stopped stretching and became aware of the audience, whom she doesn't like. That was when I had her hop back onto my arm for her security. Remember, she may not like me much, but she definitely disliked everyone in the audience much more. She was safe on my arm, and depending on her ongoing evaluation of the audience, she might never leave my arm, even after it had gone to sleep and was totally numb.

The program went well, and the seventh graders had obviously had some great teachers and also fine parents. There were three words to describe them: engaged, polite, and intelligent—the perfect audience. They asked many very thoughtful questions and occasionally even had follow-ups. One real point of interest was about the lack of a white head and tail. This was something I never expected them to be so amazed by. That was when I explained to them that the likely reason she was shot, just about fifty miles south of where we were, was not many people knew that bald eagles do not have white heads and tails for their first few years after fledging. They were amazed by that fact most of all.

After Thunder was put back in her cage, the students filed out, sang the national anthem, and then lowered the flag before boarding their buses for home. When I had the all-clear, I loaded Thunder and moved my van to the bottom of the hill and parked along a very small stream. It was about ten to twenty feet wide and had a couple of inches of water in it that was flowing, clear and clean. There were some depressions with a foot or so of nice cool water in them as well. I planned to let Thunder walk around on a fifty-foot lead after most of the staff had departed. It wasn't long before only a few were left, so I opened up the back of the van, opened her cage door, and had her hop on my arm. I walked the short distance to the creek, stooped down slightly, and had her hop to the ground. The remaining staff came toward us but maintained their distance out of respect.

Eventually, Thunder stepped into the shallow water and took a little drink before picking up rocks and turning them over. I didn't know if she was playing or hunting for food. She continued exploring up and down the stream at a snail's pace, making frequent and prolonged stops, dragging her long rope lead behind her. Finally, she reached a deeper pool and waded into it to about six inches in depth. This was about the depth of her pool that she played and bathed in. Well, it was bath time, and the remaining staff was getting a real show. She really did take a bath, a long and complete bath, submerging her head and entire body under the water time after time. Eventually, she moved to more shallow water and began the drying process.

While she was still standing in the water, very quietly, I decided to try feeding her since there was an audience. This would be the first time I had her on a long lead, standing in a creek when I offered her food. I took a ten-to-twelve-ounce trout from her food cooler and walked it over to where she was standing and dropped it in the water a few feet from her. She noted its presence and definitely knew what it was but was not particularly interested at the moment. It was getting close to 5:00 p.m. now, and the creek, situated at the base of a slope, was pretty much shaded. There was some sun just a short distance from where the trout was dropped. After a few more minutes, she began to walk toward the fish. Eagles walk funny and even run funnier. She went right past the fish and hopped on a piece of log that was in the sun, nature's feather drier. I was amazed that she was doing all this with an audience, albeit a small audience, but they were still strangers. This is what I meant when I referred to Thunder feeling safe.

The venue was great, and there was a limited threat level from the humans there. We returned to this camp for many years, and even though she got older and more experienced, she just expressed a special relaxation that she seemed to feel while exploring this tiny creek at Hervida 4-H Camp. Eventually, she dried off enough that she hopped back to the shallow water and devoured her trout. She still had visitors for this event too. I was amazed at the entire experience and could only imagine all the fun pictures they were getting. Many were firsts and exclusives.

After her dinner was completed, it was a bit after six o'clock. Since we needed to get checked in at the Lafayette Hotel and Thunder settled for the night, I thought we should head back to Marietta. It was almost a thirty-minute drive. I parked along the curb of the historic wedge-shaped building, left the vehicle running with the air on, locked it, and went inside. The staff at the front desk was waiting for us and very excited to have a bald eagle staying with them. I got the room key and went to check it out—not the biggest room but nice and quaint and more than adequate for both our needs.

I went and got our stuff and Thunder out of the van and began our trek up the access ramp to enter the building. The squeeze was very tight going through the door, but we made it. We went around and down a hallway to the lobby and elevator. We made a short stop at the elevator, and I lifted the drape covering the cage so the on-duty staff could have a peek. They were quite appreciative and in awe of her size. We hopped on the next elevator and took it to the third floor.

Down the hall to the room and through the door, we went—not so fast. I went through the door, but Thunder's cage wouldn't come close to fitting through the doorway. *Yikes*, I thought and got on the phone and called the front desk, explaining the situation to them. They sent someone up with more keys and took us down the hall to a handicapped room. She wouldn't fit in that one either. I explained that I could not leave her in the vehicle overnight, so if there weren't any larger doorways, then we would have to try to find another hotel.

When we got back to the lobby, the night manager met us, took a peek at Thunder, and asked us to describe the problem. I told him it was simple; a thirty-one-and-a-half-inch-wide cage would not fit through a thirty-inch opening. He thought a second, went back behind the desk, and immediately returned. He hailed the elevator and said to hop on. The elevators were small too, but the three of us and Thunder did fit. The manager punched B, and we headed down. We got off in the basement, walked and rolled down the hall, and stopped in front of a room that said Mississippi Queen Room. It had a small glass window. It was one of their conference rooms.

He unlocked the door, and we went inside. The cage fit. The room was nice sized, about thirty feet long and twenty-five feet wide with high ceilings. There was a big conference table and chairs set up in the middle of the room. He asked, since we fit through the door, if this space would work to leave Thunder in for the night. I told him my concern would be someone having access during the night, and he quickly assured me that he and I would have the only keys, and he would be there till 9:00 a.m. I thought that would work, and the room was large enough that we could get by with just scooting the table and chairs to one side of the room. That would give us a straight shot to the far end, where I planned to locate her cage.

He asked if I needed anything else or assistance with my setup. I told him I could handle making Thunder's sleeping area, but I definitely needed the key. He was ready for that because

I no more than put the period at the end of the sentence, and he was handing me a single key on a tagged ring. He reminded me to let him know if we needed anything else. I let him know how grateful we were for making these special arrangements, and I would make certain that Thunder could have her area of activity, including the hardwood-paneled wall behind her, completely covered with our plastic drop cloths. I explained the setup, and he was fine with that.

Before he left, I asked if there was a place to get a bit of dinner. He told me they had two restaurants and a pub area with a bar and lots of raised tables. He said that was usually the busiest this time of the evening, and they served the same menu items the restaurants served. I asked him if he would mind if I took Thunder up there for a few minutes to give the guests a little special surprise viewing. Then I asked if she could be removed from her cage. He wanted to know when I wanted to do that because he wanted to be there. I told him it might take fifteen minutes to get the room here ready, and then I would be right up. They both left smiling, and I was pleased with our arrangements here as well.

After I had the wall and carpeted floor covered and all of Thunder's items of necessity unloaded—rags, paper towels, water misting bottle, and large bath towels—we headed out of the conference room toward the elevator. Once I exited the elevator in the lobby, I glanced over toward the front desk, where I was immediately informed that the manager and many others were in the bar waiting for us. We entered the bar and migrated to an area against the wall, where they had pushed some tables closer together to give us more room. The manager took this initiative solely based on the fact that she wouldn't fit in the rooms and she was now occupying one of the conference rooms. This was a fairly big place with an old wooden bar, likely fifty or more feet long and that many high tops and tables as well.

Upon entering, we immediately had the attention of all the folks in there, so I took advantage of the opportunity, introduced myself, and told them to please be calm and that I was going to bring out Thunder. I told them that she was far from twenty-one, but it would be okay since I was older than that. I removed her in the usual dramatic fashion to everyone's amazement and delight. After she settled on her perch, I immediately got her on my arm and rotated my hand slightly so she would spread her wings. I just gave a brief history of her and our purpose here before I answered questions for about half an hour. Before the questions ended, Thunder had had enough bar life, and I put her back in her cage. We left shortly afterward and went back to our conference room. She had already eaten and bathed at the 4-H camp, so I just placed her on her perch, removed her jesses, and left. I planned to come back after dark and dim the lights to near off and leave her for the night. Her first night alone—I was a bit anxious but trusted the manager.

The next morning, I entered the nearly dark conference room and turned up the lights. I went to the small restaurant to have breakfast while Thunder got herself together. Big birds have to wake up too. After breakfast, I went down, and she was very alert. I cleaned up most of her molted feathers and packed what I could of her stuff. I then jessed her and placed her inside the cage. I had placed a towel all around the top perch so she wouldn't mess up the sheet covering the cage during the night. The towel was soiled though, just as planned. After she was covered, I moved the cart with the cage on it off the drop cloth. I removed the plastic from the wall first, piled it on the floor, and then wadded up the floor cover along with the wall cover. Remember, she ate that ten-to-twelve-ounce trout about thirteen hours ago, and a large part of it had passed through her system during the night, at least a half cup, likely more. The plastic caught it all, and I wrapped it, careful not to spill any of the runny waste before putting the whole thing inside a plastic trash bag. I double-checked for any feathers I might have missed and packed her travel box, and we headed to the lobby.

It was a bit after seven, and we were ahead of schedule, so I made my way to the lobby to return the key and say thank you to the staff. There were people checking out who wanted to know what was under the cover. This became a parting tradition where the guests present when we checked out got a brief peek of Thunder. They were always amazed.

It was time to go, so we loaded into the van and headed northwest to Camp Hervida. We arrived a bit before the buses as planned. I got Thunder's setup completed, and after raising the American flag and reciting the Pledge of Allegiance, the second half of the Washington County seventh graders filed into the building, a group just as good as yesterday's. All their questions were answered just before the horn sounded for them to break off into their separate groups to start the rotation part of the day. Thunder and I got everything loaded, said our goodbyes, and began our trip home. Before leaving, they presented us with a nice donation for the WVRRC and expressed an interest in making this an annual event. They gave me a card with next fall's scheduled dates handwritten on it. They wanted Thunder to return.

Our drive back was just under two hours, shorter than the normal drive time for us. Thunder was quiet and calm for the trip. We were both a bit tired but by no means overly so. Thunder had enjoyed her entire trip. There was not any nervous or anxious behavior from the time we left home to our return. She loved the stream at Camp Hervida, and the setup was relaxing for her as well. We probably went there ten or more years, and every time was a good experience for her and me as well. It ended up that how things went for Thunder went so for me. If she was not happy, she made sure that I was in the same frame of mind. The folks at the hotel always remembered us and had either the Mississippi Queen Room or the Rufus Putnam Room for us. We became annual fixtures, and they would inform their visitors that they should keep a lookout for us.

One thing that made the rest of our visits to the Lafayette even more enjoyable was the city park across the street from the hotel. It bordered the Ohio River, and I would normally take Thunder down by the river to enjoy her evening meal. Sometimes we would go and sit, her next to me like a puppy, watching the ducks and geese on the river. We would have very large audiences from people standing high above us on the overlooks for the river. It must have been quite a sight, and we were there so often that we were referred to as "the man and his eagle." I always explained that it was not my bald eagle; I was merely responsible for her care.

We stayed at the Lafayette Hotel on numerous other occasions while doing other programs in the town of Marietta. Things always worked well there for Thunder, and we certainly were treated with kindness and respect. So the Lafayette gets a big tip of the wing from Thunder for being her favorite home away from home.

Chapter 31

More Time and More Questions Yet Fewer Answers

Thunder has appeared as the main attraction at hundreds of educational programs, fairs, and even social gatherings since her first appearance on Earth Day in April 1995. Many have included road trips, some requiring hotel stays, while most were of a more local nature. Thunder will be twelve years old on her next hatch date in late April 2004.

Much has been learned about her during this time with me, including the realization that I will never live to learn the answers to all the questions I have. This will not deter me as I will continue to search, observe, record, and analyze. I believe that part of the "lack of information" problem stems from the little that we do know. This limited knowledge doesn't allow us the insight to search for or even ask the right questions that would allow for greater discoveries.

Research funding—or lack thereof—also plays a big role in limiting our knowledge and understanding. We have psychologists and psychiatrists who can't even agree on certain basic human behaviors, so why would one expect to understand a bald eagle that we can't even get into the office of the psychiatrist, let alone have it face interrogation on the couch?

My long and short trips and the thousands of hours spent with Thunder could hardly equate to a one-hour session on the couch, but the more time we spent together, the more bits of knowledge I acquired. So we continue on to the next new adventure, all the while hoping to make the knowledge void a bit smaller.

Chapter 32

On the Road Again

November 2003 marked another milestone in our travels. An educational tour through Tennessee and Florida was arranged during late summer and early fall. As with any of our trips, much planning and preparation were required. This jaunt would begin on Sunday, November 9, and end late the following Saturday. My sister (Mary) was a high-school teacher in Maryville, Tennessee, located not far from Knoxville. She did all the great legwork of scheduling and logistics for the Tennessee leg of the trip. So on November 8, I began packing for the trip—no, not my stuff, Thunder's.

Let me begin by telling you again that traveling on a long trip with Thunder is akin to a single parent traveling with six-month-old triplets. I've never done that, but I can't imagine it being much more work. For one, the triplets get to wear diapers; that reduces the odor and range of placement of those necessary "nasties." And second, the kids get to eat from a bottle, much neater and less odoriferous than smelly fish that's strewn about like feathers on a windy day. Included in her "necessities" are the obvious staples, such as food and water. I've often considered it to be easier just taking her into a sushi bar and "ordering up" a jumbo plate. I'm aware that wouldn't work, but it would save cleaning up the mess of uneaten skin, fins, intestines, and scales that make up that messy part of strewn leftovers.

So with that awareness, I packed a lunch—or seven lunches, in this case. A large cooler with ice was needed to keep the tasty trout fresh and desirable, as well as a five-gallon water bladder and her mini pool (holding about eight gallons) for those daily baths. I also took a fifty-foot hose for when the opportunity presented itself that she could shower if bath time and facilities were limited, a large sealable plastic tub (two by two and a half by one and a half feet) filled with paper towels, rags, a scrub brush, cleaners, deodorizers, a large roll of ten-by-twelve-foot plastic drop cloths, masking tape, duct tape, rope, garbage bags, gallon Ziploc bags, and her portable perch, which was constructed from three-inch PVC pipe mounted on a detachable base (a twenty-seven-inch bicycle tire and rim poured solid with concrete for stability for when she landed on it a bit too hard). Naturally, we'd need Thunder, her cage, and my handling gear. Spare jesses were a must. I had a difficult enough time finding leather straps around here. Oh yes, I almost forgot the reason for the trip: the two boxes of educational material and all the various state and federal permits.

I probably forgot something, but I loaded Thunder early the next morning, and we were "on the road again." Thunder was a great traveler, and I think she would say I was an equally good "big-bird hauling" driver. To qualify, you just have to remember to take turns softly, accelerate slowly, and *never* tailgate. She hated those sudden stops. The first day's trip was only seven hours, which followed the same southern route, utilizing the tunnels carved through the mountains of Southern West Virginia and Western Virginia. This trip was much less adventurous than our last one through the tunnels, her first overnight trip seven years ago.

We made one rest stop at the Tennessee Welcome Center. We got to park with the "big rigs." Parking there allowed us to hide from most of the folks. I would look for two tractor trailers with space between them. Once I pulled into the empty space, we were almost out of sight. There was a bit of noise from the diesels idling their engines, but the sound didn't bother Thunder. The first time we did this, I was curious as to the amount of the fumes present. It might have been there, but I didn't notice it. This tidbit of knowledge was very helpful on the second leg of the trip when we made a rest stop in Georgia.

When we pulled onto that particular rest area, I was certain I was seeing gnats or mosquitoes or both all around the van. When I found a secluded spot and got arranged properly in the space, I got out and was almost smothered with mosquitoes. Instantly, I got back into the protection of the van and pulled out. On the other end of the rest stop was where the trucks parked. I pulled in between two of the big rigs and got out but didn't shut the engine off in case we needed to perform a quick getaway from all the insects. I exited the van, but not a one was seen or heard buzzing around my ears. It must have been the fumes, the truck vibrations, or some combination of each. It too could have simply been that there were no mosquitoes there since there was no vegetation nearby.

Hidden as we were, we would still get spotted by a few observant travelers as Thunder stretched her seven-foot wings and flew on her line for her exercise. We usually ended up doing a mini program while keeping the visitors a good distance from her. After all, this was her rest stop too. She got her pool filled with water just in case she wanted to splash around. After about twenty minutes, if she hadn't taken a drink, I'd offer her water from her quart-sized Tupperware cup. She always bit me when I did, this but she still drank. I think the bites were part of the ritual though; if not, I'd be fingerless by now.

We made it to Tennessee, and my sister had Thunder's room all ready—almost. She had moved both vehicles out of the garage and secured or covered anything else that could possibly be a danger to her or just needed protecting. By this time in her life, Thunder made a pretty good houseguest and was content on sitting on her perch once put to bed. Mary did, however, neglect covering the floor. Not a big problem—I literally had that part covered. We made the necessary modifications, and I set Thunder's portable perch under a bit of shade in the lawn. She stretched as usual, but she had only been riding about an hour and one half after we left the rest stop at the Tennessee line. She enjoyed the light breeze and sunshine. The temperature was in the seventies, and she was just sitting there, taking in the new surroundings.

Backing up a bit—my sister's family had a Great Dane puppy named Blue, a big puppy, maybe about seven to eight months old but still as large as a small pony. She had an outdoor kennel that was enclosed and contained her little house. She wasn't usually running loose, but with the folks around, she got to hang out. She greeted me when I arrived but became bored after a few minutes, like most puppies do, and quickly disappeared. I hadn't seen her in a while, and Mary figured Blue was back in her kennel, possibly finishing her dinner, which we interrupted with our arrival. Now it was time for Thunder to be removed from her cage. She took her place on top of her portable perch and, as usual, began her stretching ritual.

My sister and her family were not unlike any other onlookers as Thunder made her grand exit from her travel cage. They all stood and watched her every move. I never was able to fully understand what was expected of Thunder while on display but whatever it was, it didn't seem to include disappointment. Even on her grumpiest of days, Thunder always seemed to spawn intense observation techniques, outward admiration for her beauty and stoic presence, and lots and lots of big smiles. As many times as we have done this since first presenting Thunder to an audience, I have never been able to completely figure it out. I did conclude that whatever it was that was expected, I was certain it was something good.

An adult bald eagle perched here in suburban America in the lawn of one family in a neighborhood of Maryville, Tennessee, was definitely not something you'd see every day. As we continued our visit, Thunder remained calmly perched outside, now for twenty minutes or more, when out of the blue—no pun intended—Blue came loping around the house from out back. She got about thirty feet from Thunder when she finally saw her. The breaks were applied with a sense of urgency, causing her to come to an instant halt. Thunder, the veteran she was now, didn't give Blue a single consideration or in any way acknowledged her presence. In fact, she did a small wing extension to adjust her feathers and immediately folded them again, followed by a small roust, where she sort of gave her entire body a back-and-forth kind of shake to put the feathers back in their proper places. Thunder still had not reacted, but now, in an instant, Blue had made a 180-degree turn and ran full speed back to her kennel and truly hid in her house.

I was surprised at Blue's feeling of terror, but after a bit of consideration and reflection, I guess I understood. After all, Blue was just a pup and Thunder an adult predator. She was more intimidating at thirteen pounds than I could reasonably imagine. My sister was a bit surprised too, thinking Thunder would be the one more frightened by Blue's speedy approach.

I then told her about a program we had done this summer for some Girl Scouts. It was held at the State Wildlife Center. Animals native to West Virginia now and in the past were kept on the vast grounds. One of the species was the elk, which long ago used to roam the mountain and valleys of wild and wonderful West Virginia. In fact, we had the program set up at the top of a hill just on the outside of the multiacre elk enclosure. I told her that as that program progressed, a few of the female elk (cows) had come very close to the fence where we were. They were likely curious and just quietly stood there, watching. More of them gathered, and the last one to join the herd was a big bull elk that had been growing a huge set of antlers all summer. The girls turned to look at them when I mentioned their presence and briefly discussed them, and then we went ahead with our program. At some point after that, Thunder felt the need to stretch her wings and did a couple of mild wing flaps. As soon as the wings were extended for the first time, the herd of elk literally stampeded away from Thunder and down the hill. The ground shook. That male weighed about seven hundred to eight hundred pounds and the adult cows close to five hundred pounds each. In total, there was likely over two tons of "on the hoof" elk frantically fleeing from thirteen pounds of bald eagle. Again, why should I be so surprised at Blue's response?

After some more playing, feeding, and showering with a hose, Thunder was ready to turn in for the night and rest for the five programs scheduled for the next two days—well, almost ready. As usual, everywhere we went, Thunder was quite a curiosity. Mary had done a great PR job for the programs, which meant that some of her special friends wanted and expected a private viewing. So they came. Thunder was tired but quite the trooper and tolerated it all very well. It too was possible, when I think about such situations, that it was I who was tired. I was a good sport too. Mary had worked hard planning this trip, so a few more minutes from the star and her mouthpiece could certainly be an equitably minimum payback. After our debt was paid, we set the big girl in the garage, closed the doors, and locked the main door. Her bathtub was filled, and I placed a nice trout on her perch next to her talons. Since it was still daylight outside, I figured we would not do lights out for at least two more hours.

By then, she would have eaten, gotten herself a drink, and splashed in the water as she felt necessary.

On Monday and Tuesday, we did our environmental education programs. All in all, over two thousand students sat quietly and respectfully in total amazement at the presence of this magnificent bird. Tuesday was Veterans Day, making the presence of our proud national symbol even more special. Thunder left with a much longer list of personal admirers. The kids were terrific and equally appreciative. The staff at each of the schools was more than the usual pleasant folks; they really were Southern ladies and gentlemen. They may have been extra nice since it was my amazing sister who had arranged the five schools to be visited in just two days. That meant three programs on the first day and just two for Tuesday. The schools being fairly close together helped, but when you figure three programs within the timeframe of a school day, well, that took planning. Each would require at least an hour for the presentation and a few questions, setting up and then reloading, plus the travel. Oh yes, and let's not forget the photo ops for the school staff. Lots of folks wanted to be included in photos with the big bird. Wow, a lot was squeezed into a day. We had to keep a schedule, and Mary saw to that. The second day was a lighter load, and that was done intentionally since we would be traveling the next day. Thunder couldn't rest as well while traveling because a certain amount of stabilization was required, even with my bird-friendly driving.

Doing these programs with Thunder was a rare privilege and honor for me, a lot of work and very tiring but equally rewarding. I rarely knew going in what Thunder's mood would be, but we eventually figured it out. With her large size, she could, at times, be much more than a handful. She had a very complex personality, but the years of learning to understand it and assessing the situations we were placed in for these programs made it so much easier than it might be. She was a pleasure most of the time.

On Wednesday, we planned to continue our trip to Orlando, Florida, where we had one program scheduled for November 13 and multiple for the fourteenth. Before that would happen, there were some serious maintenance and cleaning issues that needed to be addressed. Most of the sanitation problems were resolved with scrub brushes and disinfectants. Some deodorizing sprays were used inside the van in an effort to keep Thunder's odor from penetrating too deeply into the upholstery. As much waste as she produced in a day's time, the odor really wasn't that powerfully bad. "Once removed, it didn't linger" was how I described it to other people. If they were riding with just me and not Thunder in the van, they would ask how long it had been since she had ridden in the van. If I replied that it had been a couple of weeks, they advised me that I was merely used to that smell. Maybe it lingered more than I thought, or I actually did not find the smell that offensive. It didn't smell like a horse or cattle barn, but it was no more unpleasant. The exceptions to this were when she would get carsick, usually after dark, after having eaten some fish a few hours prior. If you were driving down the Interstate at legal speed limits and she suddenly coughed up a partially digested piece of fish, you could only hope that you could hold your breath long enough to get safely off the road and out of the vehicle. For this, I used a paper towel to clean it from the floor of the travel cage and then sealed it in a storage bag. I've smelled skunk spray firsthand, and this was an odiferous equivalent to be sure. The difference here was that the source of Thunder's odor was a piece of fish that could be instantly removed and the entire source sealed. Skunk spray was far more difficult to isolate.

I had everything cleaned and ready to be packed for an early departure in the morning. At about 6:30 a.m. on Wednesday, I put Thunder in her travel cage and loaded her and her portable perch into the van. Our hosts were there to thank us and wish us a safe journey to Florida.

These trips are exhausting but even more gratifying. Nothing is more encouraging than meeting all these leaders of tomorrow and sharing with them the experience of being in Thunder's presence. The environmental responsibilities they are being made aware of, even at this young age, will likely last them a lifetime. While it may be difficult to quantify the absolute positive effect Thunder and the accompanying narrative had on the tens of thousands of students we reached, I can say with certainty that I have met well over a hundred of these students who have since grown to adults and have recited, verbatim, the important parts of the message I was trying to convey to them many years before. It's this sharing of information and knowledge with young open minds that make all the time and effort invested so worthwhile.

CHAPTER 33

Next Stop—Orlando Florida

It wasn't long before we left the corporate borders of Maryville, Tennessee, and were driving south on I-75. This route took us through Chattanooga, Tennessee, and then Atlanta and Macon, Georgia, before entering Florida. The drive was about nine and a half hours, but we needed to add another hour and a half for the three rest stops we would make. There were two in Georgia; one was where we encountered all the mosquitoes and the last one near Gainesville, Florida. We were close to our destination when we made the last stop. We no doubt could have continued, but in the last four days, we had traveled over a thousand miles and done five formal presentations and another five spontaneous ones. This wore on both man and beast, and the little stops really did benefit Thunder, not to mention the chauffeur.

As we pulled into the hotel parking lot in Orlando, I immediately began searching for a vacant area. I wanted a place virtually to ourselves. We didn't want visitors for what we had in mind. It had been a long day, and the last thing either of us wanted or needed was another audience. This was our downtime. As I reflected on the day's trip, although a long one, it was without incident—well, almost. I remembered the rest stop with all the mosquitoes where, in that case, we managed to make lemonade from this swarm of lemons. All in all, I considered the entire long day a huge success.

The parking lot was well lit, and since we had made a stop a short while ago, I left Thunder in the locked vehicle while I checked us into our quarters. The temperature was not much over seventy degrees so I had no qualms about leaving her with just the rear-side vents open. At the front desk, I was met with a warm welcome and assured that the staff would do everything necessary to make our next three nights enjoyable.

"Let us know of any special needs for the bald eagle," they proclaimed.

With that invitation, I told them where I was parked and wondered if, by chance, there would possibly be a hose bib somewhere nearby. I explained I wanted this private area to hide Thunder so I could shower her with my garden hose. To my surprise, one of the staff was called to the front desk, who then escorted me to a hose connection not fifteen feet from where I was parked. So it looked like Thunder was going to have her own private shower area. The dumpsters for the hotel were inside a solid vinyl fence. This was tall enough to block the view from that side, and my van was parked about twenty feet to the left of the fence. Landscaping was shielding the front view, which only left the rear open. That wasn't a problem since it wasn't likely anyone else spending the night would have an eagle that would be in need of a shower.

I never thought I'd be writing about a bald eagle taking a shower in a hotel parking lot in Orlando, Florida, with a small audience. It never mattered when or where we were; when Thunder was removed from her covered travel cage and placed on her portable perch or I just held her perched on my arm, a crowd from nowhere always seemed to appear. Maybe I was too occupied with what Thunder was doing or trying to do to notice, but one moment, we were alone, and the next, we were serving tea to our uninvited guests. I really didn't mind the attention as long as it was positive. We would spend so many hours traveling, cleaning, eating, and presenting that there was little time left for rest. I could tolerate the stress as long as Thunder was relatively relaxed with the situation. If she was not, it was back into her covered travel cage. As I've said all along, stress has to be monitored, or the well-beings of all our wild raptor ambassadors would be in jeopardy. I guess I shouldn't complain about Thunder today; after all, this was what I had signed up for almost thirteen years ago. It was sort of like a married couple who chose to have children; it couldn't and never would be a matter of convenience.

I left Thunder in the van as I moved all our gear to the room. The hotel employee who showed me the hose bib brought a luggage cart along with him—great move—and for that bit of initiative, he was given the first peek of Thunder. Understated, he was impressed and excited. We loaded everything but Thunder and her dinner on the cart and took it to the room. I spent an extra ten minutes getting everything set up. I told the employee that I would not need the cart since all that remained was Thunder, who had her own cart.

I went back to the van alone and opened the side and rear doors. I set up the portable perch within the confines of our "hideout," jessed Thunder, and attached her leash before removing her from the cage. As usual, she would perch on the portable one. Her travel cage door would stay open, with the rest of the cage remaining covered with the drape. Precautions like this were done as a result of experience. Should something or someone move threateningly in her direction, I could quickly get her back into the safety of her drape-covered travel cage. In fact, her travel cage was such a safe place for her that she would make an effort to get into the cage on her own. That could only happen if she physically had a view of the cage. There had been numerous times when she was on the ground at a rest stop or other similar places or situations where she felt threatened and voluntarily, with a sense of purpose, hopped and flew right into the cage. It appeared that she had every expectation that I would be on the other end of the leash to quickly close the door and drop the drape. I was always there.

I had already attached the hose to the faucet and tested the spray pattern through the nozzle. Thunder was sitting on her perch, stretching, when I turned the hose onto a soft spray. When I would do this, she would keep her wings closed for a bit until there was a misty layer of water covering her outer feathers. Now she opened her wings, gripped the perch with her huge talons, and flapped those giant wings as though she were trying to fly away with the perch. Now that the water had been scattered over and between the outside feathers, she held her wings in an open position, allowing me to mist her front again and also the undersides of the wings. As the wings extended, the overlapping of the feathers became less and less. This allowed more feather surface to become wet. And honestly, after the front was sufficiently drenched, she actually turned around as though asking for the same treatment of the top side of the wings.

Now she closed her wings, and I pointed the spray into the air as though imitating a soft rain. She had her wings folded now and, using the control muscles for the skin, drew the skin tighter, which caused the angle of the feathers to open up, allowing air as well as water to get in between the feathers. While they were still open, she would fill the spaces with more air, making her size appear nearly double. Now she gave a ferocious back-and-forth shake (rousting), expelling large amounts of water across the feather surfaces before expelling it entirely from her body.

This was just the start of a long evening at the spa. She wasn't finished by any means, but I loaded her into the travel cage and got her to the room. Once there, she was let out of the cage and placed on the perch screwed into the cage's top. Her jesses were removed, but she wouldn't leave the perch. She would spend the next two to three hours completing her self-spa treatment. By morning, the plastic floor cover would be lightly coated with feather dander and a good many tiny feathers, most coming from the head and neck. This was molting season for that area of her body. It was possible—but I think not likely—for this to be particular to this one bird only. I would expect to see the same molting pattern for all bald eagles, taking into account the nesting season variables from North to South.

Chapter 34

Kids "R" Kids

Thunder and I were always up early in the morning when we were traveling. Today would be an easy day with only one program, which wouldn't begin until ten thirty. So we needn't rush. Thunder would have plenty of time to have her breakfast trout before we met my youngest daughter in the hotel's lobby. This program was a special fit-in for my grandson's fifth birthday. "Kindergarten audiences are not the most challenging" was a classic opinion from someone who hasn't undertaken this task. Well, I beg to differ. I had a bird that was taller than most of the children and definitely much scarier. Her wingspan exceeded twice their height, and a single flap of those wings moved air rushing past them at a noticeable wind speed and volume.

We got set up in the room, and the children were seated on the floor, with the adults scattered among them. Regardless of the audience's age, a normal response could be expected when Thunder exited her travel cage and suddenly appeared on top of it. With the preschool children, it was just a bit more animated. At the first sight of Thunder, the youngsters' eyes, fixed and wide, showed brief signs of question and possibly fear; but once the air rushed past them, blowing papers and their long hair, enormous smiles and giggles filled the room.

Children this age had limited vocabularies for sure, but that doesn't mean you couldn't find common grounds on which to teach them about their environment and this one big bird that sat atop the food chain. It too was an effortless challenge explaining just what a food chain was. One thing for sure was the students didn't go to sleep while Thunder was out and active. Just in case, though, they had just finished their morning nap before Thunder and I arrived. If they were initially impressed with the bird, as nearly everyone seeing her in person was, her size would suffice in holding their attention. If they were skeptical or even a bit fearful and weren't sure about the bird, they would be equally attentive if for no other reason than purely for survival's sake. Thunder was a pleasant and well-behaved bird most of the time, but she did naturally exhibit that furrowed brow and stern, almost unfriendly expression.

Today's program was scheduled for about thirty minutes, more than enough time to make the intended impression as well as a few points about nature and just how these little ones now fit and would fit into and affect the big picture later on in their lives. As they grew, so too would their footprints grow.

We stuck around for a bit, talking to the staff. The half-day kindergarten schedule would allow my grandson to be ready to leave with us by the time we could get away from our adult audience. They took many photos of Thunder and asked lots of interesting questions. This latter statement, as a rule, indicated how well the student body behaved during the program. If the kids were very polite and well mannered, Thunder would control the audience, giving the staff more opportunity to listen to the presentation rather than needing to keep a watchful eye on the little ones. The more rambunctious the audience, the more the staff's attention was diverted from Thunder. As a rule, though, there was not much student management required at any of our school presentations.

It was time to continue with the day's plan. My daughter and the kids, three in all, would meet us back at the hotel once I got the big bird packed. It was always easy to get Thunder into her travel cage, gather our other program-related items, and head for the vehicle.

Back at the hotel, I had Thunder sitting on her cage perch, untethered and relaxed. It wasn't much after that that my daughter and the three kids got to the room. Today was Parker's fifth birthday; his sister Taylor was now three years and seven months and the baby, Peyton, only twenty-one months old. When they got in the room, Thunder showed no concern, but the kids sure did. As always, from very early on, Thunder never seemed to even acknowledge the presence of children under seven or so. I guess she considered them too large for a meal and not large enough to be a threat.

We didn't stay long enough for the kids to get relaxed with her, and we headed back to Robin's house to spend the afternoon together. Before leaving, I made sure Thunder was settled and placed the Do Not Disturb sign on the outside of the door. Once in the lobby, I reminded those at the front desk that no one was to go into the room since the eagle was just sitting untethered on her perch. They had seen Thunder and assumed that the best method for staying out of harm's way would be to follow the instructions on the door hanger. I didn't usually leave Thunder alone for much more than the length of a meal, but every time I did, I placed a toothpick in the doorjamb near the floor on the hallway side. If it was still there when I returned I knew that the door hadn't been opened. If the door had been opened, the toothpick would be lying on the floor. In all our years of traveling, I never did find one on the floor. From that, I deduced one of two things controlled these results: respect or fear. I guess a little of each could have been a third option.

I returned to the hotel room before dark and removed the toothpick from the door before entering the room. I decided to take Thunder outside to shower and stretch before bed. I put her jesses on her and placed her inside the cage, closed the door, and pulled the cover over the door. We headed for the same vacant corner of the lot near the dumpster and water faucet. It was about dark by now, so our privacy was almost guaranteed.

I had fed her early in the morning but hoped she would eat some more now. I was planning my feeding strategy for our return trip in two days. I wanted her to be on an evening eating schedule so she would eat a big meal tomorrow night and then be able to travel the twelve hours without eating during the trip. Remember the carsick eagle I traveled with? If you were ever with her just once, you would go to your grave remembering it. Trust me.

Anyway, like a good girl, she ate a nice one-pound trout. Now it was almost eight thirty, and I was beginning to tire. Thunder, on the other hand, had been napping all afternoon. We weren't done yet; there was still the small issue of her shower. We could normally complete this in fifteen minutes as long as she didn't have to do her hair. That was a joke, one of many I would use to humor myself in an attempt to maintain my sanity. Remember traveling with the triplets as a single parent? Well, this was more of that "no rest for the wicked" parenting responsibility. I wheeled her back to the room and put her back atop her perch to spend the rest of the night doing her feathers in preparation for the next day's presentations. She primped in the dark, and I slept.

My eldest daughter was a teacher at Carver Middle School in Orlando. This was going to be the final leg of this Southern educational tour. The school programs in Tennessee were organized by my sister, and the Florida leg was organized by my two daughters, Krista and Robin. This trip was definitely a family affair, but the thousands who were part of the audience were definitely the fortunate ones. Most had never seen a live bald eagle and most definitely not one as magnificent and large as Thunder. To cap it off, this sighting would be up close and personal.

Thunder and I arrived at the school a bit after nine. I went through the normal school security protocol and was given an escort to Krista's classroom. As usual, we were a bit early, which gave us time to plan our strategy and get everything positioned to best benefit Thunder. This didn't take long, and shortly after we finished, the first of three classes began to file in.

All the students were in the seventh and eighth grades. This was probably, if you were to ask experienced teachers, the most difficult age to teach. They were at the age where they wanted nothing more than to become adults, and there wasn't much teachers or parents could say to slow this naturally occurring maturation process. Along with the desire to grow up came the natural inclination to profess having knowledge that was still far out of their reach. This might come from the fact that teenagers were now in possession of almost all their grown-up teeth. Puberty had or soon would set in, and they did actually spend more time around adults once the 'teens are reached. I was by no means a child psychologist nor do I profess to be, but I was an authority on a middle-school student's behavior in the presence of one giant, totally wild-with-manners bald eagle.

To maintain the attention of seventh and eighth graders, the teachers had to be very good. They had to be able to stay ahead of the quick-thinking wannabes while providing challenges to keep them on a desired course. Or they could just carry Thunder around with them. That was my trick, and it worked. How often have you ever seen seventh or eighth graders sitting still for ninety minutes or more? Answer: anytime Thunder was in front of them for ninety minutes or more.

Now it helped if you had a story to go with the prop, but Thunder's solid streak of wildness provided what I could never provide an audience: in a word, unpredictability. Thunder definitely provided that. The two of us had lots of mutual experience under our respective belts, and Thunder was easily controlled. Let me restate that. Thunder was easily controlled by me and me alone. She was big and strong, and if she was made uncomfortable and responded accordingly, I had been the only one large enough to handle her with any semblance of grace. As I've said before, she flapped her wings just once and blew the long hair of a young lady as though she were in a wind tunnel. When this happened, she was eight to ten rows back in the classroom. At this point, the audience might not be totally certain she could be controlled. That was the first and very natural response. After that was over, they very attentively kept their eyes glued to the large wing-flapping bird. Their ears were open just as wide, and they hoped their teenaged newfound hungers for knowledge would be partially fulfilled. This was like watching a great action movie with a great plot. These young teens really were the greatest, the most challenging to be sure but definitely the greatest. These three classes were no exception.

Another trait more prominent in some of the males would have to be the blooming and display of macho behavior. The real macho ones actually wanted to hold Thunder on their arms. I explained that it was really not as easy as I made it look since I weighed 220 pounds and the larger boys might weigh 140 pounds. I told them there were two reasons why they couldn't hold her. First and most important was that it was not legal for someone under the age of eighteen to do this. Second, I told them that they weren't physically strong enough. That got their macho blood boiling as they professed to me how strong they really were. So we did a little demonstration where I told them that if they could hold a book weighing about three pounds on the backs of their wrists with their palms turned down for two minutes, then they were strong enough to hold her. So they tried, and as the time ticked by, it was not even a minute into the demonstration that their arms would begin to shake violently until the books slid off their wrists. Had their palms been turned up, I'm sure they would have all been strong enough. The problem here was that you could only hold and control Thunder with your palm turned down.

The macho young lads ate a little crow and always admitted how hard that was, and they couldn't believe they couldn't do it. They too admitted that with Thunder weighting thirteen pounds—plus she moved around—they would not even be able to hold her. They then confidently professed that when they were of age, they would really be proud to give it a try.

This age group will always be a favorite of mine, and these three classes were even better than normal. I'm sure the teachers had a lot to do with that, but this was one of Thunder's really, really good days. She wasn't too wild, but she had that air about her when she quietly appeared invincible. A great hair day for Thunder made for a great day for the audience as well as myself. On days like this, her behavior was most definitely in spite of me, not because of me.

We did two of the classes in the morning and then took a break and finished the third one after lunch. Thunder and I weren't invited into the cafeteria, but we were very pleased with the school, the teachers, and the students we got to meet. We said our farewells, packed up, and headed back to the motel room, where we would spend one more night before leaving Saturday morning.

Chapter 35

Thunder and Blackberry 6210

Thunder and I spent the rest of the afternoon in the hotel room. I took the time to rest a bit since we would be driving for about thirteen hours tomorrow. We would get an early start in the morning so I would pack what I could now and then take a rest before I had my dinner. While I was organizing and packing, Thunder and I watched some television. Nothing seemed to interest her; daytime TV didn't have much to offer a bald eagle, especially soap operas. *The Young and the Restless?* I don't think so.

I went down to the restaurant to get myself some dinner. A young lady took me to a table not far from a couple about my age. After I had put my menu down, the gentleman at the table next to me pardoned himself and asked if I was the person traveling with the eagle. As surprised as I was, I really shouldn't have been since having a bald eagle in a hotel for three days naturally drew some attention and was the subject of much discussion. I confessed that I was indeed that person. He went on to tell me that he and his wife had been here for a few days visiting Disney World with some friends. She then added that they were from Indiana and would be leaving in the morning heading home. Then she used a phrase I've heard and completely understood hundreds of times: "I really love bald eagles. Would there be any possible way that I could see your bird? Thunder, I think, the staff at the counter told me, was her name. Would a quick peek be possible before we leave in the morning?" While traveling with Thunder, I have conditioned myself to be surprised by nothing. Thunder herself had so many possible hands to deal, and the audience, while much more predictable, tried to make their cases as well. Since I was never surprised anymore, I formulated my conditional response almost automatically.

The request wasn't new, but the restaurant, hotel and the characters were. I told them that we could possibly arrange something after I had my dinner if that would work for them. They had not been served yet and asked if I would join them. I moved to their table, and the lady introduced them and repeated where they were from. I told them who I was and where I was from, and by then, I had already forgotten their names. I did remember Indiana though.

I am terrible at remembering names, but it must not bother me since I have never done anything to resolve the issue or even improve that part of my memory to any significant degree. While I didn't believe this, I tried to convince myself that it was okay because I met so many thousands of people as a result of doing these programs with Thunder. I used to think, while hunting for excuses for my poor manners, that Thunder was such a mental distraction that I didn't really hear the names. To a point, that was an excuse since when she was out on my arm, it was hard to concentrate on anything but her welfare when the crowds closed in. It was not that bad during the presentations since the audience was just that—an audience and not a crowded mass converging on a very shy bald eagle. Admittedly, Thunder wasn't at the table with us, so all I could say was that it was all on me and my lack of concern when it came to family or given names. Maybe I'll try to do better. Let's hope.

We had a nice dinner and great conversation, almost entirely about Thunder and the WVRRC and its long successful existence with an all-volunteer staff. Somehow we had managed with no paid employees. Most folks found that amazing since our travels were even done at the volunteer's expense: their time, vehicle, and fuel for both vehicle and volunteer. I must say that they were impressed knowing that I had traveled this entire trip at my own expense. I explained that all our volunteers did this because they believed in the significance of the educational impact that we had on the audiences, especially the younger ones. I still don't recall their names, but they did donate a hundred dollars to the raptor center right there at the table. I jokingly, to myself, thought of this as a pre-event bribe.

I told them what my feeding and bath plans were for Thunder after dinner and invited them to see her just prior to feeding. I told them they could not stay for dinner or her shower. The reason for that? Thunder would most certainly not participate in those activities if strangers were nearby. Since we would have a long day tomorrow, I certainly wanted her to eat this evening as planned. They agreed, but I did tell them they could take pictures if they wanted. Since it would be in dim lighting, I assured them that a camera flash would not bother Thunder in the least. They gave me their room number, and I promised I would call when we were heading to the corner of the parking near the dumpster cage.

Thunder's food was in the fridge in the room but everything else—except Thunder, of course—was in the van. I put her jesses on and slipped her into the travel cage. I had my gloves, armguard, and leash, and her Ziploc containing her fish was put in the small cooler. I called my new nameless friends and asked them to meet us in about five minutes by my white van. We headed down the hall, where I hailed an elevator.

I rolled her cart through the lobby toward the front door. All the staff we saw spoke to us—yes, us. In fact, I'd say the greetings were intended more for Thunder than me. That was okay; after all, she was the reason we were here in the first place. I pulled the cart the long distance across the lot, and there stood the couple waiting for us. I got the cart into position where it was fairly well hidden and instructed Mr. and Mrs. X where to position themselves. As usual, the cage door was situated on the opposite side from our guests. That was done intentionally so when I raised the drape at the door, Thunder wouldn't see anything but me. Perhaps she didn't like me, but I believe she saw me as the least of all possible evils.

The door was opened, and Thunder automatically positioned herself so I could quickly hook the leash to the jesses and she could step onto my arm and be placed on her top perch. She liked routines, especially when she got something she wanted. She was on my arm now, and I asked the guests to stay still as I backed away from the cage with Thunder still on my arm. I was still squatting behind the cage with Thunder out of sight when she realized I was far enough back that she could flap twice and suddenly appear atop the cage. As she perched, she immediately gave another couple of flaps, I think, just to dramatically announce her appearance. Maybe that was not the intent, but nonetheless, those were the results she got.

The guests were more than impressed, and since it was in dim light, Thunder was as relaxed as the folks were excited. They had a nice little camera with a built-in flash. I told them earlier that the flash would be okay, but they wanted to make sure. They began taking pictures, and Thunder was striking her many poses and looks. I told them I would get her on my arm and have her extend her wings for some shots. She was very relaxed, and their excitement continued to grow. Since the wife had a particular love for bald eagles, I offered to let her have a picture taken with Thunder.

"Can I?" she asked.

I assured her we could do this if she stood still, and I brought Thunder to her. I naturally would be holding her and would be in the photo as well. I positioned her and told her husband where to stand, and I positioned myself to the lady's left, which put Thunder right next to her left shoulder. She was relatively short, so Thunder and I both towered over her. I told the husband to keep taking pictures and the wife not to move as I had Thunder spread her enormous wings, which gave the appearance that someone was about to be carried away.

I'm certain they got some great memories, but I was not certain if the husband was being kind and really did not want to impose or if he was a bit intimidated by Thunder. Either way, he declined the photo with Thunder but was genuinely pleased that his wife was given this once-in-a-lifetime opportunity. They concluded their visit with many thanks and the proclamation that this would likely be the best trip they had ever taken. I was glad but a bit disappointed for them.

Before parting, Mr. X went into his wallet and offered another hundred-dollar donation in the form of two fifties. I thanked him again, and as they walked out of sight, I proclaimed to myself that Thunder had now raised over $1,200 in donations for the raptor center. I told her that her reward would be a fresh three-day-old pound-and-a-half rainbow trout. Like she cared when and where it came from; she was hungry and devoured it in just a few short minutes. She had her little shower, and then I repacked everything in the van in preparation for tomorrow's trip, and then it was back to the room and to bed.

I was up at 5:30 a.m. and started the basic house cleaning—not everything, just control of feathers and dander. I ran down to have some breakfast while the diva had a few more winks of beauty rest. My plans were to be out of the hotel by seven o'clock.

We made it to the lobby about ten before seven. My bill was settled, but I wanted to pass along my appreciation to the staff for all they did for us. There were lots of folks checking out early. Orlando is the conference capital of the world, so lots of business folks were up and rushing off to their destinations early, not so rushed that there wasn't time for someone, waiting to check out the old-fashioned way, to ask what was under the cover. Once I gave the first person a peek, a small mob scene of interest developed. I actually got back in the corner and took Thunder out of her cage. They may have been rushing a moment ago, but no one was going anywhere now. There were about twenty people there to begin with, but the number was growing. I was explaining what we were doing here and where we were from when it happened.

A very large and tall gentleman at the counter was talking on his Blackberry to someone who appeared to be his wife. I was talking and listening at the same time, something required of you when you worked with Thunder.

I heard him say, "Yes, I'm telling you, there is a man with a bald eagle here in the hotel lobby." She likely asked if he had too much to drink last night because his next line was, "Here, I'll show you. I'm going to take a picture and text it to your phone."

With that, he turned around with his brand-new Blackberry, the version of which had just come out earlier in 2003, and snapped some pictures of Thunder and me. As I was talking, he was fiddling with his phone, which was followed by a long pause.

Then he said, "See? I told you there was a bald eagle in the lobby." Then he gave a hearty laugh and turned to me, holding his phone and trying to show me the picture he had taken as he gave me a big thumbs-up.

This was the first time—November 15, 2003, at approximately 7:00 a.m.—Thunder had her photo, as far as we know, taken and sent to another phone via a text message. And to think I thought I had a fancy flip phone. Photos and sharing photos caught on quickly, and I would not be surprised if possibly a million cellphone photos have since been taken of this magnificent bird. It didn't take long to progress to e-mails and Facebook, where everything travels so quickly on the World Wide Web. This new media mania increased Thunder's educational value exponentially. This didn't match the firsthand value to live audiences, but her Web base was so much larger, and even in that medium, she was still "large and in charge" and a proud specimen whose species represents our nation as a living symbol.

Chapter 36

Respect in the "Swamp"

Thunder, a young, injured, and yet unnamed bald eagle, came to me for handler's training in late December 1992. When she arrived, the name given to her was Spot—not very respectful, I'll admit, but you had to have been there. I knew from my readings that there was a lot to learn, not only about the species but also about this bird in particular. Even then, I had planned to document the process so that I could share what I hoped to learn until the bird was mature at age five. This was arbitrary, perhaps, but my over-the-top education and vast experience (sarcasm) told me this would be more than adequate—my first major mistake.

I began documenting everything either of us did and the results. Even then, I was positive I would write a book about it. The title didn't come until the name did, at about day 531. I was still positive that after five years, not only would she be a mature adult, but also, there would not be much more new to be learned. So I was wrong about and equally disrespectful of this magnificent bird. It has, unfortunately, taken eleven years of this bird's life and until the last chapter of this book to finally have a clear vision of the relationship Thunder and I shared. So let's end this quickly and with the utmost respect due this very special creature.

It was June 3, 2005, and Thunder and I awoke to a bright sunny morning in the United States Capitol. I also awoke to a plastic drop cloth covered with the waste from Thunder's previous dinner—not really that big of a deal, and at least I didn't have to change any diapers. The odor was notable, not that foul of an odor but definitely exhibiting a nonlingering yet memorable aroma. I think I can actually smell it right now. When I refer to it as nonlingering, I simply mean that being around it won't make the smell stick to your clothing. When we walk into a room, I don't remember noticing people sniffing as though trying to locate the source.

Actually, this was the first thing, on a priority basis, that greeted your five senses but not the most urgent early-morning duty. Your eyes didn't have to be open for your sense of smell to be functional, but they did need to be open to see the actual puddle of waste as well as the small feathers and dander covering the drop cloth. My first actual duty in an effort to help the housekeeping staff was to raise the corners of the drop cloth so all the tiny litter would become piled close to the bottom of the perch; I then got a small bit of water and flung it onto the pile. This, I hope, would be completed before Thunder decided to do a bit of wing stretching herself. Without this technique, the dander-covered plastic would be swept clean with one simple wingbeat. If I didn't beat her to the punch, I would be spending lots of my breakfast time gathering *all* the tiny feathers that would be scattered throughout most of the room. If I were to leave any of the feathers behind and they were innocently collected by some of the hotel staff, well, that could mean fines or possibly even jail time for them. Every place we stayed, I always alerted the staff of the possible consequences of collecting any part or parts of this bird. I strongly suggested to them that if there were tiny feathers that I had not been able to find, they should roll them into a ball between their fingers and then discard them in the trash. As for the dander, well, the vacuums and the room's air-filtering system would have to deal with that. Thunder's wingbeats were to these tiny particles like turning a large fan onto a very fine pile of dust.

With the number-one priority now under control, I turned my attention to the half cup of excrement that Thunder shot against the plastic-protected wall during the cover of darkness. Cleanup wasn't really that difficult since the semifluid waste was a bit oily in texture, causing it to stay together and actually pool in one place on the plastic. I simply called on my rolls of paper towels to soak it up, and then it was deposited and sealed in one of the many gallon Ziploc bags I always had handy. An engineer carries pens and pencils in a plastic pocket protector, and a bald-eagle tender carries paper towels and one-gallon Ziplocs.

Right on cue and just after I finished the feather and dander detail, Thunder did a big roust to realign her body feathers and expel any residual dander. She followed this with a couple of hearty wingbeats that indicated she was now awake and ready for today's activities. I didn't actually believe she thought this way, but I was certain that she had been conditioned to this routine, which was always followed with loading her into the travel cage in preparation for ultimately being relocated. This was a bit like when I was a kid. Any trip we would be going on, either near or far, I would be instructed to go to the bathroom before leaving. After a while, even I didn't need reminding; it had become a routine.

Thunder and I had now spent, at best count, eighty-five nights sharing the same hotel rooms, bed-and-breakfasts, and cabins or lodges beginning with our first overnight trip in 1995 to Hilton Head, South Carolina.

This certainly was a unique way to start any morning, but today was a very special morning with a very special bird in a very special place. Thunder, of all the bald eagles in the world, had been invited to the U.S. Senate grounds, referred to as "the Swamp." The invitation was on behalf of the U.S. Senate. Thunder was selected after an extensive search showed her to be the only wild bald eagle they could locate that could be safely handled in public. The purpose of the visit was for Thunder to represent and serve as the poster child, so to speak, for the success of the Endangered Species Act, which was passed by the U.S. Senate in 1973.

It was a warm and sticky day, and the staff photographer was taking hundreds of photos, both staged and impromptu. Many were taken on the lawn with us and members of the Senate. At one point during the photoshoot, Pres. George W. Bush flew over in *Marine One*. Thunder didn't like helicopters at all, not even the president's.

My favorite photo is the one used on this book's cover: Thunder returning to my arm in front of the United States Capitol, right where she belongs, as the symbol of freedom, strength, courage, and honor for this great nation. I feel somewhat ashamed that it has taken me this long to recognize the full complement of respect that is due this very special bird. Yes, Thunder is a bird but not just a bird, never just a bird. She's a bald eagle, and she represents the United States of America and all that is wild and free. I refuse to express anthropomorphisms, however profound our relationship, and I will always be the first to admit that Thunder and I are different. It's simple: I can't fly.

The End

A Thunder/Spot Poem

Liz Snyder

Now as Thunder sat perched in the sun,
she observed a new person had come,
bearing fish, rabbit, and squirrel, for the diva eaglegirl,
but of bribes, she would not take a one.

At Lake Stoney, friends of Thunder did cast
but came up with just algae and asked,
"Is it worth it or not to keep fishing for Spot
with the rain pouring down on the task?"

The human took the catch in the cooler
and schlepped through weather to see her
and then poured out the snack, in the storm stood aback,
damp and dripping under blue bumbershooter.

Thunder sat, eyeing her tub,
and then mused to herself, *Here's the rub:*
I can swoop in like lightning on the bluegill, so frightening,
or perch till the humans give up.

A bluegill, she caught; while she ate, she gave thought.
Has my human gone fishing, I wonder?

Thunders' Obituary

(from the WVRRC regarding the death of Thunder, a very special bald eagle)

The West Virginia Raptor Rehabilitation Center (WVRRC) announces the passing of our beautiful bald eagle, Thunder. She died at 9:20 p.m. on December 21 in the arms of the one who was her greatest friend and longtime partner, Michael S. Book, WVRRC founder and director. She was a resident of the WVRRC twenty-one years to the day.

Thunder was hatched in Upstate New York along the Delaware River, according to her leg band, and was shot in the thigh and left wing while migrating as a juvenile over West Virginia in 1992. She was brought to the WVRRC for rehabilitation on December 1 and into Mike's dedicated care on December 21. With kindness, patience, and lots of tasty rabbits, fish, and squirrels, Thunder made her recovery. Veterinarians determined that because of the nature of her wing injury—the gunshot basically took off all the vital primary flight feathers, rendering sustained flight impossible—she would be unable to survive if returned to the wild. So began the process of training Mike to understand the needs and behaviors of a young bald eagle with all the spirit of the wild in her eyes and heart.

Thunder became the WVRRC's most visible environmental education bird ambassador. She was the "poster child" representing the success of the Endangered Species Act. She traveled hundreds of thousands of miles through many states, making appearances before audiences of thousands or dozens, from U.S. Congress to kindergarten classrooms, delivering a message of conservation and responsible environmental stewardship, along with hope for the future. She touched the lives of three generations of children.

She will be missed beyond measure, our big bright girl, our watch eagle and creator of whirlwinds.

If you, as a Native American permit holder, are receiving a feather or part or piece of our special bird, know that she was the embodiment of all that is wild and beautiful. Treat her with the utmost respect. We loved her, and she did more for the environmental cause than any human we know. The people of West Virginia are now entrusting you with one of our most precious resources. Thank you for your prayers.

Liz Snyder, Operations Director Friend of Thunder West Virginia Raptor Rehabilitation Center

Edwards Brothers Inc.
Ann Arbor MI. USA
May 7, 2018